Breaking FREE

*A self-help guide for adults
who were sexually abused
as children*

Carolyn Ainscough
& Kay Toon

FISHER BOOKS

Publishers: Bill Fisher
                  Helen Fisher
                  Howard Fisher
                  J. McCrary

North American
Editors: Bill Fisher
                  Sean Stewart

Cover: Paula Peterson

Published by Fisher Books
P.O. Box 38040
Tucson, Arizona 85740-8040
520-292-9080

First published in Great Britain 1993
by Sheldon Press, SPCK, London

**Library of Congress
Cataloging-in-Publication Data**
Ainscough, Carolyn
      Breaking free : a self-help guide
for adults who were
sexually abused as children / by
Carolyn Ainscough and Kay Toon.
            p. cm.
      Includes bibliographical
references and index.
      ISBN 1-55561-057-9
      1. Adult child sexual abuse
      victims--Rehabilitation.
I. Toon, Kay. II. Title.
RC569.5.A28A36   1993
616.85'82239'0651--dc20
                              93-37229
                              CIP

Contents

Preface

WE FIRST MET TEN YEARS AGO when we were training to become Clinical Psychologists at the University of Leeds. During our training the words *sexual abuse* were hardly mentioned—certainly not in relation to adults who were experiencing psychological problems.

After finishing training we both took positions with the Wakefield Health Authority. There we were working with adults, referred by doctors or other professionals, who were experiencing emotional difficulties or problems coping with their lives.

These clients came to us with many different problems: depression, anxiety, eating disorders, sexual problems, and phobias. But as we talked with them, many began to tell us they had been sexually abused as children and this appeared to be a major cause of their current problems. At first we worked individually with clients who had been sexually abused and then in 1987 we set up our first Survivors group.

We had already run anxiety groups and our clients had found group work very beneficial. They were able to share their problems and experiences with others in the same situation, to help and encourage each other and to set up long-lasting support networks and friendships. We hoped Survivors would benefit similarly. Since this time we have set up a psychology service in Wakefield for Survivors.

We have led many Survivors groups as well as continuing to work individually with people who were sexually abused as children. The groups meet with us for 15 to 20 weekly sessions and then continue to meet as self-help groups. In these Survivors groups the women are able to share the pain of their experiences, work through their feelings and begin to break free of their problems.

At some point we decided to write a booklet on sexual abuse to help and encourage Survivors who were waiting for therapy. Some of the former members of the Survivors groups were eager to help by contributing the writing they had done as part of their own therapy. Many Survivors have never had the opportunity to talk about what happened and how they feel. Soon the booklet had expanded into a book and A.C.T. (Abuse—Counseling and Training), an action group of Wakefield Survivors committed to helping other Survivors and working towards prevention, was formed.

We wrote this book to share what we have learned, to reach out to all people who were sexually abused as children and to help them take their first steps in breaking free from the past. It is not intended as an alternative to professional help; we hope this book will give Survivors confidence to seek the help they deserve.

This book expresses our belief in the power of human beings to survive, to heal, and to grow. It would not exist without those Wakefield Survivors who were prepared to share their experiences with us and to contribute their writings. All the events and people described here are real. The names have been changed for legal reasons or to protect family members, but not because the women are ashamed. The women know the responsibility for sexual abuse always lies with the abuser and never with the abused child.

Note to male survivors

Most of our sexual abuse work has been with women victims and we used their stories and quotations in this book. Many men, however, were sexually abused as children and more and more men are now talking about their experiences and seeking help.

Male Survivors experience many of the same problems as female Survivors. We hope the references to women will not keep you from reading this book and taking the first step toward coming to terms with what happened to you.

Acknowledgments

The ideas in this book developed from our work with the Survivors of sexual abuse who were brave enough to share their experiences and who struggled to overcome their problems and break free from their pain and guilt. We have great respect for these women and thank them for the knowledge we gained by working with them.

We especially thank all the women who contributed their writings to this book. We also thank Margaret Ainscough, Chris Bethlehem, Alistair Cant, Sharon Jackson and Diane Skinner, who read various drafts and offered suggestions and corrections; Chris Leach for advice about writing and publishing; Jon Fraise for help with word processing and Sally Pinnell for contributions from her research on our groups.

We appreciate and are grateful to Bryn Thomas and Andrew Lister for their support throughout our writing this book. Andrew Lister also generously devoted his time in reading drafts and rewriting problem sentences.

Special thanks to Erika Reinhold for contributing her own story and for hours of typing and retyping and to members of A.C.T. for their unfailing enthusiasm and support for this project.

Carolyn Ainscough and Kay Toon
Chartered Clinical Psychologists

Survival and Recovery: Sharing the Pain

Now I feel more powerful. I'm going to take care of this power and nurture it and I'm going to take charge of my life and get out of this mess. I can see a different life. I can smell a better future. I'm not frightened anymore. I'm breaking free! *Lizzie*

Sexual abuse of children is not a new problem. Generations of children have been sexually abused in secret and remained silent. The silence and secrecy is now being broken as Survivors of childhood sexual abuse begin to speak up about their experiences and break free from their past. Survivors of sexual abuse are learning that they are not alone.

They are reclaiming their own power and self-respect. Until recently the sexual abuse of a child was thought to be a terrible but extremely rare event. In the past few years an increasing amount of attention has been given to sexual abuse on television and radio and in newspapers and magazines. As more and more Survivors dare to speak out, it is becoming clear that many people were sexually abused as children.

Many Survivors, however, have carried the secret of their abuse to the grave; others still carry the burden of that secret and suffer in silence. We may never know the true extent of this problem. The shame and secrecy that surrounds sexual abuse and keeps people silent makes it difficult to estimate the number of people who have been sexually abused.

The results of research studies vary but it is generally believed that at least 1 in 10 people was sexually abused as a child. Even the most conservative estimates indicate that sexual abuse affects large numbers of people. It is a worldwide problem not confined to any specific country, race, culture or class. This means millions of people are alive today who were sexually abused as children.

Who is this book for?

This book is primarily a self-help book for adult Survivors of childhood sexual abuse. Sexual abuse has damaging effects on children but it can also lead to problems in adulthood. This book contains information about sexual abuse, the kinds of problems it can cause and ways in which Survivors can begin to deal with these problems.

We hope that friends and relatives of Survivors and people working in the caring professions will also read this book and gain some insight into the difficulties Survivors face. However, we address this book to you, the Survivor.

The words we use

Sexual Abuse—We use the term *sexual abuse* to mean any kind of unwanted or inappropriate sexual behavior with a child. This includes sexual intercourse, oral sex, anal sex, being touched in a sexual way and being persuaded to touch someone else. It may involve inserting objects into the child's body or sexual acts with animals.

However sexual abuse doesn't always involve physical contact. Being made to watch other people's sexual behavior, or to look at their bodies or at sexual photographs or videos can also be forms of sexual abuse. Sexual abuse includes abuse by one person or by groups of people. The abuse may have happened only once or many times over a number of years. It may still be happening.

Abusers—In the book we refer to abusers as *he* because the majority of abusers are men. However there are female abusers. An abuser is anyone who has sexually abused a child. This could be a father, mother, brother, sister, other family member, friend, person in authority, acquaintance, older child or a stranger.

Survivors—We use the word *Survivors* to refer to people who were sexually abused as children. They have had to find ways of surviving the trauma of sexual abuse. But, with the help of this book, we hope they will go beyond simply surviving to living a fuller and happier life. Survivors are referred to as *she* in this book because most of the work we have done has been with women Survivors.

The personal stories are all from women. However, many men were also sexually abused as children. Survivors can come from any walk of life. Wakefield Survivors include teachers, housewives, policewomen, radiographers, health workers, single parents, the unemployed, nurses, domestic workers, caterers, clerical workers and business women.

This book is for men and women who were sexually abused as children by male or female abusers in any way .

About this book

This book is intended to help you think in new ways about your experiences and feelings and to start to work through your problems. Women Survivors share with you their own experiences of sexual abuse. They also describe the problems they've had since being abused and the ways they've found to overcome these difficulties.

Each Survivor has had her own personal struggle but has been helped by sharing her pain with other Survivors and experiencing their understanding and support. Writing has been part of their healing process. Through their writings they extend their understanding and support to you.

The book is divided into five sections. Section I, "Sexual Abuse Changes Lives," contains accounts by Wakefield Survivors of their experiences and illustrates the ways in which sexual abuse affects people both as children and as adults. Section II, "It Must Have Been My Fault," considers the feelings of guilt and shame that Survivors experience.

We look at the common questions that Survivors try to answer: "Why did it happen to me?" and "Why didn't I tell?" We also look at the signs children may show when they are being sexually abused and what happens when people tell someone that they have been abused.

Section III, "Tackling the Problems," considers some

common problems experienced by Survivors of sexual abuse and suggests ways of dealing with these difficulties. This section includes chapters on feelings, anxiety, depression, eating problems, and sexual problems.

Section IV, "Feelings Towards Others," observes the difficulties Survivors may experience with their feelings towards children, their mothers and their abusers. Section V, "Breaking Free," describes how Survivors can overcome their problems and Wakefield Survivors write about what has helped them.

We also look at ways of working towards the prevention of further sexual abuse. In most chapters there are exercises to try and a list of books you might like to read. This book is a first step towards healing rather than a final solution. We hope it will give you the confidence to break free of your past by sharing your experiences with others, contacting other Survivors of sexual abuse and getting professional help. The Resources Section at the end of the book gives details about where you can seek further help. The damaging effects of sexual abuse can be overcome.

How to use this book

You will gain the most benefit from this book if you read through the chapters slowly in the order they appear, completing the exercises at the end of each chapter before moving on to the next one. The chapters build on each other and follow the sequence we've found most helpful for Survivors of sexual abuse. It is particularly important to read Section II on guilt and self-blame and do the exercises in these chapters before trying to deal with the more specific problems in the rest of the book.

Getting support

You will need time to understand and accept what you read and to deal with your emotional reactions. You'll probably find some of this book upsetting. Don't try to push your feelings away. Accept your emotions and allow yourself to cry or feel angry.

Set aside time to read the book. Read it in a place where you feel safe and comfortable. It is not a book you can read casually in a spare moment. If possible, try to find someone you trust who will support you and talk with you about how you are feeling while you are reading this book. Getting help and support from others is a useful and practical way of dealing with your problems, not a sign of weakness and failure.

Writing

Most chapters contain exercises, many of which ask you to write about your feelings and experiences. Many Wakefield Survivors discovered that writing played a very important part in their recovery and they describe how it has helped them in chapter 17. Some Survivors find the idea of writing very threatening and may also feel that it won't be helpful. Writing can bring back memories and feelings that have been blocked-off and make the reality of what has happened very clear. This can be frightening but bringing back the memories and facing up to the reality is an essential part of the healing process.

At first when I wrote things I always tore them up or burned them immediately. I was pleased when I could read through them again. I'd pushed it all down inside me. I started writing down all the things I couldn't cope with or talk about. *Lucy*

Writing isn't the same as just thinking things out. Many Survivors recall memories and feelings and begin to understand themselves better once they begin to write.

I'm not sure what to put down. I just write whatever comes into my mind at the time. I only remembered where I'd been abused when I'd written it down. There are quite a few things I've remembered this way. *Mavis*

I wouldn't have believed how writing it down could have helped so much—it was incredible. I could see it much more in black and white. Seeing it written down you think "Yes, that's how I feel." Without writing you don't always recognize exactly how you feel. *Jocelyn*

Spelling, grammar and style don't matter. It is your thoughts and feelings that are important and need to be written down. The education of many Survivors suffered because of abuse during childhood. If you have trouble writing, speak into a tape recorder or get someone you trust to write as you speak. The writing is for your benefit. It's not necessary for anyone else to read it.

If you are worried that someone else might find your writing keep it in a safe place or leave it in a sealed envelope with someone you trust. Writing is a good way of communicating your experiences and feelings to other people without having to talk, so you may want to share your writing with someone else. Sharing your writing also helps to break the secrecy of your abuse.

The healing process

It is possible to break free from the damaging effects of sexual abuse but this can take time. You may have had problems over many years and they won't just disappear overnight. Many people try to cope with sexual abuse by burying their memories and feelings. This is one of the few ways in which children are able to cope, but as an adult this strategy has disadvantages. It doesn't work completely and it doesn't last.

Bad feelings and memories escape as nightmares, panic attacks, fears, depression, sexual difficulties, flashbacks and many other problems. These problems are the symptoms. The underlying cause is sexual abuse and this needs to be dealt with before you can overcome your problems

Dealing with sexual abuse is not about wiping out the past. You can never do that. Neither is it about blocking-off the past by burying your feelings or building a wall to keep the memories away. It is about dealing with the way the abuse has affected your life and the way you feel about yourself. You will never be able to forget about the abuse—but you will be able to release your feelings of guilt and reclaim your self-respect.

This book aims to help you deal with the underlying problem. To do this you have to dig up memories and feelings. Here is what Claire said about her experience in group therapy:

Things seemed to get worse as they were stirred up and brought up to the surface. But then it got better. You get a bit worse before you get better and when that happens you get frightened and feel you want to quit but suddenly you change. Then you look at yourself and see the difference. *Claire*

You may feel reading this book is making you feel worse at first as you begin to face the pain of your past but keep going and you will begin to feel better. Clearing out the memories and bad feelings from your mind is like cleaning a closet. You pull everything out all over the floor and it looks worse than before. However as you keep going, throwing some things away, cleaning and moving things and putting them back in a new order, everything begins to look much better.

If you begin to feel distressed take some time out from reading and take care of yourself. Try to relax and ask for support from other people. Do something you enjoy such as having a bath, going for a walk, talking to friends or listening to music. When you feel ready, go back to the book and go on reading. Kate attended a Survivors group. After time and effort spent working through her bad feelings and difficulties this is what she has to say:

Maybe I did lose my childhood but I managed to find the little girl in me and now take care of her. I feel so great now. No longer is there an ugly monster looming at the back of my mind, rearing its ugly head and constantly affecting my life. Now I am in control. *Kate*

This book could be the first step in helping you regain your own power and strength. Meeting other Survivors or getting further help from an experienced therapist could be the next.

2

Survivors Speak Out

IN THIS CHAPTER JANE, EILEEN, ANITA, PAM AND DOROTHY speak out about the sexual abuse they suffered and how it affected them as children and adults. Each Survivor's story is different but many of the feelings and effects are similar. These stories are powerful and at times distressing, but also hopeful and positive. You may be concerned for the person whose story you are reading but often it will be your own memories and feelings that are surfacing.

Use these stories to reflect on your own experiences and feelings. If you can, find a friend with whom you can talk about how you are feeling. Read the chapter slowly and stop when you want to. Do not feel you have to read all of these stories before going on to the rest of the book. Leave them and come back to them later if you wish.

Jane's story

I am in the bathroom staring at the light. I am lying on the floor next to the scales. I don't remember what my daddy said to me beforehand but I remember as he lay down on top of me. I wanted to push him away but he held my wrists to the floor on both sides of my head. I remember his clothing rubbing against my naked skin. The contact hurt, the pressure hurt as he rubbed himself up and down over me. I remember his brown silk tie flapping in my face.

Afterwards he stood me in the bathtub. He told me not to tell, that my mother would not understand, it was our secret. The threats came later. That was the first time my stepfather sexually abused me. I was seven. My parents split up when I was four. My natural father had always been a distant figure, and then for three years I had very little contact with any men. When my mother remarried we became a real family. My little sister and I had a daddy.

As the family became older my stepfather became more threatening and domineering. As I became older I felt I was walking a tightrope between my two lives. I wanted to be liked and loved as me, but what if people knew what I was really like, what I allowed to happen, what I was involved in? My stepfather was very well liked, he used to help old people, pick up prescriptions for the sick, stack wood for people and shovel snow. So I thought it must be me that was really bad. I must be responsible. Who would believe otherwise? My stepfather rewarded me with money sometimes, more money than my mother could spare.

So I felt even more guilty. I felt that if my mother found out her marriage would break up. It would be as if she was being punished, not me, whose fault it really was. Sometimes I would screw up all my courage and refuse him but whatever tactics I employed he would outmaneuver me. He would appear to go along with me and then he would begin to be really nasty to the family. He would give my mother less money to run the house. He'd threaten to throw us all out of the house. He would go to a bar right after work and be late for meals. He would either totally ignore one of us or pick on all the children for minor things and blow them up out of all proportion. He had total control over the TV and would change the channel five minutes before the end of a program we were all watching. He'd say, "Hey, I pay the rent," and that caused a lot of hurt.

Then he would come back to me and ask again. This would continue until I gave in. I felt guilty for giving in to him and I felt guilty for causing all the misery to my family. When I began to menstruate I wanted to beg my mother not to tell him. I felt ashamed again, not in control of my body, but I didn't feel I had the right to ask her not to tell him. I wondered if this would change anything, but I guess since penetration wasn't involved nothing did change. I still had nightmares about becoming pregnant through clothing.

Once I developed breasts (a word I didn't like as he used to tell me I had beautiful breasts) I only had to strip to my waist. He would change into nylon trousers and then push his nicotine-stained tongue into my mouth and ears, and play with my nipples with his hard cracked fingers. I would be on the floor and as I silently cried the tears would collect in my ears. I could never understand why the sight of tears didn't turn him off. I would clench my fists on the floor and grit my teeth against his tongue and try to imagine myself out of my body. I lived in constant dread—I knew what would happen whenever I was left alone with my stepfather.

Being ill and staying home from school was not much fun at our house. Keeping this big secret made me feel I was different. I had to pretend that I was normal and the same as everyone else. I kept very much to myself, not daring to risk close friendships or to draw attention to myself in any way. I deliberately didn't take an active role in the classroom at school. I had friends at school but no best friend, no one to come over for refreshments after school.

The more I pretended the more guilt I felt about the deception, and the more certain I became that people liked the pretend me—not the real me. The friends that I did have were mainly boys because they were happy to play outside rather than inside and they weren't interested in being 'gossipy'. I found them less socially demanding. This became a problem with my stepfather when he began to see them as a threat. I was about 14 at the time. I have always been alone.

I don't think I ever considered telling. I knew of no one who could cope with sharing this awful secret. Now I know that it wasn't my secret and I no longer feel isolated. Having met other Survivors I feel sad for what they have been through but it has helped me realize that being abused wasn't my fault. I don't have to be ashamed. I know now I am not alone, that the feelings that I had were not abnormal, and that I am not crazy. Now I am free and I am in control of my life. I know who I am. I am full of hope for the future.

Eileen's story

I think that my uncle must have sexually abused me from the age of two or three. I was told that I began to be a naughty child about this age. I was continually disruptive after that. I thought that if I did something really naughty someone might find out that uncle was putting his hand down my panties and hurting me with his fingers. I played dare games with my friends in the hope I would get hurt and would be taken to the hospital and away from my uncle. My father was fighting the war and mother was still suffering from the death of my younger sister and didn't notice anything beyond my attention-seeking behavior.

I started school on my fourth birthday, one year earlier than the usual age in those days. Being sent to school early was a form of rejection to me and I resented being there. As soon as the teacher turned her back I ran away and got home before my mother because I took a shortcut. This was a daily routine for almost three years. The resentment built up in me even stronger as I was punished regularly. We lived one and a half miles away from school and my mother spent most of her day walking back and forth between home and school determined to get me used to it. I eventually did. My mother and I visited my grandparents almost daily and I was regularly sent to deliver messages and to do errands for my uncle who lived on the same street.

My earliest memories are of knocking on uncle's door. The door would open and I would be quickly pulled into the house. He would lock the door and push me against the wall beside the window and put his hands down my panties and touch me.

He told me that if I told anyone what was happening I would be punished for what I had done wrong. The feelings of guilt and fear increased in me. I felt very confused, helpless, dirty and disgusted. There was no one to talk to. I was very much alone and very lonely. I was desperately unhappy and cried silently for help but no one could hear me. There was constant pain and soreness in my genitals but no one noticed that either.

By the time I was eight he was partially penetrating my body with his penis. Although he did not climax at this time he gained great pleasure from the abuse. At ten I was suffering from gross anxiety and displaying more behavior problems than ever. I had nightmares of his overweight stocky body, his thick spectacles and his aggressive manner in his excitement. His heavy breathing and his sweaty hands as he held me down repulsed me.

I would wake up at night crying, afraid and shaking with fear. I began to have frequent bouts of vaginal pain when I urinated. I was unaware at the time that I was suffering from cystitis and that this was connected to the abuse. By the time I was 11 my feelings of guilt and unhappiness were enormous. I cried every night and lived in constant fear of the next attack.

My personal hygiene became an obsession in order to cleanse my mind and body of the dirty feelings from the abuse which was forced upon me. I hated him for abusing me and gaining pleasure from it and causing me pain and misery. My vagina was constantly sore and the thought of his sperm seeping from my body following intercourse nauseated me. He obviously never stopped to think how I felt and was only concerned for his own selfish needs.

My school work suffered despite my struggles to learn. The abuse was always prominent in my thoughts and learning came second. The school teacher encouraged me to take an examination to go into the seventh grade. She said I had the ability but didn't apply it. I failed the exam miserably, possibly due to lack of knowledge, but mainly through lack of concentration.

I constantly hoped that the teacher would guess the reason for my misery and poor school work. I was too young to realize that no one has a crystal ball in their head to read unspoken words and thoughts. I thought no one would want to help me, even if they could, as I was dirty, disgusting and unworthy of help. I was not even fit to be a human being because of the disgraceful things I did.

My abuse continued until one day at 14 he attempted to attack me as though it was his lawful right. He tried to pull me to the floor and started to grope his hand up my skirt. I began to struggle and fight, hitting him anywhere my fist would reach while avoiding his hands. He was shocked at my reaction at first but soon recovered when I hit him on the face with one hand and at the same time pulled his hand away from tearing at my underwear. It was a hard struggle as he was a very strong man but miraculously I managed to get away from him.

When I reached home I burst into a flood of tears and quickly told my father what had happened. He went to see my uncle. I never discovered what action my father took to straighten out the situation but the abuse never occurred again. My parents obviously thought it was a one-time incident. I was never asked and I didn't tell them otherwise. Possibly the reason they didn't ask me was that the abuser was a family member. So it was kept quiet and covered up.

I carried the secret for 50 years as even in my adult life there was no one I could trust with my story. In the past years the press has publicized stories of rape and abuse and the females have often been accused of provocation and of being the guilty party. Based on that I felt no one would believe me either. I had pushed the experiences of the abuse to the back of my mind and pretended it had not happened—or so I thought. That is, until the nightmares and flashbacks brought it flooding into my mind again.

Whenever child abuse was publicized I always felt very sympathetic towards the abused and extremely angry at the abuser. It never occurred to me that I understood because it had happened to me. It would have been too painful to remember my childhood experiences and associate them with others who were suffering the same. I felt unworthy, dirty, disgusted, ashamed and unfit to be a human being. I felt depersonalized, detached and I had lost my personal identity. I became a victim of life.

Wrestling throughout my life with the emotional misery and torment of abuse has been very difficult but with determination and group therapy I have overcome the major difficulties in the emotional side of my life. The abuse has changed my personality and I have often wondered what or who I would have been without the traumatic experiences.

I have been burdened by the misery of my emotions all my life up to the present time. I often think of the other me and what it would be like to have had not only a happy contented childhood but also a peaceful and happy transit into adult life. Now I have been to a Survivors group and have told my story, maybe one day I will find the real me.

Anita's story

As I look back on my life and recall events leading up to my abuse I have no happy memories at all. I'm sure there must have been some good times, but I really can't remember any. I had never felt loved and secure as a child. My father was forever drunk and became very violent and abusive towards my mother. I was terrified of him. My mother was always tired and overworked and I can't remember ever seeing her smile.

Neither of them ever gave me love or affection and I was desperate for a little love. I tried so hard to make them love me but I always got everything wrong. I was a shy, clumsy child and I was constantly humiliated and ridiculed at home and at school. As I grew older I became more and more shy and insecure. I had no friends and was desperately lonely. Eventually my father left home and moved in with a girlfriend. At first he came to see us but gradually visited us less and less.

My older sister moved out to live with him and that was the last I saw of both of them. By this time my mom was working every hour God sends and I never saw her either. As I was now the oldest girl at ten, I came home from school to an empty house, did all the housework and made a meal for my older brother and younger sister.

Around the same time I became very ill and was diagnosed diabetic. I spent two months in the hospital with no desire to get better. The only visitor I had in all that time was my mom and she found it really difficult to visit because she had to work. Because of this I felt very guilty.

My mom had had a terrible life and now that it was starting to improve, I had to go and get ill and become an even greater burden than I was already. While I was in the hospital my mother remarried and when I came home my stepfather made a terrible fuss over me. I felt so special, because I had never had attention like this before and I loved it. In fact I made a point of showing off to my brother and sister. "I'm his favorite." I'd say. "He really loves me." I threw myself at him.

Every time he sat down I'd jump on his knee and throw my arms round him. He'd kiss and hug me and I felt so special. I immediately began to call him daddy and was sure at last I did have a real daddy who really loved me. I soon began to realize that I didn't get hugged so often when other people were around, but I put this down to him not wanting to make my brother and sister jealous.

He began taking me for long rides in his car. He'd park in a lonely spot and then start to kiss me but somehow the kisses weren't the same. They were sloppy and wet and I didn't like it. I didn't dare tell him though. He also started touching me all over my body. This made me feel uncomfortable as I really didn't understand it. It was a really funny feeling and I wished he wouldn't do it. Each time we went out he did this more and more. He also started breathing funny and I began to feel terribly frightened.

My mom now was working most nights and he started telling me to see him after the others went to bed. He told me he loved me, but I was not to tell anybody, because no one would understand and I'd get into trouble. We'd keep these special times secret just between us because he loved me so much. 'And you do understand, Anita, it's because I love you so much that I do these things to you. Don't be frightened. I won't hurt you. You'll like it, I promise. I do love you.'

But he did hurt me. It was horrible. He did terrible things to me and I was so frightened. He talked to me all the time telling me how wonderful everything was. "It's good, isn't it, Anita?" "You like this, don't you? I told you you would, didn't I?" I was so scared I couldn't move. My body was stiff and tears were rolling down my cheeks. Yet still he seemed to be in a fantasy world believing I was really enjoying it.

He was so perverted and I feel sick at the thought of the things he did to me. As he became excited he began to slobber and dribble all over me and he'd grunt just like a pig. I tried so hard to cry out, I opened my mouth but nothing happened. I had now become quite ill and withdrawn. All the teachers thought this was due to my being diabetic. I didn't bother at all about my diabetes and purposely made myself sick. Several times I became so ill that I was rushed to the hospital for tests and to restabilize the diabetes. This was the only relief I ever got.

When I was 14. I had become such a freak at school I was a constant source of fun for the other kids. One day a couple of girls were making fun of me, referring to the fact I had never had a boyfriend and trying to embarrass me by asking me all sorts of silly questions about sex. Had I ever tried this or had that done to me? I became so fed up with it I broke down in tears and told them all to leave me alone because in actual fact I had had more experience than all of them and knew more than they'd ever know.

One girl, though, persisted and wanted to know what I was talking about, so I told her. She was shocked and then insisted on dragging me off to our school counselor. I couldn't really tell the school counselor anything, only that my stepfather had done things to me which is all I ever said to anybody. He then told my mother. I was terrified of facing her, I felt as if I'd wrecked her life once again. Her first words to me were "Why didn't you tell me? Why did you tell someone else?" This seemed to have really hurt her and I felt guiltier than ever.

She promised me it wouldn't happen again and that was an end to it. It wasn't mentioned again. It did stop for a couple of weeks and then one day he came in to tell me how sorry he was. He began to cry and he put his arm around me, as he did so he began all over again. I later told my mother he had started doing things again and she said she'd make him stop. By this time he seemed to have realized he could get away with anything and so now he didn't even wait for my mom to be out of the house. I never knew when he was going to appear next. I'd be certain he was out of the house so I'd risk taking a bath and he would just appear from out of nowhere. My life was a nightmare. I decided the only answer to my problems was to end it all so I overdosed on my insulin and put myself in a coma. Of course I was saved, and sent to a child psychologist who told me all my problems were due to being called "matchstick legs" as an infant.

After this episode I was really desperate and one day I decided to try to get a drink in a bar. With a little make-up and the right clothes, I looked quite attractive and easily got served. This provided a way of numbing myself. I couldn't make the problem go away but at least I could make it bearable. I stopped going to school. I'd just disappear into the park with a bottle of vodka. The teachers never even noticed.

I started going out every night. I'd just walk into a bar and someone would always buy me drinks. I was 15 by this time and I'd just stopped caring. I started getting invited to parties and the first time I went to one I stayed out all night. When I got home he was waiting for me. He began to hit me and I thought he would never stop. He told me I'd worried my mother to death and how dare I do this. After that first time it was much easier. I told my mom I was going out and I didn't know if I'd be home and she seemed to accept this.

I went out almost every night. I was always drunk and I slept around. I just didn't care. I smoked dope and took LSD, anything so I didn't have to feel. Then one guy I'd spent the night with seemed to have fallen in love with me and asked me to marry him. I was now 16, so I said yes. My mom agreed and that was that. A month later we were married. Soon afterwards I was rushed into the hospital with acute liver damage and was told to treat alcohol as poison. I didn't take a drink for three years. Instead I became obsessed with having a baby and eventually after losing a couple I had a baby. This was the unconditional natural love I'd been waiting for all my life and it was all I wanted.

Our marriage was a joke. There was nothing between us, we each led separate lives, and I wouldn't have sex unless I really couldn't get out of it. I made excuse after excuse. Luckily the first time we did have sex after our daughter was born I got pregnant again and so didn't have to bother until after the birth of our second child. After our son was born I had a lot of illnesses and used this as an excuse. I eventually had to have a big operation. When I got over this my husband became very impatient. He came home drunk one night and raped me. As a result, our third child was born and immediately afterward my husband walked out and left us.

After this I became obsessed with dieting and after a short period of anorexia I became bulimic (binging on food and vomiting) and this took over my life. It's the only way I have of coping with life, as deep down I really detest myself. I am desperately lonely and unhappy and I just can't wait for life to hurry up and finish. I've had a couple of disastrous relationships since the breakup of my marriage. I just can't seem to make them work. I hate sex and men and find it difficult to make friends generally with anybody. I keep trying hard to make my life work.

I adore my children and I don't think I give them what they deserve, but I keep on trying and maybe one day I'll get it right. It seems everything I try I fail at and the harder I try the bigger mess I make. I moved to another house and tried to make a new start shortly after the breakup of my marriage. The first time I gave in and accepted a little practical help from a man, I ended up being held prisoner in my own home for three days, being repeatedly raped and abused.

I then got into a relationship with a man so manipulative and possessive it was like reliving my childhood. After so many terrible experiences I wonder if maybe it's been me that's caused it all along. My own daughter was molested when she was four-years old by a man at a summer camp. I wonder if all men are abusers. Maybe they're normal and I am the one with a problem. I recently found a faith in God which has kept me going and helped me believe in myself more. I am now gaining confidence gradually and hopefully beginning a whole new life.

Pam's story

My mom and dad had to get married as I was an unexpected early arrival. All through my childhood I felt this was the reason they both treated me so badly. They never bought me clothes, shoes, school uniforms, etc. They made me babysit my brother and two sisters and I had to do the housework, washing and ironing. I was a stand-in housewife in more ways than one.

One Saturday in August when I was 12-years old, my mom went shopping and as usual my father was left to look after us all. I went upstairs to wrap my mom's birthday present. I couldn't do it by myself so my dad came upstairs into my brother's bedroom, supposedly to help. As I was walking out of the door my dad grabbed me, pulled me onto the bed and ripped my shirt out of my skirt. I began to shout and scream and kick. Nobody came to help me. He started fondling my body and sucking my breasts and then he pulled my pants down. I was still shouting and screaming and kicking.

My brother came upstairs demanding, "What's going on?" My dad threatened him with a beating, so my brother went back downstairs none the wiser. My dad kept trying to shut me up. He said I would enjoy it. After he had finished he walked off leaving me crying into the pillow. He came back fully dressed shouting, "Hurry up and get dressed before your mother gets back." I walked into the bathroom. My father came in and pulled my bra back down and then left me.

For years my dad had made sexual comments to me, and tried to put me on the pill as soon as my periods began, but this was the first time he'd raped me. It went on for another two years. I had nightmares and daymares all the time. I became withdrawn, defiant and irritable. I felt as if my whole body was crawling. I felt so dirty and used.

The same sort of thing had happened to me before, but with a different, older, member of the family. This left me wondering if I was different from everybody else. I was all alone. Fears of becoming pregnant constantly ran through my mind. I mentioned the rape to the child-protection officer who was visiting our family at the time. He wasn't interested. My mother commented on my changed behavior, so I told her. She said I was a liar and should have been drowned at birth. Nobody was willing to help, so I ran away and took an overdose, but it didn't work and I ended up back home.

At 17 I met and fell in love with my first husband who was 12 years my senior. I left home to live with him and we eventually got married, but he couldn't accept what had happened to me and also decided he didn't want any children. He turned out to be just like my father, he beat me regularly so I left him and filed for divorce. After my divorce my faith in men disappeared completely and the nightmares continued. Then 18 months later I met my second husband who guessed there was something wrong between me and my father, so I told him the story. He was the first person whom I had told and who had understood. Six months later I was pregnant and we had a son. One year later we married. Then I started suffering from depression and agoraphobia. [Fear of crowds and public places.]

I thought this was a build-up of trying to cope with a baby, work full time and falling out with my parents. After seeing my doctor I realized my problems were because of the sexual abuse. She referred me to a psychiatrist, who wasn't much help as he was a man. But he referred me to a clinical psychologist who ran a group for women who had been abused as children. During the group session emotions ran high. I relived all the horrible episode again, often beating my husband in my sleep, shouting and screaming at my father in my nightmares. I became very depressed.

After about ten weeks with the group I confronted my mother and father. I locked them in my house and told them how much I hated them and why. At last my mother believed me. As soon as they had gone home I felt so much better for getting it off my chest. Now the healing process could begin. I am now in control of my emotions. I don't have nightmares anymore and my marriage is even better for having gone through this trauma. I don't think I could have done it without the love, understanding and thoughtfulness of my husband whose love and devotion spurred me to get treatment in the first place. I have now forgiven my father, although I will never forget. He knows this, my mom knows this and now we get along OK. We understand each other, and keep our distance. My life has meaning for the first time and I can honestly say, there is life after abuse.

Dorothy's story

Dorothy has never attended a Survivors group. She only came to
see us once, after she had taken an overdose. Then she sent us
her story. She wrote, "I am sorry that my spelling is so poor,
that's what comes from having very little schooling. I began to
tear this letter up but decided it may be helpful to others." We
think so too. We found her letter so powerful we asked if we
could publish it in full. Here it is.

As far as I am concerned, my life began at the time my
daughter was conceived. If I go back to my childhood or my
teenage years I am only filled with sadness. I would rather die
than live those years again.

I have been told that I was a perfect baby and a very bubbly
child who loved being around people. I was a tomboy who
enjoyed school and was very bright and always eager to please. I
was a chatterbox with a constant giggle and was loved by everyone. Around seven or eight years old I suddenly changed and
became sullen and withdrawn. I was always alone and would not
talk to anyone or smile. I wouldn't go to school. I played hookey
or if I did go to school I was disruptive.

I ran away a lot and spent most of my time alone in secluded
fields and isolated areas. I began to have fits and blackouts and
memory loss. No one could understand why my personality had
changed so suddenly—no one but myself and my older brother.
He was the one who abused me time after time after time. I
never told anyone what was happening to me and I grew more
insecure and afraid as time passed.

I now remember exactly what my brother did to me. I
remember the cold bathroom floor, my hands tucked tightly
under my chin and the fear and silent tears. I remember well the
pain as things were pushed inside me, things left inside me and
the blood between my rigid legs. I remember the penis in my
body and in my mouth, I remember the taste. I remember the
throbbing inside my head and my ears and I remember always
waking up under a pile of coats in a dark hall.

I think the teens were the worst. In my early teens I wanted
to be like the other girls, who all seemed to have boyfriends. Lots
of boys asked me out and I did go with one or two, but as soon
as a boy touched me I froze. I would just run, often for miles
without stopping only to fall down in a dead faint. I soon became

known as Miss Ice or Miss Fits. I found it difficult to cope with life and would often try to hide from it by running away and sleeping under hedges. Even though my brother had married and was no longer at home, I still hated being at home and I would do anything to get away from it.

I even pretended to be asleep in other people's houses, in the hope they might let me sleep over. I hated my body so much that I cut it with glass and razor blades. I put pepper into my eyes so I wouldn't have to look at anyone. I withdrew more and more and I seldom left my bedroom. I started writing stories but the stories took on a sordid side. I wrote about little girls being sexually abused and I drew pictures to go with the stories.

When my parents found my stories they forbade me to go to my room until bedtime. I hated not being able to go to my room, having no place to hide away, to feel safe and at peace. I ran away and ended up in another town where I sat all day in a church.

Eventually I was found collapsed in the middle of a busy road and taken to a hospital late at night. Two days later when they discovered who I was, I was transferred to Wakefield Hospital.

Eventually I got a job very close to home, as a nanny to a seven-month-old boy. The baby became very dependent on me as he seldom saw his parents. I loved this baby and was very happy. I had my own room with a lock on the door and my own warm bed. I loved the job and I was never ill all the 14 months I was there. Suddenly it ended. The baby and his parents moved to the coast. They wanted to take me with them, but my parents said No. I was depressed at the thought of going back home and I missed the baby more than I ever thought possible.

Once back home I withdrew again and the fits started. At 17, I met and married a 17-year-old boy. We found a cozy little house and made it really nice. I loved that little house and cleaned and polished it all day long. I loved to cook and try new dishes but soon my sparkling little house was gone and my bubble burst. Within the year the marriage was over, it was never consummated and had no real love in it. I was back home and my parents sold all our household goods.

I couldn't take it anymore. I had had enough of life and hated fighting it all the way. I felt my life was meaningless and would never go anywhere. I took a massive overdose and ended up in a coma. I lost most of my hair and became more depressed than ever. I ended up in a Psychiatric Hospital where I was given more electric-shock treatments. Then I was taken to Mansfield Infirmary and put into some sort of sleep that let me go back in time—back to being a little girl. I got to the age of eight and went into convulsions and this treatment wasn't used on me again. No one ever knew what had happened to me, though doctor after doctor tried in vain to find out. I must have put up a block and no one could get through to me, not even the best doctors. From the age of 14 to the age of 19 I had lots of electric-shock treatments and so many doctors that I never got used to one.

Still I told no one and still the fits continued, the depression, my attempts to kill myself. My fear of men grew stronger and I grew more and more withdrawn; until I seldom ever left the house and only spoke when spoken to. One night I woke and heard my mother talking to dad. She was wondering what would become of me and how it was a shame I'd been born. Dad said I would go into a home when they were old. I couldn't believe my parents had given up on me, even though I'd given up on myself.

Over the next few weeks I began to try to do better, by baking and sewing and going for walks on my own. Soon after, my mom introduced me to the man I married. He was 15 years older, needed to be taken care of, very lonely and very undemanding. I made a good wife and was determined to prove to everyone that I could make it. I had to show them that I wasn't abnormal like they thought, that I wouldn't end up in some home, that I was capable of doing anything other women did. I knew I could cope, I had to show others too.

My husband had everything. He had little sex drive, so we had no problem in that area. We made a nice home and I was fairly happy. I longed desperately for a child. As a young teenager my mother took me to several doctors, who always gave me an internal examination. I never knew why and I never asked, but I always blacked-out before the examination was completed. Now I was married and longing for a child, but it wouldn't happen.

I went to my doctor who gave me yet another examination. This time I didn't blackout but I nearly did when he told me I'd never be a mother. I couldn't accept this. I wouldn't give up hope. I cried every month when I had my meaningless period. I would go through anything for a child and so asked for more medical help. In the hospital I underwent very long and almost unbearable examinations. I was told I'd never be able to conceive and also asked if I'd been sexually molested as a child. I went home in tears and for the next two years I went into every church I could find.

Eventually I got pregnant. While I was in labor I had flashbacks. I saw pictures of myself as a little girl. I was frightened and I tried to push it away but with each pain came a picture so clear it was lifelike. I saw myself on the bathroom floor and my brother too. By the time my daughter was born I'd completed the jigsaw puzzle but I was so happy with the gift of my child that I put it in the back of my mind again. I just wanted to concentrate upon this perfect extension of my life.

Later when my daughter was less dependent upon me, I began to reflect again upon my childhood pictures and my jigsaw. I began to analyze myself and my problems. I realized that I had never been abnormal, just a victim of circumstance. What my brother had done to me had left me scared and insecure. I couldn't trust those who were close to me and couldn't trust men. I had never been hugged, kissed or touched by my father. In fact I had never felt really loved by any man, not even my husband who was never romantic, never loving or warm. He was a selfish man and cruel in many ways to my daughter and myself.

After my daughter's birth I was told never to become pregnant again, but 12 years later I gave birth to a son. Things had been getting worse with my husband and when our son was just two-years old I left him. The next two years were a nightmare. I've never felt so isolated. I moved to a new house and a new town so I didn't only lose a marriage, but also my friends and family. My son was constantly ill and I knew no one. Now four years later I have a happy home full of warmth and love and laughter.

My daughter is almost 18 and my best friend. She's engaged to a good boy and I look forward to having him extend my family by becoming my son-in-law. My daughter works hard and enjoys life. She thinks a great deal of her five-year-old brother. It's not easy to be a mother to a young boy when you reach middle age and have no man in your life, but it's an adventure I wouldn't want to miss. My son is full of energy and loves to bring me snails and worms and gets me to climb trees with him, and put on my boots and take him fishing. My daughter and my son are the reason I live and my reason for ever being born. I've so much love from these two young people that I could never want for love again.

The sexual abuse was very dirty and painful and so I associate pain and fear with sex and with men. I blacked-out because I didn't know how else to deal with it. I became distrustful of all people and I've isolated myself most of my life. Now at 43 and alone, it is harder and I do get lonely. I often wonder what it would be like to be held by a tender loving man. To be able to do what others take for granted.

I would like to have confidence and be able to walk out of my home without feeling the whole world is looking at me. My brother is free and he had his childhood and his teens, his marriage and he got no punishment. I am a prisoner in my own body. I was denied my childhood and my teens and I've lost two marriages. I sometimes hate my brother and wish him dead most of the time

I just feel nothing towards him. I try not to think about it all, but every now and then I have nightmares, always the same. I'm always sobbing, always bleeding, always in pain with him forcing things into my vagina. I understand myself now, I was abused terribly for some years, damaged in mind and body, I needed my parents but they weren't there. I have been paying all my life for my brother's crime.

Further reading

Other accounts of sexual abuse can be found in the books below.

Autobiography

Angelou, Maya. *I Know Why the Caged Bird Sings,* Bantam Books, Inc., 1983.
Armstrong, Louise. *Kiss Daddy Goodnight: Ten Years Later.* Pocket Books, 1987.
Danica, Elly. *Don't. A Woman's Word.* Cleis Press, 1988.
Petersen, Betsy. *Dancing with Daddy: A Childhood Lost & a Life Regained.* Bantam Books, Inc., 1992.
Somers, Suzanne. *Wednesday's Children: Adult Survivors of Abuse Speak Out.* The Putnam Publishing Group, 1992.

Fiction

Harrison, Kathryn. *Thicker Than Water.* Random House, 1991.
Morris, Michelle. *If I Should Die Before I Wake.* Dell Publishing Company, Inc., 1982.
Pearce, Flora. *Essie.* Ulverscroft Large Print Books, Ltd., 1991.
Vachss, Andrew. *Shella: A Novel.* Alfred A. Knopf, Inc., 1993.
Walker, Alice. *The Color Purple.* Pocket Books, 1990.

3

The Damage Caused by Sexual Abuse

IN THE LAST CHAPTER Jane, Eileen, Anita, Pam and Dorothy shared their own experiences of being sexually abused as children. Each woman's story is different. They were abused in different ways, by different people and for different lengths of time. Linking each woman's experience, however, is the pain they suffered, the damage done to them, and the ways they have struggled to survive. Each woman is at a different stage of working through her difficulties, but each has found courage and hope and has come to realize that, as Pam says, "there is life after abuse."

After the first meeting of a Survivors group, the group members say that they feel relieved and surprised to find they are not alone. They and other people have had similar experiences and have suffered similar problems as a result of being abused. By the beginning of the second meeting each woman has usually found some reason why she thinks she is still different from the rest of the group and why she shouldn't be there:

- I was only abused once.
- I was abused by a woman.
- The abuser didn't have intercourse with me.
- I was a teenager when I was abused.
- It started when I was a baby.

- The abuser wasn't a family member.
- I've never tried to kill myself.
- What happened to me doesn't seem as bad as what's happened to everyone else.

Many Survivors feel frightened and distressed when they see how sexual abuse has damaged other Survivors. They may try to convince themselves that they haven't been as badly affected by focusing on the differences between their experiences and other people's. Survivors often feel guilty, ashamed and worthless, so emphasizing these differences may be a way of saying "I don't deserve to be helped." Feeling different is also a lifelong habit for many Survivors.

All of the women in chapter 2 were abused by male family members (a father, two stepfathers, a brother and an uncle). However, abusers can also be women, friends, strangers, older children and people in positions of authority. Abuse includes many different types of physical acts or may not even involve physical contact. The physical acts of abuse described in chapter 2 include exposing genitals, fondling, masturbation, intercourse and penetration with objects. The acts are different but they are all acts of abuse. Sexual abuse may also involve animals, group sex, rituals and torture. Sexual abuse can occur on a regular basis over many years or it may happen on only one occasion.

Jane, Eileen, Anita, Pam and Dorothy have all had different experiences but all were sexually abused. Try to remember what you were thinking as you were reading chapter 2. Were you emphasizing the differences between your experiences and theirs? Your story may be quite different from theirs but if you have had an inappropriate or unwanted sexual experience you have suffered abuse.

The women in chapter 2 were all affected both as children and as adults by being sexually abused. Some Survivors develop serious problems in many areas of their lives and are unable to cope. Others may appear to cope very well on the surface, but are struggling with fears and insecurities underneath. Table 1 shows the most common long-term effects of sexual abuse. Frequently Survivors do not realize the extent to which they have been affected by being sexually abused.

Before I joined a Survivors group, I felt confused—did the abuse really happen? I even thought I'd come through it unscathed; it hadn't really affected me. I was narrow-minded, everything had affected, me, my personality, my sexuality, my relationships with everyone—parents, adults, friends, male and female. Who was I? Who am I? *Jocelyn*

Before Jocelyn joined a Survivors group she felt that sometimes getting depressed, having feelings that she couldn't cope with and not liking to make close friendships was just part of her personality. She was amazed to find that the other women in the group had similar feelings and difficulties. Gradually the patterns began to appear and she realized that her present difficulties were connected to her childhood abuse. Like Jocelyn, Survivors often think:

• That's just the way I am.
• I'm not very lovable, that's why I keep having disastrous relationships.
• I'm not very bright, that's why I didn't do well at school.
• I'm a loner.
• I'm a weak person.
• I'm not very nice.
• I was a difficult child.

Many Survivors find it difficult to accept that being sexually abused as a child can continue to affect them many years later. It may seem too fantastic, or too frightening an idea to believe. David Finkelhor, a U.S. researcher, has tried to explain how sexual abuse affects a child and leads to long-term problems. He suggests four ways in which childhood sexual abuse causes problems:

• Traumatic sexualization
• Stigmatization
• Betrayal
• Powerlessness

Wakefield Survivors found this model very useful in explaining how sexual abuse can fundamentally affect a person's life. Take a closer look at this model below.

Finkelhor's model:
Four ways in which sexual abuse causes problems

Traumatic sexualization

Children usually feel frightened, confused or distressed when they are being sexually abused and may also experience physical pain. Their early experience of sexual behavior and sexuality are traumatic and inappropriate. The physical and emotional pain involved in sexual abuse means that sex becomes associated with bad feelings. These feelings can continue into adulthood and lead to fears and phobias about sex, and a dislike or avoidance of sex, touching or intimacy. Survivors may have difficulties in becoming aroused or reaching an orgasm, and may experience flashbacks to the abuse during sex. In chapter 2 Anita and Dorothy describe their dislike of sex and the ways they tried to avoid it.

However, not all children experience such distress at the time they are being abused as not all abusers are brutal. Anita loved the kisses and hugs she received from her stepfather at the beginning. Sometimes children enjoy parts of the touching and many experience sexual pleasure and orgasm.

My father would put his hand between my legs and rub my clitoris (I didn't know what it was then). I would always feel a great deal of shame afterwards because what he was doing felt nice. *Sandra*

However non-brutal the abuse is, when children are sexually abused they are exposed to sexual experiences which are inappropriate or too advanced for their age or level of development. They are also given confusing and incorrect messages about sexual behavior.

Survivors grow up confused about their own sexual feelings and normal sexual behavior. Their sexual experience, knowledge and identity is not allowed to develop naturally. This leads to sexual difficulties in adults ranging from fears and phobias about sex to preoccupation and obsessions with sex. Sexual difficulties are discussed in more detail in chapter 12.

Stigmatization

Children who are sexually abused usually feel there is something wrong and shameful about it even when they don't understand exactly what is happening. The abuser may blame the child for the abuse, tell her to keep the abuse secret and frighten her into silence. This secrecy makes the child feel that she has something to be guilty and ashamed about. Other people who are told or find out about the abuse may be shocked and blame the victim or put pressure on her to remain silent. This can add to the feeling of shame. Jane and Dorothy kept the secret of the sexual abuse all through their childhood. Although no threats were used they felt the stigma of the abuse and knew they had to remain silent. Adult Survivors often continue to keep the secret for fear of other people's reactions and because they feel ashamed.

Many Survivors blame themselves for the abuse and continue to feel responsible and guilty for anything bad that happens to them or to other people they know. Survivors often feel bad about themselves and different from other people. Because of this they isolate themselves from other people and avoid making close friendships. Eileen has spent most of her adult life feeling dirty, disgusted, ashamed and unfit to be a human being. She has never made close friends and has always felt different from other people. The feelings of shame and guilt can lead Survivors to abuse and punish themselves with drugs, alcohol or through self-mutilation and suicide attempts.

Dorothy's feelings of stigma and shame were so great that she mutilated her body with glass and razor blades and by putting pepper in her eyes so she wouldn't have to look at anyone. She also tried to kill herself. Dorothy still keeps her distance from other people and feels the whole world is looking at her when she leaves the house.

Some Survivors feel so different that they see themselves as outsiders in society, unable to care about what happens to them or what they do. Survivors who feel like this may start to behave in criminal or antisocial ways and end up in court or prison.

Feelings of guilt and shame are dealt with in section II.

Betrayal

When a child is abused, especially by a relative or someone she knows and likes, her trust in that person is betrayed. Abusers often build up trusting relationships with a child and may make her feel wanted and cared for before abusing her. They manipulate her trust and vulnerability and disregard her well-being. The child may also feel betrayed if other non-abusing adults do not support and protect her.

Anita was vulnerable, she received very little attention from her real parents and was overwhelmed by the affection shown to her by her new stepfather. She soon trusted him but the kissing and hugging turned to abuse. Anita's trust was betrayed.

Furthermore Anita's mother betrayed Anita by failing to protect her from the abuse. Jane's stepfather also betrayed Jane's trust in her family and her new daddy by abusing her. Despite Anita's and Jane's tears and obvious distress, their abusers continued to abuse them. Their well-being was disregarded and they were treated abusively by the very people who were supposed to love and protect them.

Betrayal can be experienced as a feeling of loss—loss of a trusting and loving relationship. This leads to feelings of grief and depression, or anger and hostility. Fear of betrayal can lead to mistrust of others, especially men, and cause Survivors to withdraw or feel uncomfortable in close relationships. In chapter 2 Dorothy describes her grief at not being able to trust and to form intimate relationships. At 43 she has resigned herself to being alone. On the other hand some Survivors become extremely dependent and clingy.

Betrayal by the very people one would expect could be trusted can result in Survivors having difficulties in judging how trustworthy other people are. Trustworthy people may be mistrusted, and trust put in those who do not merit it. This in turn makes the Survivor vulnerable to further abuse and exploitation of herself and her children.

Pam married at a young age and was physically abused by her first husband. Anita experienced further physical and sexual abuse as an adult. Survivors do not ask to be abused again and are not responsible for the abuse. However, sexual abuse may leave Survivors more vulnerable to further abuse, especially if they are unable to judge trustworthiness or feel compelled to cling to bad relationships. Relationship problems are discussed in section IV.

Powerlessness

A child experiences an intense sense of powerlessness when she is sexually abused. Her body is touched or invaded against her wishes and this may happen again and again. The abuser may

Table 1—Effects of sexual abuse

fears	not remembering	unable to get close
anxiety	what has happened	to people
phobias	for hours or days	marrying young to get
nervousness	(blanking-out)	away from home
nightmares	binge-eating	marital problems
sleep problems	self-induced vomiting	unable to love or
depression	compulsive eating	show affection to
shame	anorexia nervosa	children
guilt	no interest in sex	excessive fear for
feeling like a victim	fear of sex	children
lack of self-confidence	avoiding specific	alcohol problems
feeling different from	sexual activities	drug problems
others	feeling unable to say	employment problems
feeling self-conscious	no to sex	being re-victimized
feeling unable to take	obsessed with sex	criminal involvement
action or change	aggressive sexual	needing to be in
situations	behavior	control
feeling dirty	flashbacks (feeling of	delinquency
obsessed with	reliving parts of the	aggressive behavior
cleaning or washing	past)	bullying
constant worrying	hearing the abuser's	abusing others
thoughts	voice when he isn't	clinging and being
suicide attempts	there	extremely dependent
self-harming	seeing the abuser's	anger
(i.e., slashing arms)	face when he isn't	hostility
blackouts	there	distrusting people
fits	confusion about	difficulty in being able
	sexual orientation	to judge people's
		trustworthiness

trick or force the child into abuse. Even if she tells someone else she may not be able to make them believe her. The child repeatedly experiences fear and an inability to control the situation.

Many children attempt in their own way to try to control the situation and stop the abuse but their attempts are often useless. Jane sometimes managed to say no to her stepfather but he then treated all the family badly until she gave in. Jane felt no one would believe her if she tried to tell what was happening because her stepfather appeared to be such a nice man. She was trapped.

Anita's mother stopped the abuse for two weeks but then it started again and continued even when Anita's mother was in the house. Anita had nowhere to turn, she was powerless. Pam had been unable to stop the abuse despite shouting, screaming and kicking, nor could she get her mother or the child-protection officer to believe her.

The powerlessness experienced in sexual abuse can lead to

long-term feelings of being unable to take action or change situations. Survivors thus feel powerless to prevent further abuse and may end up feeling like victims all their lives. Powerlessness also results in fears, anxiety, phobias and nightmares. Survivors may try to escape from their fears and feelings of powerlessness by running away from home or from school, or by withdrawing emotionally. Emotional withdrawal can take the form of depression, blanking-out or blacking-out, or living in a fantasy world.

Many of the women in chapter 2 described their tantrums, bad behavior, and running away from school or home as a child. Dorothy ran away from home and skipped school. She suffered from anxieties and nightmares and later retreated into depression, fits and blackouts. Pam suffered from nightmares, depression and agoraphobia. Pam's healing really began when she confronted her parents and was able to feel powerful and effective again.

Survivors may also react to feeling powerless by attempting to take control and by making themselves feel more powerful in some way. Eating disorders often involve a desperate attempt to exert some control, by controlling food intake and body weight. Some Survivors try to feel more powerful by aggressive behavior, or by bullying, being abusive and controlling other people.

It has been suggested that women Survivors usually react passively to this feeling of powerlessness whereas male Survivors frequently react by trying to exert their own power. If this is true we would expect more women Survivors to become anxious and depressed and more male Survivors to become controlling, aggressive or abusive. Anxiety, depression and eating disorders are discussed in Section III.

Making the connections

Survivors are often affected by being sexually abused not only as children but also in adult life. Many Survivors do not realize that their present problems are linked to their past experience. David Finkelhor describes four processes by which sexual abuse causes problems. Some of these processes are common to other types of abuse or trauma. Physical abuse by a parent can also cause a child to experience a sense of powerlessness, betrayal and even stigmatization. In accidents and disasters victims frequently experience an overwhelming sense of their own powerlessness and, without help, this can develop into a problem or difficulty. This is being recognized more and more as post-trauma stress.

When disasters happen, counseling services are usually brought in to help victims and rescuers deal with the terrifying experiences they have been through. Being sexually abused is like being involved in a disaster, a disaster that may be a one-time incident or may be repeated over many years. Sexual abuse also has the added impact of traumatic sexualization not found in other types of abuse or disasters. Survivors of sexual abuse need counseling, support and help, just as much as victims of disasters. Sexual abuse has immediate and long-term effects. Without help these problems can continue indefinitely. With help Survivors can and do overcome these problems.

Survivors are damaged to different degrees by their experiences. This does not depend on what has happened physically. A Survivor who has been raped will not necessarily be more damaged than a Survivor who has been touched. The degree of damage depends on the degree of traumatic sexualization, stigmatization, betrayal and powerlessness, the child has experienced. This in turn depends on a number of factors such as:

- who the abuser was
- what took place
- what was said
- how long the abuse went on
- how the child felt and how she interpreted what was happening
- if the child was otherwise happy and supported
- how other people reacted to disclosure or discovery of the abuse
- how old the child was

This book aims to help you understand how your problems are linked to the abuse and how they can be overcome. For now, just try accepting that being sexually abused will have affected you in some way. This isn't making excuses for your problems; it's a way of trying to understand them and overcome them. You deserve that understanding and help. No matter how small your problems are they are worth working on; no matter how big your problems are you can overcome them.

For many Survivors accepting the link between sexual abuse

and their present difficulties can be distressing and frightening. They don't want to believe that after all these years the abuse is still affecting them. Accepting the link, as Jocelyn found, can also be enlightening and hopeful. Problems that could not be explained become understandable and with understanding comes the possibility and hope of healing.

Exercises

Before doing these exercises read notes on writing in chapter 1.

1. Look at the effects of sexual abuse listed in Table 1 and check any that apply to you.
2. Write an account of how you feel you have been affected as a child and adult by being sexually abused. It is impossible to know for certain but use what you have read to re-examine your life and make the connections between the sexual abuse and what has happened since.

Further Reading

Finkelhor, David. *A Source Book in Child Sexual Abuse.* Sage Publications, 1986.

4
Why Me?

Many survivors have asked themselves the question "Why Me? Why did he choose ME to abuse?" They often answer this question by blaming themselves for what happened:

- I must have been flirting.
- It must have been something bad in me that he could see.
- Maybe I led him on.
- I was big for my age and well-developed.
- It was because I was the youngest/oldest.
- I sat on his knee and hugged him, and liked it.
- It's my fault because I was so quiet and shy—it wouldn't have happened if I'd been noisy and sociable like my sister.

Sometimes the abuser has given a reason for the abuse:

- It's because you don't show your feelings—I'm teaching you.
- You look like your mother.
- You're too friendly with your girlfriends—I'm stopping you from becoming a lesbian.
- I'm punishing you for being naughty.

A child might believe such excuses and the adult Survivor may go on believing them and blaming herself for the abuse. These beliefs keep the Survivor silent and add to her feelings of guilt and shame.

Elaine's story

Susan, Anne and Elaine are sisters. All three were sexually abused by their stepfather when they were children. At the time, each one thought she had been specially chosen to be abused. They didn't realize it was happening to all of them. Susan thought she had been abused because she looked like her mother. Anne had been told by her stepfather that she was frigid and he was teaching her about love. Elaine, the youngest of the sisters, blamed herself for being so quiet and shy: "If I'd been more confident and sociable like Susan it wouldn't have happened." Each girl felt she had been singled out to be abused because of her looks, her behavior or her personality. None of them talked about what was happening to them.

When Elaine was 27 she became deeply depressed and tried to kill herself. For the first time in her life she told Susan what had happened to her. She couldn't believe what Susan said—that it had happened to her too. When they discovered that Anne had also been abused by their stepfather, all three sisters began to look again at why it had happened to them. They began to think it might not have been their fault after all and to see that it was their stepfather who was responsible for the abuse. Survivors usually blame themselves for what has happened. But sexual abuse doesn't start with a child, it starts with an abuser. There's nothing special or strange about a child who is being abused. It could happen to anyone. So why does it happen to one person and not another?

Finkelhor's model: Four steps before abuse occurs

We have already looked at David Finkelhor's model about the effects of abuse. Finkelhor has also studied the situations in which sexual abuse occurs and found that four things must happen before a child is abused:

- There is a person who wants to abuse.
- The person overcomes inhibitions about abusing.
- The abuser gets the child alone.
- The abuser overcomes the child's resistance.

We will discuss each of these steps below.

There is a person who wants to abuse

First, and most importantly, a victim must have come into contact with a person who wants to abuse a child. It is still not known why certain people want to abuse children. Some abusers have authoritarian and controlling personalities. They do not see children as other people, but as objects which they can use for their own benefit.

An abuser may be someone who feels socially and sexually inadequate and insecure with other adults. He wants to abuse children to get sexual gratification without risk of rejection. Some abusers are sexually aroused by children. Studies have found that some child abusers show a greater sexual response to photographic slides of children than to slides of adult women. An abuser may be someone who has been sexually, emotionally or physically abused himself as a child or adult.

He may try to make himself feel more powerful by victimizing someone else. The above are ways of trying to understand why a person wants to abuse a child—they are not excuses or justifications. The abuser is still responsible for the abuse. It is probable that a variety of factors combine to produce a person who wants to abuse but as yet there are no clear answers.

What we do know is that it is not a case of a person coming into contact with a certain child and suddenly becoming an abuser. Before the abuse occurs there is usually a period where the abuser fantasizes about what he is going to do to a child. The abuser's desire to abuse is not created by the child—it is there before the child appears.

The person overcomes inhibitions about abusing

People who want to abuse know that it is wrong to abuse children. At the very least they know it is illegal. Before they can put their fantasies into action they have to deal with any thoughts they may have that abusing is wrong.

There are a number of ways in which abusers attempt to do this. Many abusers drink alcohol before abusing. Alcohol lowers inhibitions and people then do things that they already want to do but might not have dared to do when sober. It has been found that in 30 to 40 percent of abuse cases abusers have drunk alcohol before abusing and 45 to 50 percent of child molesters have had drinking problems.

Drinking alcohol does not cause a person to sexually abuse a child. But if he already wants to abuse, drinking alcohol or taking drugs may release his inhibitions and allow him to act out his fantasies. Many abusers try to justify what they are doing:

- I'm just loving her.
- It's not intercourse so it's not abuse.
- It's sex education.
- He's too young to remember anyway.
- I'm not hurting her.
- He enjoys it.
- The law doesn't understand the special relationship I have with my daughter.
- She's my stepdaughter not my real daughter so it doesn't count.
- I'm keeping the family together.
- I was abused and it didn't harm me.
- She seduced me.

They manage to convince themselves that what they are doing is acceptable. They often justify their behavior in the same way to the child they are abusing and may even convince the child that they have a good reason for abusing. Whatever an abuser says, there is no good reason for abuse. Abuse does not benefit the child. In certain groups of people or families the sexual abuse of children may have become so common that it is thought to be normal.

Child pornography, although illegal in Canada, Great Britain and the U. S., is available in videos, books and photographs. Looking at child pornography, discussing it and exchanging it with friends encourages people to think that it is acceptable to use children for sex. Pedophiles (people sexually attracted to children) have publicly argued that sex with children should be legalized and that children are capable of giving informed consent to sex at the age of four. In this climate a potential abuser can convince himself that sexually abusing a child is a form of sexual liberation.

Child abuse is sometimes highly organized. Abusers know each other and may abuse together, either in families or in groups of friends. Abusers sometimes help and support each other by protecting each other, swapping information, and helping each other get jobs where they have access to children. They create an environment for themselves where child sexual abuse is seen as acceptable.

The abuser gets the child alone

For abuse to occur the abuser must get a child on her own or at least away from adults who would protect her. For fathers, stepfathers and other family members this is easy—bathtime, bedtime or when mothers are out at work or shopping. Abusers often plan ahead to get children on their own. For example, they take the child shopping or out to eat or encourage the mother to go out for the evening. Children may be especially at risk if one of their parents is absent or ill for a period of time or if their mother is in the hospital having a baby.

The abuser is often a trusted person, a family friend or family member so it is usually easy for him to get the child alone without anyone being worried or suspicious. Abusers often work on becoming a trusted person by befriending the family and gaining their confidence as well as the child's. Research has shown that approximately 75 percent of abusers are known to the child and 43 percent are family members. Many children may have come into contact with abusers but have not been abused because the abuser did not get the opportunity. Children who are abused are unlucky enough to have been alone with an abuser or away from people who could protect them.

The abuser overcomes the child's resistance

The child does not come into this situation until the end. The scene has already been set. The person is ready to abuse as soon as the right opportunity arises. He only has to make sure he can overcome any resistance the child might show.

It isn't difficult for an abuser to make sure the child does as he wants. Many children are taught that adults know best and that they should do as they are told. They don't attempt to resist. It's very hard for a child to object to what is happening or to disobey.

The child may not even understand that what is happening is wrong. The abuse may start at a very early age when the child is too young to comprehend what is going on.

Abusers make sure that children don't try to resist by using persuasion ("It's our special secret."), rewards (money, candy, gifts or simply not being in a bad mood) or threats ("You'll be put into a home."). When the abuse has happened once, this in itself can be used as a threat ("I'll tell what you've done.").

Physical violence may be threatened and in some cases used.

Children soon learn to lie still if the choice is between being sexually abused or being sexually abused and beaten up. Some children are given alcohol or drugs before they are abused.

Why did the abuse happen to me?

You may blame yourself by feeling you caused the abuser to abuse you or because you think you should have stopped him. A child does not cause abuse, an abuser does. For abuse to happen there must be an abuser who wants to abuse and who has overcome any misgivings he has about it. He must then find a place and time when he can abuse undisturbed and frighten or persuade the child into doing as he wants.

When Ron married Elaine's mother he came into daily contact with three young girls. He fantasized about touching them and carefully planned how he could put his fantasies into action. One night he had a few drinks, his wife was working a late shift and it was easy to get Elaine alone in her bedroom.

Afterwards he told himself he hadn't hurt her and she wouldn't remember anyway so he hadn't done anything wrong. He told Elaine not to tell anyone or she'd never see her mother again. Elaine hadn't been chosen because she was quiet and shy. She was abused because she was unlucky enough to find herself on her own with a man who had a desire to sexually abuse children. As Susan, Anne and Elaine talked to each other they began to realize that they hadn't caused their stepfather to abuse them. He was an adult who knew what he was doing was wrong. He was responsible.

"But I have been abused by three different people so it must have been my fault"

Survivors who have been abused by more than one person often feel that this proves that it's something about them which caused this to happen. However, it is not unusual for Survivors to have been abused by more than one person. Half the women in the Wakefield groups have been abused by more than one person and research has found that approximately 43 percent of abused women have been abused by a number of different men. Steps three and four in Finkelhor's model show why it is so common for a child to be abused more than once.

Step three—The abuser gets the child alone

The child's situation may make it easy for abusers to get access to a child. Jocelyn's parents took in roomers. She lived in close contact with a succession of men and this made her vulnerable to abuse. Having parents who are regularly absent or ill can also increase the danger.

Step four—Abuser overcomes the child's resistance

As discussed in chapter 3 children and adults who have been sexually abused are often vulnerable to further abuse. Sexual abuse results in a child feeling powerless and unable to protect herself. It is easy for another abuser to control a child who has already learned to do as she is told and remain silent. Some children feel so helpless and have been abused so often that they begin to accept abuse as a normal situation which has to be tolerated.

"It must be my fault because he didn't abuse my sisters and brothers or anyone else"

Abusers do not usually select one special child to abuse and then stop. They keep on abusing children whenever they get the opportunity or can create an opportunity. As Elaine's story shows, sisters (and brothers) may each spend years believing they are the only one in the family who has been abused. If one person has been keeping the abuse secret, other people have probably been doing the same thing. Survivors frequently discover that other family members have been abused by the same person. Thirty years after her own abuse Sandra discovered that three of her brothers had also been abused.

I have learned that three of my four brothers were also abused. So for all those years I kept quiet, my brothers did the same. Maybe if we had shared our secret, then we might have been able to work together to end the violence that was inflicted on us. We have all had difficulties in forming lasting relationships and now we all lay the blame at our father's door. *Sandra*

Discovering that other family members have been abused can be distressing but it does show that one person wasn't specifically chosen to be abused.

I was sexually abused by my uncle from the age of six or seven (maybe earlier) and I was convinced, until the age of 21, that I was the only person he had abused. I always wondered why he chose me to abuse and presumed that it was because I was the oldest. My sister was two years younger and almost always in the same bed while the abuse took place, but I always thought she was asleep and knew nothing of it. I thought that perhaps my uncle was under the impression that I enjoyed what was happening. I was glad when the abuse stopped. I thought he would never abuse again in case he was found out.

He then sexually abused my sister and my cousin. I found out about what had happened to my sister when I was 21. Everything came into the open when I was 22 and my cousin told me what he was doing to her. It broke my heart because I felt I could have done something earlier to prevent it from happening to her in the first place. *Sonia*

In the Wakefield Survivors groups at least 40 percent of the women's abusers are known to have abused other children. Finally this is how one Survivor now answers the question "Why did it happen to me?"

I was young, I was vulnerable and I was in the wrong place at the wrong time. I am not ashamed of what happened. I was not to blame. *Jocelyn*

Exercises

1. We have seen that Survivors usually think of reasons why they were chosen to be abused, such as, "I was quiet and shy." Write down any reasons why you think you might have been to blame for being abused or why you might have been specially chosen.
2. Abuse starts with a person who wants to abuse, not with a child. Write down your answers to these questions (see Finkelhor's steps 3 and 4):

• How did the abuser manage to get you on your own or in a position where he could abuse you?
• How did he get you to do as he wanted?

Finally look at your answers to question 1 again and ask yourself if you really are to blame for being abused.

Further Reading

Finkelhor, David. *Child Sexual Abuse: New Theory and Research.* Free Press, 1984.

5

Why Didn't I Tell?

Most survivors feel ashamed and guilty about the sexual abuse they suffered as children. They may feel especially guilty if it went on for months or years. Kate was sexually abused almost every week by her father from the age of two until she left home to get married at 18.

By the time I was 12 I knew it was wrong but I still didn't tell anyone. Why didn't I stop him? It must have been my fault. *Kate*

Many adults who were sexually abused as children believe they should have stopped the abuser, but how could they? A child is powerless in relation to an adult. Adults are physically more powerful than children and can resort to physical violence if necessary. Even if the abuser is the child's brother or a child of a similar age there are many reasons why she doesn't stop the abuse. Abusers rarely need to use physical force to coerce children into sexual relationships.

Children are brought up to obey and respect adults and so all adults, especially relatives, have sufficient authority to make children do whatever they want. They are also able to manipulate the child's feelings and use threats and promises to gain access to the child's body and to keep the child quiet. If it is impossible for a child to stop the abuser herself then her only way out is to tell someone else.

"Why didn't I tell ?" is one of the first questions Survivors ask. Some Survivors were abused on only one occasion but many

Survivors were abused repeatedly for periods ranging from a few months to over 20 years. Repeated abuse can lead Survivors to believe they must have been at least partly to blame because they allowed it to continue for so long and didn't stop the abuser themselves or tell someone else what was happening.

Why don't children tell?

If a child cannot stop the abuser herself why doesn't she tell someone else about the abuse? The child may have no one to tell, she may not know what to say. She may be frightened about the consequences if someone does believe her. She may feel so guilty and confused that she doesn't dare tell anyone because she feels it is her fault that it is happening. Table 2 lists some of the many reasons why children keep the secret and continue to suffer the abuse. We will look at some of these reasons in the rest of this chapter.

Who to tell?

I didn't tell—I had no one to tell. Nobody listened or noticed what was happening. Of course I never said anything out loud. I cried and I always had "tummy ache." I ran away from school, I even begged not to go out with the man who abused me, but none of these things altered anything. Circumstances stopped the abuse, not me, I couldn't stop it. *Jocelyn*

A child may be worried and distressed about the abuse she is suffering and decide to tell someone about it. Who can she tell? She can't just tell anyone about something she finds so confusing and shameful. The only people who may be able to help are parents, a trusted adult or someone in authority.

I don't really think I would have told anyone other than my mom because the secret was so big. *Jane*

Some children tell their mothers when they are being abused. Other children do not have a mother or close caregiver to whom they can talk about the abuse. The mother may have left home, be ill, dead or in a hospital. Mothers who are physically present may be preoccupied with their own problems or not have the time or patience to listen. Some children do not

Table 2—Why Children Don't Tell

Reasons why Survivors didn't tell when they were being abused.

1. Who to tell?
Parents dead, ill, absent.
Parents involved in the abuse.
No trustworthy adult around.
No opportunity to talk alone with a trusted adult.
Care-givers do not listen, involved with their own problems.
Frightened of parents.
Parents discourage talk about sex.
No friends.
No one to tell.

2. What to say?
Child too young to talk.
Child doesn't know how to describe what's happening.
Child is too embarrassed and ashamed to say what has happened.

3. Fears about the consequences of telling
(a) Threats from the abuser
No one will believe the child.
The child will be put into a home.
The child will not see her mother again.
The family will be split up.
Affection and love will be withdrawn.

Family and friends will reject the child.
No one will want to marry her.
Threatened or actual physical violence to the child, her family or pets. The abuser will kill himself or be put in prison.

(b) Fears concerning other people's reactions
No one will believe the child.
Mother will feel guilty.
Family will be hurt.
Mother will reject the child.
Other people will think the child is to blame.
Other people will think the child is dirty, contaminated or disgusting.
The child will be rejected and the abuser supported.

(c) Fears for the abuser
He will be hurt and rejected.
He will be put in prison.
He will get beaten up.
He will kill himself.

(d) Fears that telling won't help
Nothing will change.
No one can stop it.
Events will get out of control.
Fear of the unknown.
It might get worse.
The abuser is too powerful for anyone to stop him.

4. The child's confusion: Feelings and thoughts which prevent children from telling include:
Feelings of guilt, self-blame, shame and embarrassment.
Confusion—is it really happening? Is it wrong?
Thinking the abuse is normal.
Not understanding what is happening.
Believing she is the only one this has ever happened to.
Feeling dirty, contaminated, polluted.
Trapped by the secrecy.
Feeling she is being punished and deserves it.
Hoping the abuse won't happen again.
Blocking-off all memories of the abuse.
Feeling sorry for the abuser.
Not wanting to betray the abuser by telling.
Feeling it's her fault because she took candy, money, toys or other rewards from the abuser.
Enjoying the sexual stimulation.
Enjoying the affection, warmth or closeness.

have an adult with whom they have a close and confiding relationship.

Looking back with 20/20 hindsight, I know I would not and could not
have told anybody. The reasons I kept quiet were very real ones. The
relationship I had with my parents was not stable or loving enough to
give me confidence and trust in them. They would have considered
themselves and others first; what was best for me would not have
crossed their minds.
     My father would go crazy over minor, needless things. What would
he have done faced with this? My mother never listened to us. That
stands out in my mind. When I was crying and pleading with her not to
send me out one day with the abuser she said, "Why? Don't be silly, go
on, go!" Never, never listened, would ask "Why?" and then not wait for
an answer. *Jocelyn*

Even if the child has a good relationship with her parents
there are many reasons why she might not tell them about her
abuse. In some households sex is a taboo subject and the parents
are very strict so children are too frightened to bring up the
subject of sexual abuse. Embarrassment alone prevents many
children from talking; the shame and stigma that surrounds
sexual abuse makes it a very difficult subject to talk about.
Children who are being abused often withdraw into their shame,
distrust people and avoid getting close to anyone in order to
stop their secret from being discovered. They don't have a friend
to tell.

What to say

Even children who do have a good relationship with a trusted
adult may and it impossible to tell them. How do you tell? What
do you say? Many children are abused from a very young age, too
young to talk or too young to know what is happening to them.
Older children may not know how to talk about what is happening to them. They may blurt out, "Daddy keeps touching me."
They know what kind of touching they mean but the adult they
are talking to does not and may assume it is tickling or some
innocent form of touching.

I never told anyone of my abuse although at one point (when I was
approximately 11) I decided to do something about it because my
uncle actually tried to have intercourse with me and I couldn't take it
anymore. I tried to tell my mother but all that came out was that I

didn't want to stay at my uncle's anymore (I stayed at least once a week usually). I told her he used to come into the bathroom while I was undressed or in the bath and generally made me feel uncomfortable. I never actually revealed that he had touched me although I tried to give hints. *Sonia*

Even teenagers find it very difficult to talk about their sexual abuse. They may feel too ashamed and embarrassed and not know how to introduce the subject. They may not have listened to any sex education because of their bad associations with sex and so they do not understand what is happening or know how to talk about it.

Fears about the consequences of telling

I have often asked myself, "Why didn't I tell anyone about my sexual abuse?" Now I can actually think of a number of reasons. I didn't tell through fear of what might, or according to my abuser, what would have happened. I was always being told that I'd be put into a home and that once word got around no one would ever want to have anything to do with me. More so, I would never ever have a boyfriend.

According to the abuser my mother would not want to have anything to do with me, and as I didn't have a very good relationship with my mother I didn't find this hard to believe. I believe deep down that if I had come out with what was happening in a no-nonsense way to my mother the result would have been just the same. I am beginning to realize that I have been torturing myself with the question for no reason. I only wish I had realized a lot sooner. *Joanne*

Even if a child does have a trusted adult she can talk to, and does know how to describe what has been happening to her, she may still not tell because of her fears about what might happen. These fears are discussed below and include threats from the abuser, fears that she might not be believed, fears about other people's reactions, fears about what might happen to the abuser and a fear that nothing will change.

Threats from the abuser
My dad would say "You'll be sent away and I'll be sent to jail if you tell." Dad also said, "It will be our secret. Mommy and daddy will not love you anymore if you tell." So part of my fear, why I didn't tell mom, was because it would upset her and the family would split up. I cared about my mother and I couldn't bear to upset her. I had nobody else that I could tell at that time and I was frightened. *Lucy*

Children of all ages fear being rejected by, or separated from, their mothers. The abusers, especially fathers and stepfathers, play on this fear and often tell the child it will be her fault if the family is split up or if her mother is upset. The child is left feeling responsible for keeping the family together and saving her mother from being hurt, even though it is the abuser who is causing damage to the family.

Other threats can be equally powerful. "No one will want to marry you if they find out what you've been doing with me (Joanne's abuser)." Abusers often tell children that if they tell anyone they will be rejected, blamed and not believed.

Kirsty's stepdad often beat her and her brothers even when they had done nothing wrong. Kirsty was therefore very frightened when he began forcing her to have sex with him and threatening her with violence if she told anyone.

At first I was afraid to tell because he said if I told anyone I would be taken away from my mom and she wouldn't want to know me. Then came the threats and the beating, and if you knew what type of violent man he was then just the threats are enough, never mind the hitting itself. I think the reason why I couldn't tell was that I was scared of what he would do to me and also I couldn't stand the thought of being taken away from my mom. *Kirsty*

Some abusers use physical violence to force their victims to have sex with them. Others threaten violence towards the child, or towards other people. The abuser may threaten to beat the child's mother or brothers and sisters or to torture or kill her pets. "If you tell anyone what is happening you will never see your dog again."

An abuser may even frighten the child by threatening to kill himself if the secret is revealed. Violence and threats of violence are easy ways to frighten children into silence, although threats concerning the consequences of telling for the child or the family are more common.

Fears about other people's reactions

Children often do not tell about the abuse because of their fears about how other people will respond. The most common fear is that they will not be believed and this is often reinforced by the abuser. It is a child's word against an adult's and the adult may be well-liked and respected in the community.

Nowadays, because of television and newspaper coverage, people are aware that child sexual abuse does happen. Only a few years ago it was thought to be a rare occurrence, so even if there were trusted adults around for a child to tell, the adult would probably have found it difficult to believe and would have had little idea what to do about it. Children often fear that telling will hurt other people, particularly their mothers and families. They may also fear that other people will think of them as dirty and contaminated and will not want to know them anymore. Their own feelings of guilt and shame cause them to fear that they will be blamed and that others will support the abuser, not them.

Fears for the abuser

Many children love their abuser despite the abuse and do not want their abuser to be hurt by the abuse becoming known. They are concerned that their mothers and families will reject and punish the abuser. Children also fear that if they tell about the abuse the abuser might be put in prison, be beaten up or even kill himself. They continue to put up with the abuse rather than put their abuser in danger.

Fears that telling won't help

The child may feel that even if she does tell, nothing can be done to stop the abuse.

Our family lived with my grandfather and an aunt in a very small apartment. I had to share my mother's bed for the first five years of my life. My brother, the abuser, slept in the same bedroom as my parents and me. Because there was no space for either him or me to move out of our parents' bedroom I saw no way the abuse could stop. When bedtime came and he wanted to abuse me I was there. There was nowhere to go. Pretending to be asleep did not help either. No way out—he said he'd kill me if I told anyone. *Ingrid*

Ingrid believed the sleeping arrangements at home made it impossible for anyone to stop her brother abusing her. In chapter 2 Anita and Pam described how they told their mothers and others about the abuse but no action was taken to stop it. The child's own feelings of powerlessness may also make her feel that no one else could change the situation.

Many children only want the abuse to be stopped and are

frightened that they will make the situation worse if they do tell. They fear that they will have no control over what happens next. Other people may be told, Child Protective Services may need to separate family members, the police may be brought in. They fear that they will have no say in what happens and that the situation could get worse.

These are rational and realistic fears. Often children do not tell about the abuse because they fear the consequences. Many of these fears are rational—the child may not be believed, she may be put into a home. Often, though, it is the child's perception of the abuser's power that stops her telling. She believes that nothing can stop the abuser, that he will punish her and that everyone will be persuaded to believe him. The abuser used his adult authority and cunning to manipulate the child into a sexual relationship which leaves the child feeling powerless and unable to protect herself. It is difficult for a child in this situation to understand that other adults may not be powerless in relation to the abuser.

The child's confused feelings

I wondered if what was happening was normal or if I was imagining it all. *Jane*

A child who is being abused is put in a frightening and confusing situation. They may never have heard of anything like this happening. Nobody has told them it is right, but nobody has told them it is wrong. Everyone may like and respect the man who is doing these things. It may be daddy.

They may think, like Jane: "Maybe it isn't happening at all, maybe I've made it up" or "Everyone else likes him so he can't be bad—it must be me." Children are brought up to trust adults (especially the family members and friends) and to do as they are told. Abuse puts the child into a state of confusion.

One of the main reasons why I felt that I couldn't tell anyone was that I had lived for the first seven years of my life trusting my mom and doing as I was told. Now there was a man who was my new daddy and whom mom said that I could trust. A major factor for me was the confusion I felt between doing what I was told by him, being obedient and not telling my mom; and being disobedient and telling my mom. I had in the past kept secrets for my mom and she had been proud of me for doing so. Perhaps this was another secret to be kept. *Jane*

I never told anyone because I was told it was a secret. As a trusting small child, I believed what my Granddad (the abuser) said. *Polly*

Abuse often begins gradually, an affectionate hug progressing over weeks or years into touching, intercourse and oral sex. Children may enjoy and encourage the initial warmth and contact but then feel frightened and guilty as the abuse progresses and they find it unpleasant or realize it is wrong. In this situation children often feel they have encouraged the abuse. They feel they have implicated themselves and only got what they've asked for. How can they tell when telling will mean revealing their own guilt? If the abuse starts suddenly children are often too frightened or stunned to say anything. They hope it won't happen again. But when it does how can they tell when they didn't tell before?

When it began I was prevented from telling by the initial guilt, shame and confusion. The longer it continued the more incriminated I felt. *Jane*

Other ways children have of coping with the trauma of sexual abuse is to block-out their thoughts about it, to pretend it isn't happening, or to retreat into a fantasy world.

I don't remember how the abuse began, I was too young. I think it must have happened gradually, otherwise I would remember the first time. But when it became more serious, before I entered school, I needed to find a way out for me to escape the abuse. I could not physically escape, but while there was nowhere to go for my body, I could send my mind away. Again I do not remember how it started but I clearly remember how I developed my own fantasy world in which to escape while I was being abused. This fantasy became as real to me as if I was physically there. During the abuse I sent my mind where I was liked by everyone and felt safe and I left my body behind to be used. Sometimes the deception was so great that I could hardly feel what was happening to me. *Katarina*

Children can't tell if they've convinced themselves the abuse isn't happening. Children can block-off the abuse so completely that they do not think of it at all when it isn't actually taking place.

I blocked-out the whole thing as if it had never happened so I never told anyone because in my mind it hadn't happened. That is until a few years ago when I started to have flashbacks. I can't remember if I was blackmailed or threatened or told it was a secret. I somehow felt detached from it all as though I watched and it wasn't really me.
Margaret

After the abuse has ended many people block-off the memories and forget about it until something triggers the memories again. Some abusers give candy, money or other rewards to the child after the abuse and this confuses the child even more. She feels it was her own fault because she accepted a reward and so she cannot tell anyone. Mary was given some marbles after she was abused—she didn't dare tell her mother about the abuse because she wasn't allowed to play with marbles. Shirley was abused by a store owner who gave her candy afterwards. She couldn't tell her mother because she knew she shouldn't take candy from strangers.

Giving a child money or presents often leaves the child feeling confused about her role in the abuse and makes it difficult for her to tell anyone about the abuse. For some the sexual contact is not always an unpleasant experience. Children who get enjoyment from the sexual stimulation often feel that because they felt some pleasure they encouraged the abuse and therefore cannot tell anyone.

Children do not enjoy being sexually abused but they may enjoy some of the things that go with it. They may enjoy the attention or affection, especially if they get very little elsewhere. They may enjoy the physical stimulation before it goes too far or before they feel confused and guilty about what is happening. Sexual abuse, however, involves more than affection, attention and physical stimulation. It also involves betrayal of the trust a child has in an older person, the manipulation of a child's feelings and inappropriate sexual contact.

The feelings of guilt and shame surrounding sexual abuse are enough to prevent most children from telling anyone what is happening to them. They may feel dirty and polluted. They may feel guilty because they initially enjoyed the physical contact or the attention or because they accepted money or candy. The child's attempt to make sense out of a situation she does not understand usually leaves her feeling confused and ashamed and unable to tell anyone about the abuse.

Breaking free from the guilt

You may have been feeling ashamed and guilty for many years because you have been blaming yourself for not stopping the abuse. After working through this chapter you may begin to realize it was impossible for you to stop the abuser yourself and that there were many good reasons why you couldn't tell someone else about the abuse.

Understanding your reasons for not telling will not make the guilt and shame disappear overnight because you have been carrying these feelings for a long time. You may understand intellectually that you couldn't stop the abuser but may still feel guilty. It can take a while for your feelings to catch up with your thoughts. Work through the exercises at the end of this chapter and do them again every time you start to blame yourself for the abuse. In time the feelings of shame and guilt will fade. Here is Anita's description of why she didn't tell:

At the beginning I was very young and I didn't understand what was happening. As I grew to realize things weren't right I felt more and more uncomfortable. I didn't know how to tell. At first I thought maybe I was imagining things then I thought nobody would believe me because it was all so fantastic. Things like this just didn't happen. As I got a bit older and now knew for certain it wasn't my imagination, I wanted to tell but it had now gone on for some time, and I'd let it.

At first when my stepdad hugged and kissed me I'd longed to feel like I did. I missed my daddy so much and my mom had never been affectionate. I kissed and hugged him back and felt really special, but when the touching started I felt uncomfortable but I couldn't tell as I felt so ashamed and guilty. I'd craved love and attention and I had finally got it so therefore I'd brought it all on myself. It was all my fault and I deserved to suffer. My mom had already had one bad marriage, now she was happy with my stepdad and I couldn't spoil everything by telling her what he was doing to me.

Time went on and things got worse and worse: he'd appear from nowhere, he'd seem to be everywhere at once, every corner I turned in the house, everytime I passed his hands would be touching me. Each time I was alone he'd be there and each time he'd do more and expect more and more. Every time I swore to myself it wouldn't happen again. I'd tell, but how, what could I say, where would I start? I would hurt my mom so much and probably make her hate me. He'd also started telling me I must never ever tell because no one would ever understand and lots of bad things would happen to both of us if I ever did. *Anita*

Exercises

Doing these exercises may help you deal with the feelings of guilt, self-blame and shame.

1. You may wonder why you didn't stop the abuser. Adult Survivors often forget how small and powerless they were in comparison to their abuser. Doing this exercise helps you remember the differences in physical size and strength between you and the abuser at the time of the abuse.

- Find photographs of yourself and (if possible) the abuser at the time the abuse began.

or

- Draw a picture of yourself and the abuser at that time.

or

- Compare the difference in size between adults and children of the age you were when the abuse began. Would it be physically possible for a child to prevent a bigger child or adult from harming them? Remember that the difference wasn't just one of physical size and strength but of power and authority too.

2. Look at the list of reasons (Table 2) why children don't tell that they are being abused. Check any reasons that applied to you. You may be able to add to the list.
3. Write your own story of why you didn't tell anyone at the time the abuse was occurring.

6

Silent Ways of Telling

THE LAST CHAPTER LOOKED AT HOW CHILDREN are usually unable to tell anyone that they are being sexually abused. They try to hide their dreadful secret and suffer in silence but they are usually experiencing very strong feelings inside: feelings of fear, depression, guilt, shame, anger, confusion, helplessness and despair.

It's hard for a child to hide feelings like this completely. These feelings tend to leak out in some way, in changed behavior or moods. People may notice the changes without realizing that they are signs of distress, signs that the child is being sexually abused. Instead, the child may be thought to be going through a phase, to be bad or even crazy. We have called these signs *silent ways of telling* because, although the child remains silent about the abuse, the signs are there for anyone who is able or willing to read them.

Today, with more knowledge of sexual abuse, we are learning to pay attention to children's bad or strange behavior and ask "What are they trying to say?" Looking back at their childhood the women in the Wakefield Survivors groups are now able to understand their own behavior. Many of these women had thought they were difficult children but now realize they were reacting to the abuse, attempting to protect themselves, and silently telling about the abuse.

Some of the signs children show at the time they are being abused or in the years afterwards are shown in Table 3. Some

Survivors showed few signs or experienced only mild problems as children, while others showed a whole collection of severe problems and symptoms. It is important to recognize that children who are not victims of sexual abuse may also experience some of the difficulties described in Table 3.

This table is intended only to help Survivors recognize the signs they were showing in their own childhood rather than as a method of diagnosing sexual abuse In this chapter we discuss some of these signs in more detail. Many of the behaviors that abused children develop to protect themselves or release their distress continue into adulthood. Looking at why certain childhood behaviors developed can help an adult Survivor understand and accept the child she was and the person she is now.

Eating and excreting

Children who are sexually abused experience a sense of powerlessness. Their bodies and feelings are invaded and they are unable to protect themselves or control what is happening to them. Feeling out of control is usually a frightening experience and people often react by attempting to take back control in some way.

Children have few ways of taking control, but eating and excreting are two ways in which they can control their bodies. Mothers of young children know all too well that battling with children over food and potty training is rarely successful. Disturbances in eating and excreting are therefore obvious ways in which children can consciously or unconsciously attempt to take back control over their bodies and show their resistance to adult authority.

The part of our nervous system which controls digestion and excretion is affected by stress, depression, fear and anxiety.

Symptoms of depression and anxiety include lack of appetite, overeating, gastric problems, nausea, diarrhea and constipation. Changes in eating and excreting patterns are common signs of distress.

Excretion problems

These problems include bedwetting, daywetting, soiling, constipation and retaining urine. All children wet and soil themselves when they are young. Remaining dry at night may come very slowly to some children. However, wetting and soiling which

Table 3—Silent Ways of Telling: Childhood Signs of Sexual Abuse

The following signs suggest a child is being sexually abused:
Displaying too much sexual knowledge for their age.
Inappropriate sexual behavior, i.e., tongue kissing.
Writing stories about sex or abuse.
Drawing pictures about sex or abuse.
Sexually-transmitted diseases.

The following signs do not necessarily mean a child is being sexually abused. They indicate that something is upsetting the child:
Eating problems
Refusing to eat
Overeating
Compulsive eating
Binging

Binging and vomiting (bulimia nervosa)
Abusing laxatives
Anorexia nervosa
Excreting problems
Wetting
Bed-wetting
Retaining urine
Soiling
Constipation
Diarrhea
Retaining feces
Smearing feces
Changes in behavior or mood
Withdrawing from people
Fearful of being alone with certain people
Not making close friendships
Depression
Anxiety
Phobias
Nightmares
Difficulty sleeping
Constantly tired
Suicide attempts
Obsessional behavior or thoughts

Tantrums
Clinging to adults
Acting younger than their age
Running away from home
Disruptive behavior at home
Disruptive behavior at school
Truancy
Under achievement at school
Over achievement at school
Bullying
Fighting
Aggressive or violent behavior
Stealing
Frequent illnesses, i.e., stomachache, rashes, sore genitals
Frequent accidents
Self-mutilation or self-abuse, i.e., slashing, scratching
Alcohol/drug abuse

reappear after a period when the child has been dry and clean, or goes on for an excessive length of time, often indicates some form of distress.

When the child is being sexually abused, wetting and soiling can also be a conscious or unconscious attempt to keep the abuser away by making herself dirty and smelly. Adult Survivors sometimes still experience problems with bedwetting.

Eating problems
Eating problems include refusal to eat, undereating and overeating. In teenagers this can develop into eating disorders such as anorexia nervosa, bulimia and compulsive eating (see chapter 11). Eating helps to blot-out bad feelings and memories, As the

food is swallowed down so are the feelings.

Overeating is an attempt to use eating to cope with bad feelings. As with wetting and soiling, overeating can be a conscious or unconscious attempt by the child to protect herself from the abuser. She may feel that, if she makes herself fat and unattractive, she will be left alone.

The look of disgust on my brother's (the abuser's) face when he looked at me is still fresh in my mind. So I thought "If he hates me fat, then maybe he will not abuse me anymore if I get fatter." So I began to eat huge amounts and gradually put on weight. It didn't stop the abuse but it increased the humiliation. *Katarina*

Not eating can be a way of attempting to regain control but can also be an attempt at self-protection—becoming too thin to be attractive, fading away, ultimately dying.

Inappropriate sexual behavior

Young children usually have very little knowledge of sexual behavior. Children who have been abused sometimes act out what has happened to them with their toys, with other children, with adults, or they show it through their paintings and stories. If this is not recognized as a sign of sexual abuse the child may be blamed and thought to be rude or abusive. When Kate was four-years old she was caught acting out the sexual behavior she had learned from being abused and was accused of sexually abusing a boy of her own age. Dorothy (see chapter 2) wrote stories and drew pictures about sexually abused girls and was punished for her bad behavior by being forbidden to spend time in her bedroom.

Sudden changes in behavior or moods

When a child is being sexually abused her behavior may suddenly change. The outgoing child becomes quiet and withdrawn; the well-behaved child becomes disruptive; the easy-going child becomes sulky and moody.

Adults who do not understand that this is a sign of distress may criticize or punish the child. Children can come to believe that they really are bad and so deserve to be abused and these feelings may continue in the adult. Some of these changes in behavior and mood are discussed in more detail below.

Withdrawing

Sexual abuse by a known person is a betrayal of a child's trust. This results in the child being unable to trust other people and keeping herself separate so she cannot be hurt by anyone else. Many sexually abused women describe being loners as children or getting friendly with other children and then dropping them when the friendship started to get close.

I would make friends quite easily but I would soon start to avoid them. I didn't want to get close to anyone. I didn't want to open up to anyone. *Jocelyn*

This barrier is also created because the child feels different from other people or even dirty and ashamed. The child does not allow anyone to get close to her in case they find out what she is really like or discover her secret. For some children, withdrawing is the only way they know to cope with the trauma of their everyday lives and the burden of the secret they carry.

Emotional problems

Many sexually abused children suffer from depression throughout their lives and into adulthood. Anxiety, phobias and a general nervousness and watchfulness may also result from being abused Suicide attempts may be a way of trying to escape from the abuse and pain, or of drawing attention to the problem.

I think I was about seven the first time I tried to kill myself. I tried to cut my wrist but the knife I chose wasn't very sharp. I didn't really want to die, I just wanted to be loved. I tried to cut my wrists about three or four times when I was at elementary school. I've still got one scar although it's really faint. I think I needed to cut deeper, not just the little veins I could see under the surface. After my abuser died I was raped by someone else. Five months later, when I was 15, I tried to hang myself. I hung myself from the window with the cord that's used to open it. The other kids laughed at me so I got down. *Paula*

A child's anxiety or depression may not be noticed or she may receive inappropriate treatment without the real problem ever being uncovered. In chapter 2 Dorothy describes how she attempted suicide and received five years of psychiatric treatment, including many courses of ECT (electroconvulsive therapy) without anyone discovering that she had been abused. Chris was put on Valium at seven because she stabbed her father when he was abusing her. Like Dorothy and Chris, some Survivors were abused further by the mental-health system.

If emotional problems are not recognized or are treated inappropriately Survivors may reach adulthood believing themselves to be strange, unstable or even crazy. This sounds like a very bleak picture. However, some children experience only mild emotional problems and heal themselves with the help of family and friends. Others receive good and appropriate help and don't carry their problems into adulthood.

Difficult or disruptive behavior

The sexually abused child may show behavior which is interpreted by other people as difficult or disruptive. The child may simply be trying to avoid being left alone with the abuser. Kate tried to avoid going out with her father (the abuser) by having screaming tantrums and by pretending she was frightened of their car. Kate was told she was difficult and naughty.

Tracy recalls clinging to her mother at the bus stop and then screaming and holding on to her when she attempted to get on a bus without Tracy. The bus conductor had to help fight Tracy off. Often this kind of behavior is interpreted as the child being clinging, demanding or willful. Difficult behavior is often simply an expression of the anger and upset the child feels.

It wasn't until I was older, in my early teens, that I feel my behavior may have been an attempt to ask for help. I remember having bad tantrums which were considered temper (taking after my real father who had a violent temper) but were always in a non-confrontational situation. These attempts were at home and were always ignored by all the members of the family. *Jane*

Survivors frequently continue to believe as adults that they were silly, difficult or disruptive children. Moreover Survivors learn from this experience not to trust their own feelings. As children their strong feelings had been disregarded or treated as trivial. As adults, Survivors often keep on disregarding their feelings and dismiss feelings of anger, distress or pain with, "I'm just being silly."

Aggression and violence

Difficult behavior and tantrums are an outward expression of anger and distress, unlike depression where the feelings are turned inward and not expressed. For some Survivors disruptive behavior can turn into violence and aggression. Chris' story shows how anger can turn to violence and continue into adult life. Chris was abused every Sunday by her father from the age of seven or earlier.

I ran away when I was ten. I was only out one night and I was found 16 miles away from home. I just walked and walked. But I still didn't tell anyone. I always used to be fighting at home with everyone. I had urges where all I wanted to do was kill people, get revenge. I remember loads of bad things that used to be said to me. Then I'd carry out my revenge by waiting and waiting. I always got revenge. *Chris*

Chris started getting drunk and fighting at school. Then she attacked her mother, smashing her head into the fireplace and fracturing her skull.

This got me in trouble with the law. I used to do all sorts of awful things. I was always in court for one thing or another. Then I got locked up on my 13 birthday and that was it. From then on I went crazy. I was always in trouble and locked in a special cell. *Chris*

She was constantly fighting and then running off. She was sent to reform school where she stayed for two years. As soon as she was let out she attacked someone else to get revenge and was sent to prison. When released, she stabbed someone else and was sentenced to three more years in prison. Finally Chris was sent to a Secure Unit for mentally disturbed offenders and was eventually released from prison at 23. In ten years, there were only five months when she hadn't been locked up.

School problems
Signs that a child is being sexually abused may occur at school even when there is no real problem with the school. Truancy from school is common.

I used to run away from elementary school. I used to have tummy ache but my mom would still send me to school. I'd then ask to go to the restroom, I'd grab my coat and run. I can feel myself running, trying to get away—away from everything. I always thought (or maybe it's because I was always told) that I ran away because I didn't like the nuns who taught us, but now I realize it was because of the abuse. I can feel myself as a child confused and wanting to do something and not knowing what I could do. Running away was the only step I ever made towards telling or doing anything. *Jocelyn*

School may be the only place the child can let out the anger and distress they feel. This can result in the child being badly behaved or disruptive, arguing with teachers or other children, and fighting.

I used to drink after playing sports for the school and I used to get drunk all the time. At school I fought with anyone who stood in my way. I eventually got sent to a special school. *Chris*

In elementary school I was reprimanded on several occasions for biting other children. At high school I had a lot of fights in the first few years. I was often teased about my hair and clothes and fighting was the only way I knew of defending myself. Funny, I don't ever remember putting up a fight against the abuser. *Paula*

I played hookey from school. I terrorized other children at school. I locked one teacher in a storeroom and spit on another one. I set fire to the girls' bathroom because a male teacher came into it. Looking back I now realize that my abuser had such a hold over me that I had to be in control. I wouldn't allow anyone to have any power over me. I rebelled against anyone who tried to control me or pin me down. *Carla*

Bad behavior at school also interferes with school work and gives the child a bad name. School work may get worse as the child becomes unable to concentrate or ceases to care what happens to her anymore. Survivors may give up, believing they are stupid because they didn't do well at school. On the other hand some sexually abused children are excessively well behaved at school and clingy with teachers, in an attempt to get the love and protection that is lacking at home. Some children become overachievers at school as they strive to escape from the pain of their feelings by concentrating their mind on work.

Frequent illnesses
Children who are being sexually abused may frequently be ill or complain of feeling sick. Illnesses may result from sexual abuse in a direct physical sense, for example, urinary infections from sexual contact. Illness can also be an indirect result of sexual abuse arising from the stress and trauma of what is happening.

Children commonly complain of stomach pains when no physical cause can be found. Headaches, skin problems and failure to grow properly are also reported. Jane lists a whole range of physical problems which she now thinks might have been related to the abuse:

Not long after I remember the abuse starting I developed tonsillitis which ended up with me having my tonsils out. I then developed persistent earache. I was referred to the Ear, Nose and Throat clinic where my doctor told me that it was all in my head. About this time I was found to have a slight Scoliosis and referred to the orthopedic clinic. They recommended that I should have very hot baths which, unfortunately, my stepfather (the abuser) oversaw.

After this, apart from feeling generally lethargic and tired and being checked for anemia on different occasions, I cannot recall any illnesses until I was 17 when the situation was bad again, mainly due to my stepdad stopping me from going out with my friends. I went to my doctor and told him the surface problem. He prescribed antidepressants which I didn't take. I had also been to see my doctor on a few occasions for period pains. During my X-ray training I felt unable to cope and, due to my symptoms, mononucleosis was suggested although not proved. *Jane*

Physical well-being is closely linked to mental and emotional health. If children are emotionally traumatized they are unlikely to remain physically well.

At about the same time as the abuse started (I was about four years old) I developed asthma and eczema. I have only vague memories of the asthma but I remember it being really bad at times. I don't remember having any treatment. However, the eczema was bad. I developed it in my wrists and the backs of my knees. I was only five when I had to have my tonsils out. The constant taste of pus in my mouth is still with me. The surgeon later said it was the worst case he had dealt with in years. *Ingrid*

Sometimes children pretend they are ill to keep someone with them to protect them or to avoid being sent to see the abuser.

Frequent accidents and self-abuse
Similarly, children may hurt or injure themselves on purpose to protect themselves from the abuser. Mary recalls getting on her bicycle and deliberately riding it down a hill and into a lamppost. She knocked herself out and fractured her skull. She was kept in the hospital where she felt safe.

Lucy had an appendix operation when she was 12. Although the operation was successful her wound didn't heal for two years. She realized later that she had been opening the wound in her sleep. While the wound remained open she was not sexually abused. Ingrid scratched her eczema open whenever it began to heal.

Bedtime for me meant having bandages put all over my hands, arms and legs, and gloves put on to stop my fingernails from reaching the wounds. I even remember some nights when my hands were tied to the bed frame to stop me from reaching the wounds in my sleep. I always got free and literally tore the flesh off again. I still remember the tears and the pain.

My mother would sit with me and hold my hand for about three or four hours every night. She stayed until I was fast asleep and often then, when she tried to loosen my grip to get away from me, I woke up and she had to go through a long wait again. But because of my mother's devotion to helping me to avoid scratching the wounds (which by the way I never did during the day) I was not available for abuse when my brother came to bed in the same bedroom. I found a way out. *Ingrid*

Self-injury and self-abuse are also expressions of self-disgust and forms of self-punishment. Children who are ashamed and blame themselves for the abuse may slash themselves with knives, burn themselves, hit or smack themselves or bang their fists or heads against the wall. Physical pain can bring relief from emotional suffering.

I broke a glass jar and slashed all my arms and neck. I'd slash myself until the physical pain was more than the pain I felt inside. *Chris*

In her pain and anger, Fiona smashed her fist through glass windows on many occasions. A third of the women in the Wakefield Survivors groups have harmed themselves in some way.

Summary

Children often do not tell that they are being abused. However, they usually show signs that there is something wrong and we have called these signs *silent ways of telling*. Adults frequently do not understand these signs and instead of offering help and care, they label the child as naughty, silly, difficult, stubborn, crazy or bad. Sometimes outside services such as mental-health workers are brought in to help. In the past, when sexual abuse was little understood this has sometimes resulted in a further abuse and labeling of the child by the system.

Many Survivors give up, believing the labels, believing they are crazy or bad. Today we are becoming more sensitive to children's emotional problems and their causes. Unfortunately, adult Survivors have rarely been treated with such care in the past. Once the links have been made between the childhood behavior and the sexual abuse, these labels can be left behind.

The behavior of sexually abused children is not crazy or bad it is simply a way of coping with strong feelings of fear, distress and anger which cannot be expressed directly. The exercises below are designed to help you look back over your childhood and understand and care for the child you were.

Exercises

1. Look at the list of childhood signs of sexual abuse in Table 3 and check any that you showed.
2. Write down what you think the adults around you thought about your behavior as a child. Include parents, teachers, social workers, psychologists or anyone else who is relevant. What did they say or do to you? Did they think you were distressed or think you were difficult, bad or crazy?
3. Write an account of how you felt as a child and the ways in which your behavior was affected by being abused. Try to understand and accept the child you were, rather than judging and criticizing yourself.

7

What Happened
When I Did Tell

In THE LAST TWO CHAPTERS WE LOOKED AT the reasons
why children don't tell anyone when they are being abused and
also at the silent ways they show their distress. Some Wakefield
Survivors told someone about the abuse when they were children and they all told someone when they were adults. They
often got negative reactions from people which made them feel
more ashamed and afraid to tell anyone else. Ultimately,
someone reacted positively, enabling them to get help and take
the first step by breaking the silence.

The children who tried to tell

Until recent years very few people had heard about the sexual
abuse of children even though it was happening to many children. It was still a closely-guarded secret. Survivors who are now
adults sometimes tried to tell someone about their abuse at the
time it was happening but they were often not believed; no one
spoke about sexual abuse and people just didn't believe it happened, especially to someone they knew.

I didn't realize it was wrong. I thought it happened to everyone. I told
my school friends in conversation and they called me a liar. When they
acted shocked and were going to tell the teachers I realized it was
wrong and so pretended I'd lied because I was frightened. They acted

disgusted and shocked. It frightened me and I never spoke of it again to anyone. *Margaret*

Some children, like Margaret, tell other children who don't believe it because it is outside their own experience and who are too young to be able to help. Katarina told a seven-year-old play-mate who probably could not even understand what was being said to her.

The first time I remember clearly telling anyone was while my brother was still abusing me. I was about eight when I told a friend of mine. For weeks I had prepared in my mind what I was going to tell her. She was the little sister of my brother's best friend. When I did tell her about the abuse I expected her to be shocked and show some sympathy. Because of my brother's threats I knew the abuse was something wrong. My friend did not say she didn't believe me, she said nothing.

But while I was still telling her about what was so important to me she just shrugged her shoulders, turned and went off to play with some other children. I was in the middle of a sentence when she walked away and I felt for the first time the feeling of total emptiness inside me. *Katarina*

The response to children's disclosures is often that children make up fairy stories, have very active imaginations, or will do anything to get at their parents. Children can make up stories but so can adults, and adults make much better liars than children. Young children have no knowledge of sexual activity unless they have come into contact with it in some way. They cannot make up stories about something they know nothing about. Pam approached two trusted adults when she wanted to talk about her experiences:

I told someone when I was 12, around the time my father raped me, I tried to explain to my mother what I thought she already knew. But she refused to believe it. She said I was lying—did I realize it was my father I was accusing? She said I just wanted some sympathy and attention. She threatened me and told me not to tell anybody else about this absurd lie as she referred to it. I also approached my child-protection social worker who was no better. He tried to worm his way out of the situation by pretending it never happened. When my parents found out I'd told the child-protection officer I got a good whipping. After that I never told anybody, I kept myself to myself. I closed myself and my thoughts within a cocoon. *Pam*

Often when people are told about sexual abuse they cannot

cope with the information. They don't want to believe it's actually happening or they don't know what to do about it. What mother wants to believe her husband, father, sister or son are abusers? Sometimes it's not that people don't believe the child, rather that they dare not believe the child because then they would have to do something about it. Pam says that her mother, "refused to believe me." Pam's father was a violent man and her mother was probably too frightened to stand up for her daughter and against him.

This is not justifying her mother's actions—Pam was left unprotected in an abusive situation—but it indicates some of the pressures her mother may have been under. Pam also says that the child-protection officer justified not taking any action by pretending it never happened. Doctors, teachers, psychiatrists, psychologists or anyone in the helping professions may also not want to believe that it's true. Believing may mean having to take action; rocking the boat; having to deal with the pain of the victim and the reaction of her carers; and having to confront one's own pain and anger. At least one in ten adults was sexually abused as a child. This includes all kinds of people—mothers, doctors, teachers, counselors, clergy—all of whom may hear confessions. They may disbelieve a Survivor's story because they are still denying what happened to them. As human beings we have the ability to persuade ourselves that what we don't want to be true isn't true.

When I was little I did tell my sisters that I didn't like my Granddad because he stuck his fingers up my bottom—at which I was smacked in the face by my sisters and told never to say it again. *Polly*

Polly's sisters did believe her but they reacted like this because it was happening to each of them too. They'd all been told to keep it secret—Polly had broken the promise.

It was then that my two sisters realized it was happening to all of us. One of my sisters told my stepdad what Granddad was doing to us. He came up to reassure me and promised me it would never happen to me again. He would protect me. It continued to happen. He didn't protect me. He also said that we must not tell my mom as it would upset her. I believed him and never mentioned it. Perhaps if I had told my mom it would never have happened again and I would have gotten help earlier on and not be the mess I am today. I might even have liked myself. *Polly*

Many children who do manage to talk about their abuse are either not believed, like Pam and Margaret, or are believed but remain unprotected, like Polly. Some children get a more positive response and are believed and protected. A child who is disbelieved when she tries to tell can feel very frightened and confused. As we have seen in chapter 5 Survivors may already doubt themselves. Did it really happen? Have I made it up? Did I dream it? To be met with disbelief strengthens these doubts.

Abusers often act quite normally after the abuse, as if nothing has happened. This adds to the child's feelings that she must be mistaken. Disbelief also adds to a child's feelings of helplessness and vulnerability. How can she ever stop it if she can't get anyone to believe her? If a child is disbelieved, by implication she is being accused of lying. Sometimes the child is told outright that she is lying and her disclosure is met with anger and insults. The sexual abuse is therefore compounded with further abuse and the child may feel betrayed by the lack of support.

The adults who tried to tell

Even as adults, Survivors may not be believed or taken seriously when they try to tell.

The first person I told was my first husband. I don't think he thought it was true. He said, "Well, it's past now." He made me feel as though it was my fault for letting it happen. When I told my mom I think she felt helpless and maybe guilty. She didn't really want to know. She must have been blind not to be able to see what my dad was doing all those years. *Rachel*

Many people find it very hard to cope with a disclosure of sexual abuse; sometimes because they don't know what to do to help. Pam's parents-in-law avoided her when they were told:

When Brian told his folks about my abuse they didn't call or visit for months. They thought it couldn't happen to anybody so close to home. Now they understand why I hate my mom and dad so much. *Pam*

Joanne was abused by her stepfather throughout her childhood. As an adult she made sure her own children didn't come into contact with him by avoiding visits to her mother's when he was around.

Around four years ago my mother asked why we didn't visit her with our children while my stepfather was in the house. At that time he had just been released from prison after serving a sentence for abusing his natural daughter.

I was so angry when my mother told me that my stepfather himself was asking as well. My anger made me tell my mother what my stepfather had been doing to me throughout my childhood. We both stayed remarkably calm under the circumstances. She looked surprised or rather shocked at my disclosure although I believe she already knew and was merely acting shocked.

The next week when we saw her she even seemed protective towards my stepfather saying they hadn't actually had a big fight over it and, to my amazement, "He doesn't want any trouble at his time of life." *Joanne*

Joanne's mother believed her. Joanne believes she even knew about the abuse while it was happening. She knew he had abused his natural daughter. The mother chose to support the abuser and protect her own lifestyle, leaving Joanne upset and betrayed. Disclosure of sexual abuse may also be used to blackmail Survivors. Lucy disclosed her childhood sexual abuse to her psychiatric nurse. He used the information to keep her silent about the sexual abuse he then inflicted on her.

Why do people react in these negative ways?

Many Survivors, adults and children, received negative responses when they talked about their abuse: disbelief, not being taken seriously, being believed but not protected; shock and disgust, and being ignored. People react in negative ways because they find it hard to believe that sexual abuse really happens. They have not dealt with their own sexual abuse, or are frightened of the consequences if they believe and support the Survivor.

Emotional problems caused by sexual abuse can be made worse by these negative responses to disclosure. Polly felt betrayed again when a trusted adult (her stepfather) failed to keep his promise to protect her from her abuser. Margaret felt guilty and ashamed after her school friends' reactions of shock and disgust. Pam felt powerless when neither her mother nor her child-protection officer responded to her cry for help.

Positive responses

It is possible to get useful and supportive responses from people too. Sometimes it may take some persistence. Although Rachel got unhelpful responses from her mother and her first husband she was not discouraged from trying again.

After I got divorced I met Paul and I thought I would tell him from the start so that I could try to sort out my feelings. He was really understanding and has backed me ever since. I also told Paul's mom. She was very understanding and helped me try to see things in a different light. I also told a really good friend.

She has helped me a lot and made me realize just what problems I had because of the abuse as I always blamed my unhappiness on other things. I told my sister and she was understanding and told me she has always felt abused by my dad as well.

I think other people didn't believe me in the past because they questioned whether things like this really do occur. It always happens to someone else. *Rachel*

Pam had not been believed when she told as a child. She went on to have an unhappy first marriage and a divorce, then she met Brian.

I didn't tell Brian about what happened to me in my childhood but to my surprise he told me he had already guessed what had happened to me. From his own job he knew the symptoms, reactions and effects too well not to notice. So I spilled the beans. Since then he has been my mainstay. Without his support I would have been a wreck. He is understanding, considerate, compassionate, sympathetic—everything I need. *Pam*

Why tell anyone?

Many Survivors had bad responses the first time they told someone about their abuse. Why then encourage victims to tell? How will they benefit? A child or adult who doesn't talk about their abuse is still keeping the abuser's secret and suffering in silence. All Survivors deserve the opportunity to release the heavy burden of the secret and to learn to feel better about themselves.

When I finally did tell I cannot describe the amount of relief I felt the next day. I was sitting quietly at my desk at work and I remember realizing that I'd actually told someone at last. I'd told my boyfriend, my husband-to-be. I marveled at the fact that nothing terrible had happened. *Joanne*

Sharing the secret can be a first step to getting help for yourself and breaking free from the shame, guilt and pain.

I did tell my husband and he really tries to understand. Telling the bulimia group (eating-problems group) was the most useful thing for me as now I can get help and feel that I am not going to spend the rest of my life as a victim of people who want to use me. *Shirley*

Being able to tell people who listened meant Shirley could get help for herself and learn to deal with abusive situations in her adult life. Telling the right person can result in feelings of relief and liberation and be a start on the path to overcoming your feelings about the past and your problems of today. Many Survivors have received treatment for years of depression, eating problems, nerves, etc., but any improvement rarely lasts without getting to the root of the problem. There are many triggers that make Survivors decide it's time to talk about their abuse. Some decide to talk about their abuse to protect other children from the abuser, or to help themselves deal with their worries about their own children.

Often they meet a sympathetic partner and want to come clean and have an open and honest relationship. When you feel ready to talk about the abuse be aware that, for different reasons, the person you tell may not react sympathetically. The important thing is to persevere. Nearly all the Survivors we have worked with have received unhelpful responses until they found someone ready to listen and to help them find a way to overcome their problems.

As Survivors stop feeling ashamed and blaming themselves for the abuse they begin talking about it to other people. Surprisingly, many of their friends and family tell them that they too were sexually abused, even by the same abuser.

Nowadays the sexual abuse of children is in the news. More people know about it, more people are ready to listen and act to protect children and help adults. There are still people around who won't listen, won't believe, will deny it, won't protect, and will abuse. However, there are more and more people around who will help. Try to find one of these people.

Ingrid's story

Ingrid first told a childhood friend about the abuse and wasn't believed. She continued to tell different people for over 30 years until, at last, she got a sympathetic response and some help for herself.

I think I may have told some friends at school when I was still a child, but the memory of that is not clear. I know that I later told my first husband before I married him when I was 17. I didn't like sex and felt that it may have had something to do with my past. He believed me, but didn't really care that I had been abused.

He beat me and took me in a sexual way that showed no love, no concern, no care for me. And so during my seven-year marriage to him, my problems increased. At times I became introverted and tried to analyze my problems to find a way to solve them. I failed on my own and knew that only outside help could rid me of the memories of the past, which still haunted me.

Very early in my marriage I realized that I would get no help from my husband, so I went to my doctor in Germany and told him, asking him to help me. His words were, "Too bad, but forget about it, it's in the past." I had trusted him completely before, but when he could not fill my need—not even see my need, I lost that trust. It took a few months for me to recover from the shock of telling someone I trusted and being brushed aside as if what caused me pain was of little importance.

My husband had many affairs which made me feel even more inferior and again I realized that I needed to sort out my life before I could sort out my marriage. I made an appointment with a marriage guidance counselor, not to complain about my husband's behavior, but to tell the female counselor about the abuse and my consequent dislike for sex. She said it was not important what I liked or didn't like, if I wanted my husband to remain faithful I had to satisfy him in bed.

She thought it was silly for me to make such a big fuss over something so long in the past. And again I walked home feeling empty and degraded. I spoke to two more people in the medical profession, people who should have known that professional help was needed. Always the response was, "Forget about it. He won't do it anymore, so why do you worry about it?"

I had by then realized that more problems had come into existence, not only my distaste for sex. Every time I tried to tell someone who might be able to help, I also explained the effects the abuse had had on me. I got no help. Maybe I told the wrong people?

I asked my brother to help me, begging my abuser to help me overcome the damage he did, by keeping out of my way. I was trying to avoid him. He didn't help me. He came to my house when he wanted to. As my first husband had become friends with him and the lover of my brother's wife (with my brother's approval) I saw him frequently.

I could not tell my parents. I felt the need to protect them from the knowledge of what their son had done. But I talked to my sister, two cousins and an aunt and told them what he had done. They may have believed me, I don't know, but they looked at me in disgust and said "He's got his faults, but he's also got his good features, you can't always see bad in people. He is your brother!" I was made to feel ashamed for telling the truth. I withdrew into myself for a while and wondered if it was worth the bother.

By belittling something that I felt had destroyed the value of my life they belittled me. One problem increased—the feeling of being worthless and not important. Not even my closest family seemed to care about my pain and nobody was willing to help me. I stopped telling anybody for about two years after my divorce while I tried to find out who I was and what direction to take in my life.

When I met my second husband and knew I was going to marry him, I told him about my childhood experiences. But he is a man who cannot talk about feelings, cannot help me because he does not understand why I have a problem. If he ever has a problem he ignores it and pretends it then goes away. He believes me but is completely unwilling to even listen to me talking about the past or my problems. So again no help.

As my regular doctor in Wakefield was not available I saw someone else in his office when I went with a minor health problem. I had not spoken about the abuse for about three years except to my second husband. It was time to try again because I realized that I needed help. I didn't want to risk another divorce because I was an unfeeling partner during lovemaking. I don't think the doctor even heard what I was telling him. He never even looked up from writing a prescription.

He didn't say a word. I'd learned by then if I ever wanted to tell someone about the abuse I had to put all those years, all the pain and all the effects the abuse had on me, into two or three sentences because I never had more time to talk about it. I was always interrupted with some patronizing remark. This time I didn't wait to recover from being rejected in my need for help.

Within days I saw a female doctor in the family-planning clinic and told her the same story. Her advice to overcome my dislike of physical contact was to satisfy myself or to use a vibrator, if I couldn't find pleasure with a man. To a victim of sexual abuse who looks on sex as dirty and degrading this is the most unhelpful suggestion possible.

Every time I told someone the emptiness in me grew. I was so eager to find some response, someone saying "Tell me about it, I'll help you." I knew what my brother did was wrong, I wanted reassurance that it was wrong, someone reinforcing my belief that it was his fault that I wasn't feeling the way other women feel. I tried to talk about it a few more times to people, mostly friends. They hardly acknowledged what they heard, none of them was supportive.

Then I gave up. I resigned myself to never being able to enjoy sex;

always having thoughts that I was less worthy than others; never losing the fear that my son would abuse his sisters; and all the other problems that I knew resulted from the sexual abuse I suffered as a child. Suddenly I had some personal tragedies which had nothing to do with my past. They came within a few weeks of each other and I became depressed. After three weeks I went to see one of the doctors at the health-maintenance organization (HMO).

I told her about my depression, expecting to get some drugs to help. I gave her all the reasons why I thought things were getting too much for me. Again I mentioned in two sentences that I was abused as a child. For the first time in my life someone looked at me with sympathy, encouraging me to go on talking about it.

We talked for about ten minutes and never before was I allowed to say so much about how I felt it had affected me all my life. She told me about the Survivors groups and asked if I would be interested in joining them. I almost cried with relief. Yes, I was interested.

A new group had just started so I had to wait three months before I could join but from that day on I felt protected. I saw that even though over 30 years had passed since I first looked for help, it was not too late. We can change our lives no matter how long it takes.

The hardest part for me was always the moments just after telling someone, when I was not believed or told to forget it. But whenever I felt close to giving up I thought that somewhere, someone must care. I just had to find that person. Now I think that perseverance was the right way for me. If I had given up trying, I would not be the woman I am now. I am happier now and more fulfilled than I have ever been before. *Ingrid*

Perhaps each of us can also be ready to listen and believe if someone (male or female, child or adult) chooses to tells us about sexual abuse.

Exercises

1. If you've had a bad response when you talked about your sexual abuse, try writing down what happened and why you think the person responded in this way.
2. Think about talking to someone about what has happened to you. The Useful Addresses section at the back lists people you can call or write to get help. If you call a help line you will be listened to and you will be believed. If you don't get an appropriate response, find someone else to talk to.
3. If you want to know how to respond if a child or an adult discloses sexual abuse to you, or if you suspect abuse, see chapter 17 on Working Towards Prevention.

8

Buried Feelings

THE ABILITY TO EXPERIENCE AND EXPRESS many different emotions—happiness, sadness, anger, grief, love, hate, fear and joy—is a natural part of being human. Sometimes, however, feelings are too intense or painful to be experienced or expressed directly. Problems that Survivors have in adult life can be caused by the ways they have tried to cope with their painful thoughts and feelings about the abuse.

They may consciously try to forget and find ways to push their memories and feelings away or unconsciously cut off altogether so that they are unable to remember what has happened or have no feelings about the event. The capacity to cut off protects people from fully experiencing the horror of their situation.

Burying feelings and memories

Abused children often hide their anger and distress from other people so that no one will suspect that they are being abused. They may also keep their feelings rigidly under control while they are being abused to protect themselves from feeling their distress and pain or because they do not want the abuser to see how much he is hurting them. Many adult Survivors continue to cope by burying their feelings and trying to forget about the abuse. However, the feelings and memories that people try to bury usually surface in some form and cause either physical or emotional problems. Remembering can be painful, but facing the memories and feelings is the only way to overcome them. Below are some of the ways that Survivors consciously or unconsciously bury memories and feelings and the kind of problems this can cause.

Avoiding

Survivors often find ways to avoid thinking about their childhood abuse or to avoid their feelings about what has happened. They may keep themselves busy and distracted or make sure they are never alone so they don't have time to think. Some Survivors do the same thing again and again when their memories and feelings begin to surface, for example, washing themselves, cleaning, counting or checking things.

Survivors often try to avoid anything that might remind them of their abuse and cause their feelings and memories to surface. They may particularly avoid anything to do with sex or sexual abuse (television programs, conversations, books) or anything that reminds them of their childhood (photographs, people, places, children).

Some years ago I got out all my childhood photos. My brother was on many of them. I tore up the parts of the photos with his image and destroyed everything that reminded me of him. Yet the memories remained. *Katarina*

Some Survivors avoid people who are expressing strong emotions, for example people crying or shouting, because they fear it will bring up their own feelings. They may or may not be conscious of what they are doing. Some Survivors describe mentally locking away their memories and feelings in a secure box. Often Survivors are encouraged to behave like this by friends or advisers who say that the best thing they can do is put the abuse behind them and get on with their lives. However, the memories and feelings do not go away; they are still there. For a time they may be less accessible and less troublesome but this method of coping can lead to many problems. Avoiding memories and feelings by keeping busy, finding distractions or repeatedly counting, checking or cleaning can be very stressful and lead to high levels of anxiety and to phobias and obsessions.

Adult Survivors often become so expert at cutting off from distressing feelings that they do this automatically.

No matter what bad thing happened in my life, I could not cry. I could not feel any emotions. For most years of my adult life I was emotionally dead. I was neither happy nor sad, neither depressed nor angry. I simply felt nothing. Even when I was almost daily abused during my first marriage it did not cause me the pain it should have. Most of the time it did not bother me. I was too frightened to accept feelings of any kind. *Ingrid*

Fiona had learned to avoid her feelings about being abused and later realized that she had cut off from all kinds of bad feelings.

When I was talking to my daughter about giving up I started telling her about when I was 17 and my mom left home. Something suddenly hit me. I had never really noticed that my mom had left my life. It was as if I didn't care. I must have been so hardened to pain or pushed my emotions so deeply away that I couldn't feel the full extent of the hurt. Looking back now I get the stab of emotions, the emptiness, the betrayal. My sadness now as a mother myself could be the scars I bear from the kind of emotional upsets I suffered giving up. I never really grieved about a lot of things, like the death of my granddad. I missed my granddad. I couldn't stand the emptiness I felt inside. I often wanted to cry but most times I wouldn't let myself. Even today I do the same. I feel ashamed to cry. I feel I'm seeking attention and feeling sorry for myself so I get angry with myself and afraid about what people will think. *Fiona*

Physical tension
Feelings and memories can be held back by physical tension. Children learn at an early age to hold back tears by tensing their chest and face muscles. Anger, grief and rage can also be held in by tensing any part of the body. We talk about people becoming rigid with rage or bowed down with grief. These sayings illustrate how unexpressed feelings can affect the physical body. It requires a great deal of physical tension and mental energy to hold back feelings and memories. Tensing the body can also become an automatic response. It saps energy and can lead to chronic tension, headaches, aches and pains and many other physical problems. It also keeps the body in a heightened state of stress and makes people more vulnerable to anxiety, panic attacks, illness and injury.

Food, alcohol and drugs
Food, alcohol and drugs can be used as ways of blotting-out bad

feelings. Eating food can bring immediate comfort and enable people to distract themselves from their feelings and eventually blot them out. Alcohol and drugs (both legal and illegal) work in a similar way by allowing people to block-out the pain and cut off from reality. Alcohol, drugs and food can seem very attractive ways of dealing with distressing feelings, memories and situations because they are easy to take and quick to work but they are only short-term ways of blotting-out distress. They may also become problems in themselves.

Blanking-out

Blanking-out, or dissociating, is another way people can escape from their painful thoughts and feelings. They separate part of themselves from what is happening and from their distress and pain. Children may learn to blank-out when they are being abused. They separate, or dissociate themselves, from their bodies so they do not feel the physical or emotional pain. Some children describe stepping outside their bodies and watching themselves being abused without experiencing any of the pain.

Others invent a fantasy world into which they can retreat every time they are being abused. Blanking-out is a way in which children cope with continuing to be abused and in which adult Survivors cut off from the painful thoughts and memories about the abuse. The Survivor may not realize that this is what is happening. Blanking-out can become an automatic response to any bad feeling, however minor.

This coping strategy then becomes a serious problem over which the Survivor has no control. Sometimes adult Survivors go into a blanked-out state for hours or days at a time. When they come out of this state they are often confused about what they have been doing or how they got to be where they are. Often they have been going about their everyday tasks but may have appeared a little vague or different from usual.

Sometimes people in blanked-out states are thought to be drunk or on drugs. Survivors who dissociate themselves from physical pain as children may find that they cannot feel pain as adults. Blanking-out can be a very frightening experience. Survivors may feel they are going crazy or that there is something seriously physically wrong with them. Many are sent to see neurologists or to have other physical examinations.

Blacking-out

Some Survivors blackout when there is no physical reason for this to occur. This may have happened to them first as a child during the abuse. Blackouts often happen to adult Survivors because something triggers memories and feelings about the abuse. By blacking-out they are put into a state in which they can no longer consciously think or feel. When they come to they may have no memory of what caused the blackout. Blackouts can be frightening experiences and physically dangerous. Lucy blacked-out when anything reminded her of the abuse or her abuser.

She was protected from her emotional pain but her black-outs became more and more frequent and she often injured herself. Eventually she was unable to work or lead a normal life and was referred to a neurologist. When the neurologist found nothing physically wrong with her she was referred to a psychologist. As she began to deal with her sexual abuse her blackouts became less frequent.

In addition to the methods mentioned above, Survivors also often cut off their memories and feelings by compulsively caring for others, by sleeping or by injuring themselves. All these coping strategies can develop into problems in themselves.

Memories and feelings surface

Survivors cannot be sure of always being able to hold back memories and feelings if the underlying cause, the sexual abuse, is not dealt with. Memories and feelings may come back through dreams and flashbacks or surface unexpectedly. Feelings about the abuse may be transferred onto other people and situations.

Dreams are a way in which hidden memories and feelings can come back into consciousness. Sometimes Survivors have nightmares about exactly what happened when they were abused. Often they have nightmares which aren't directly about the abuse but relate to their feelings and memories about it, for example, nightmares about their childhood, the abuser, death, sex, being chased or trapped.

Flashbacks are vivid memories in which a person feels they are re-experiencing past events. During a flashback the Survivor feels as if she is a child again and is reliving her abuse. Flashbacks are a way in which buried memories and feelings surface. They can happen at any time; the Survivor has no conscious control over them. Flashbacks are triggered by reminders of the abuse and therefore often occur during sex.

Many things can remind Survivors of their abuse and they may not always be able to avoid this. Survivors who try to push away their memories are vulnerable to being suddenly reminded of the abuse and may find themselves taken unaware by memories flooding back. This can happen in situations where it is very difficult to deal with them; Dorothy's memories came back when she went into labor

Painful feelings can also come flooding back. Fits of rage or floods of tears for no apparent reason are frequently described by Survivors. Survivors may be taken by surprise by their feelings and be unable to understand where they are coming from and what they are about. Many believe they are at the mercy of their hormones, suffering from premenstrual tension, post-natal depression, the menopause or some chemical imbalance. Survivors may be treated for these problems, or for anxiety and depression, for many years without making the connection between their feelings and being sexually abused.

Feelings can also surface and be transferred onto other people or other situations where they can be more easily expressed. Survivors who feel very little about their own abuse may find themselves weeping profusely at a film or book, or crazy with rage at an injustice that has been done to another person. They may find themselves getting angry at people for trivial reasons.

I was angry but I didn't know what at and so it was directed at my husband, the dog, anyone close to me. *Jocelyn*

Difficulties in relationships and sexual problems are also often the result of feelings about the abuse or abuser. The Survivor's buried feelings about the abuse surface and are transferred onto a current relationship.

Facing buried feelings—when and why

Recent research has shown that 50 percent of women and 23 percent of men receiving psychiatric help have been sexually abused. As we have seen, many mental-health problems such as anxiety, depression, phobias, sexual problems, eating disorders, drug addiction and tension can be the result of buried feelings and memories about the sexual abuse. Survivors have often received many years of treatment for these surface problems before the underlying problem of the sexual abuse was uncovered and dealt with.

Eventually Survivors come to a point where the old coping strategies are no longer working or are becoming serious problems in themselves. Feelings and memories may be surfacing despite attempts to bury them. It is at this point that Survivors may decide that they have to get help and that they need to disclose the abuse. They may have carried their secret for 10, 20, even 50 years before this happens.

In some cases specific events cause memories and feelings about the abuse to surface.

Last year I had a little girl who only lived an hour and then died. I thought I'd coped with it quite well but my mother had been no help whatsoever—she only came to see me once. I felt as though she'd let me down—everything accentuated how I'd felt for a long time about myself. I didn't like myself at all. I was really depressed and one day I told my visiting nurse that I'd been sexually abused as a child. I hadn't thought about it a lot but then I realized that was my problem. The death of my little girl brought back that my mother wasn't there for me, all those years ago, she didn't protect me then either. That's what triggered my depression. *Jocelyn*

Jocelyn was abused by two men 22 years earlier. She'd struggled with her feelings all those years. But it took the death of her baby and the lack of response from her mother to trigger her memories and feelings about her abuse. This prompted her to tell about her sexual abuse and then get help by joining a Survivors group.

I don't think I could have gone for help before. There's a point when it's right to go—for me it was my mom letting me down again and I could see it this time. Before, although I felt so bad, I didn't realize I needed help or that anything could help. *Jocelyn*

Survivors may have to reach a stage where they feel absolutely desperate or attempt to end their life before they start to talk about the abuse.

I was getting suicidal. I felt I was totally losing control and that I didn't have the right to make decisions. I always used to feel in control at

---

Table 4—Events that trigger memories and feelings about childhood sexual abuse

Birth of a girl
Birth of a boy
Child reaching the age the
  Survivor's abuse started
Death of the abuser
Death of the mother
  or caretaker of the
  Survivor
Meeting or seeing a person who
  looks like the abuser
Revisiting the place
  of the abuse

Hearing or reading about another
  person's abuse
Feeling vulnerable, ill or under
  stress
Any situation in which a Survivor
  once again feels: stigmatized,
  i.e., falsely accused
  of stealing; betrayed, i.e.,
  husband has an affair;
  powerless, i.e., fired; sexually
  traumatized, i.e., rape.

---

work but now this was starting to crumble as well as everything else. I went to see my doctor for a referral to a Clinical Psychologist. *Jane*

Lucy had kept her memories and feelings buried by blacking-out, but when this coping method became a serious problem in itself she decided to get help.

I kept having blackouts and being admitted to the hospital. They could not find anything physically wrong with me and referred me to a psychologist. I was so desperate that I either had to do something and get it right or kill myself. I decided it was time I really got to the bottom of it. *Lucy*

Like Lucy some Survivors eventually get psychological help after they have been through a whole range of physical tests and investigations. Their physical problems (blackouts, fits, numbness, pains, gynecological problems) are found to be a result of emotional distress caused by being sexually abused.

I never used to cry or even get upset, I'd always blackout. During one Survivor's group meeting I burst into tears. Crying made me feel better and I felt as if I could talk about the abuse. Feelings of anger also came out in the group. Before I was always fine and didn't need help but I kept having blackouts and I think I would have killed myself if I hadn't got help. Now I can say "I'm not all right" and I don't have to put on a brave face. *Lucy*

Some of the problems that result from buried feelings are

discussed in more detail in the following chapters. We discuss ways of dealing with these particular problems, but to overcome them you also need to face the underlying feelings and memories about the sexual abuse.

When powerful feelings and memories begin to return it can be frightening and disturbing. However, it does mean that these memories and feelings are not lost. So they can still be experienced and dealt with even if the abuse happened many years ago. Allowing your buried feelings and memories to surface is the first step. Being truly in touch with your feelings not only helps to heal the past but also allows you to experience life more fully and openly in the present.

Exercises

1. Write a list of any ways in which you have tried to bury your memories and feelings, i.e., avoiding (places, people, thoughts); keeping busy; distracting yourself; obsessively doing something (counting, checking, cleaning); using alcohol, drugs or food; sleeping; blanking-out; blacking-out.
2. Look at Table 4 and check any events which have brought back your memories and feelings about the abuse.
3. Many Survivors have lost touch with their feelings. In order to help you make contact with your feelings again, during the next few days keep asking yourself "What am I feeling now ?" Do this regularly every day and make a note of your feelings. Put a colored Post-it ™ (piece of sticky paper) on your watch (or on something else you look at regularly) to remind you to make a note of your feelings every time you look at it.

9

Anxiety, Fears and Nightmares

When I had my first panic attack I didn't know what was happening. I just felt a fear that I had never experienced before. I was scared to tell anyone because I thought I was cracking up and they would think I was really stupid. *Polly*

Not being able to eat in front of people came on gradually—it just seemed to get worse and worse. It was as if everybody was watching me. *Mavis*

MANY SURVIVORS OF CHILDHOOD SEXUAL ABUSE feel tense and nervous much of the time. Some can't travel alone, avoid busy shops, can't eat in front of people, have panic attacks or think everybody is looking at them. Others have intense fears of specific things like being in the dark or older men. These are all anxiety problems. While many people suffer from anxiety, it is a particularly common problem for people who suffered abuse in childhood. They experienced so much fear as children that even as adults their minds and bodies are still in a state of fear.

Anxiety

When people feel anxious their minds and bodies are in a state of fear although they are not in danger. Anxious people are usually very tense and may describe themselves as jumpy, nervy or wound-up. Anxiety has three parts: physical symptoms, changes in behavior and negative thoughts. Table 5 contains a list of the more common symptoms of anxiety.

Physical symptoms

Anxious people experience the same physical reactions as people do when they are in danger. When people are in danger their bodies increase the production of stress hormones (adrenaline and cortisol). This is known as the *fight or flight* response, which helps people deal with dangerous situations by preparing the body for action. Anxious people, however, experience these bodily reactions even when they are not in danger. Many of the physical symptoms of anxiety, such as palpitations, butterflies in the stomach and dry mouth, are caused by the body's natural response to danger.

People often begin to breathe quickly or gasp for air (hyperventilation) when they are afraid. This rapid breathing causes changes in the chemistry of the blood creating physical changes associated with anxiety (such as feeling short of breath, pins and needles, and dizziness). People also tense their muscles in response to fear and this can become a habit resulting in aches and pains in many parts of the body.

Negative thoughts

When people are anxious they have negative thoughts about themselves or other people. They often assume that something dreadful is about to happen; for example, "I'll never see my children again." Anxious people often have negative thoughts about harmless events. They may, for example, notice somebody looking at them and think, "Everyone is looking at me, they can see what I'm really like." The negative thoughts may be connected to the physical symptoms of anxiety.

Physical symptoms	Negative thoughts
Feeling dizzy	"I'm going to pass out."
Tingling sensation	"I'm having a stroke."
Blurred vision, things look unreal.	"I'm going crazy—I'll end up in the mental hospital."

This kind of thinking is called *catastrophizing;* in this case making a catastrophe out of the harmless (but uncomfortable) physical symptoms of fear. Negative thoughts make anxiety

Table 5—The symptoms of anxiety		
Physical symptoms:	surroundings seem	obsessional cleaning,
tension	unreal	counting or checking
palpitations	nausea	
(becoming aware of	poor concentration	**Negative thoughts:**
your heartbeat)	dizziness	I'm going to have a
butterflies in stomach	churning stomach	heart attack.
trembling, shaking	headache	Everyone can tell
pins and needles		what I'm really like.
feeling short of breath	**Behaviors:**	My children are going
loss of appetite	drinking too much	to have a bad acci-
poor sleep	eating too much	dent.
sweating	eating too little	I'm cracking up. I'm
chest pain	taking drugs	going to end up in
dry mouth	(prescribed or	the mental hospital.
weak legs	illegal)	Everyone is talking
aches and pains	avoiding going places	about me.
vomiting	escaping from places	People think I'm dirty.
diarrhea	where you feel	
blurred vision	afraid	

worse by making the person become more afraid, which in turn produces more physical symptoms and starts a vicious circle of increasing fear.

Behavior changes

When people feel anxious they often change their behavior in order to cope with their feelings. If they feel anxious in a particular situation they may have a strong urge to escape and sometimes they run away. They may avoid that situation in the future because they fear they will become anxious there again. People also try to cope with feelings of anxiety by eating more, taking pills or drinking alcohol. However, avoiding facing up to fear by using any of these coping strategies actually *increases* the fear. Unfortunately, all these ways of trying to cope with anxiety can become habits and, in time, develop into problems themselves such as agoraphobia, compulsive eating, tranquilizer dependence, alcohol abuse and obsessional behavior.

Connections with sexual abuse

When people are anxious they have often been in danger or experienced a great deal of fear in the past. Their bodies have continued to respond with the symptoms of fear even when they are no longer in danger. A child who is being abused may feel fearful for much of her childhood: afraid she will be sexually abused again; afraid the abuser will do something worse; afraid she is being physically damaged by the abuse; afraid she will get pregnant; afraid that people can tell she is being abused; or afraid of the consequences if someone finds out.

When a child experiences fear like this for long stretches of her childhood it is unlikely this fear will just disappear when the abuse stops or she becomes an adult. She has learned to be fearful and will probably continue to experience the symptoms of fear until she understands why she is anxious and learns how to control her fear.

Nightmares

Survivors often become anxious when they start remembering or thinking about their sexual abuse and their fears may be expressed in the form of nightmares. Rachel felt so terrified by her nightmares that she made her fiancee walk the streets with her at night so that she could avoid having to go to sleep. Nightmares often illustrate fears and memories that are too frightening or painful for Survivors to face up to when they are conscious.

Survivors often have nightmares about death, perhaps expressing the idea that the sexual abuse had killed something in them. Remembering her own sexual abuse may make a Survivor anxious about the safety of her children, and this may come out in her dreams.

My fears were really coming out in my nightmares. I dreamed that I was in town and suddenly realized that I had left my young daughter in someone's care where my abuser could get to her. I desperately tried to save her before he abused her. However fast I tried to go I couldn't seem to reach her. The abuser was getting nearer to her all the time, right up to him opening the door to where she was, then I woke up screaming. *Kate*

Dreams can be terrifying but they can also be a useful way for Survivors to get back their memories about the abuse, to express their fears and to explore more difficult feelings.

Panic attacks

I had to go to the hospital to see a doctor. I got a taxi there and sat in the waiting room. The clock seemed to be ticking really loud and every-thing seemed very noisy. I was called into the doctor's office. He was talking to me but I just couldn't hear what he was saying. I started sweating and felt very hot. My hands were trembling and I couldn't stop swallowing. My chest felt tight and I felt the room was coming in on me. I just had to get out. *Polly*

Panic attacks are an extreme form of anxiety, usually triggered by thoughts or memories. They are very frightening because the physical symptoms are powerful and unexpected. People often react by thinking they are going to have a heart attack or die. These thoughts make people even more frightened and so increase the physical symptoms and the tension. This in turn leads to more negative thoughts and causes the panic to build up and up. When people have panic attacks they experience a very strong urge to run away and may do so. Survivors may have intense and sudden attacks of anxiety when they think about their abuse or are in situations associated with their abuse.

The first time that I can remember having a panic attack was when I was about ten years old. I was at a Christmas party at my grandma's house. Three of my abusers were present at the party. I remember feeling very frightened and very dizzy. My heart was thumping very hard, I could feel all the pulses in my body going and I started shaking all over. I felt very faint and weak. At the time I didn't realize what was happening. I didn't realize I was having a panic attack. *Wendy*

Some Survivors, like Wendy, started having panic attacks as children but many develop them for the first time as adults.

At the time of my first panic attack I was having flashbacks and nightmares about the sexual abuse by my grandfather. I tried to push the memories down and get on with my everyday life but the panic attacks kept happening. *Polly*

Fears and phobias

Some Survivors are not only generally anxious but also suffer from phobias—irrational fears of specific things or situations. People can develop phobias about situations where they have had traumatic experiences: people who have been involved in a car crash may become phobic about traveling in cars; or a child who is bitten by a dog may grow into an adult who is phobic about dogs. Some people, though, are not aware of how their fear began.

People often develop phobias about situations (being in a supermarket, in a group of people, near a particular animal, in the dark) where they have felt anxious or had panic attacks. The initial fear can develop into a phobia if the person avoids getting into that situation again, thus allowing the fear to grow. Being sexually abused is usually a traumatic experience and Survivors may develop fears and phobias. In this section we describe the phobias which are most commonly associated with sexual abuse.

Agoraphobia

The first panic attack I put down to being tired and under stress but they kept happening to me. They made me so frightened that I was scared to go out or do anything for fear of having one. If I went out I would start feeling really shaky and my heart would be thumping. I would sweat and I felt dizzy like I was going to pass out. I had to leave wherever I was. I just needed to run and get away, preferably home where it would go away. I gave up work and became like a hermit. My friends and relatives all tried to help but I wouldn't admit to them what was happening to me. I made excuses: too tired, headache, felt sick, anything to get out of going out. I tried going back to work but I was really nervous. I seemed to cope for a while and then again from nowhere I had another panic. I stopped work and became really depressed, thinking I was cracking up and would end up locked up in a nut house. *Polly*

Agoraphobia is an intense fear of being away from the safety of the home, being in busy places and feeling trapped. People who suffer from agoraphobia often fear traveling on public transport, standing in a line of people, being in a busy place, being alone, or being out of the house. Some people with agoraphobia feel safe enough to go outside if they are in or near their car or if they have someone else with them.

Some Survivors of sexual abuse, like Polly, develop agoraphobia. They may feel threatened and anxious when they are outside their own homes and therefore develop a fear of leaving them. Survivors have often felt trapped and out of control during the abuse and these feelings may return whenever they are in situations which they cannot leave immediately, for example, waiting at a supermarket checkout stand. Some Survivors do not feel safe when they are alone as the feelings and memories about the abuse return.

Social phobia

Social phobia is a fear of meeting people or being in situations where there are other people. Many Survivors suffer from social phobia. They feel very self-conscious and think that other people are looking at them. Survivors often have negative thoughts that others can see how guilty or dirty they are inside, or can see that they have been sexually abused. They may feel particularly self-conscious when they are eating in public. Some people feel they have a lump in their throat or they are going to choke.

Survivors may have coped with the abuse by isolating themselves from other people and so feel uncomfortable around others. They may avoid other people because they are afraid of being abused or betrayed again. After Joan was abused by her sister's boyfriend in the bathroom of her parents' home she had to go back into the living room and face her family. She felt ashamed and guilty and felt sure they would be able to tell that she had been abused. As an adult Joan was shy and self-conscious, often blushing and trying to avoid being the center of attention.

She was too embarrassed to go to a restroom when she was at work or in restaurants and other public places although she didn't understand why. When she came out of a restroom she thought everyone was staring at her. She felt guilty, anxious, embarrassed and unsteady on her feet. She coped with this by drinking as little as possible when she was out so she wouldn't need to go to the restroom. Eventually she stopped going to the toilet all day at work and avoided going to restaurants or other social gatherings. Joan started off with a fear of restrooms but eventually developed social phobia.

Fears associated with the abuser

Survivors often have fears that are associated with the person who abused them: fears of body hair, the smell of alcohol, cigarette smoke, being kissed by older men, people with glazed-over eyes, men generally.

Survivors who have been abused by men may, as adults, be frightened of all men or a specific group of men, i.e., older men, men with beards. Kate was abused by several men and as an adult was frightened of being alone with a man.

When I went into a store I hated having men serving me. Sometimes I wouldn't go into a store at all unless I thought a woman would serve me. *Kate*

Some abusers seem to go into a semi-trance while they are abusing. Survivors often describe the glazed look in the eyes of their abusers before or during the abuse and often as adults become fearful if they see someone with eyes that look glazed over.

Fears associated with the abuse

Some fears and phobias develop because of their association with the situation where the Survivor was abused or with objects used during the abuse. Survivors often have fears of bathrooms, being in a room with a closed door, the dark, being touched, washing their hair or being alone at night. Abuse often occurs in the dark or behind closed doors. Many children are abused in bathrooms; abusers who are family members often take advantage of a child taking a bath or washing their hair and use this as an opportunity to abuse them.

Survivors develop fears of being touched in certain ways, on certain parts of the body or by particular people; these fears are usually associated with the touching they experienced during the abuse. Survivors may have fears relating to objects used during the abuse: knives used to threaten the child, bottles or other objects that were inserted into the child's anus or vagina. Lucy blacked-out whenever ice cream was mentioned; her abuser had smeared her with ice cream. Some Survivors are manipulated or forced into sexual acts with animals. Maria had been forced into sexual acts with a dog and as an adult was very afraid of them.

Before therapy I couldn't go near a dog without cringing and turning away, but now I can actually bathe my friend's dog without feeling ashamed and guilty because I touched him. *Maria*

Claustrophobia (fear of being in an enclosed space) can also develop from being locked in or feeling trapped during the abuse.

Fears associated with the abuser's threats

The threats used to silence some children are so terrifying that they develop lasting fears that the threats will be carried out.

Sophie was raped on a grave when she was seven. The abuser said that if she told anyone the rotting man in the grave would know and would find her. This threat was so terrifying for Sophie that she blocked-off all memory of the abuse and, even as an adult, had nightmares about rotting bodies coming to get her and a phobia of dead bodies.

Lorna's abuser said he would know, and would kill her if she ever told anyone about the abuse. This threat was so frightening to Lorna that as an adult she was very anxious. She was unable to talk about the abuse because she believed she could actually see her abuser in the room with her and could hear him threatening her. Adult fears which may seem to be irrational, can often be traced back to an association with the abuser, the situation the abuse occurred in, or to the threats which accompanied the abuse.

Obsessional problems

Some anxious people suffer from problems with obsessions. They may feel they have to clean their house for hours every day, count things, do something a particular number of times, or check that the doors are locked over and over again. There are usually repetitive thoughts that go along with the actions, i.e., "If I don't check the doors six times my son will have a terrible accident," or, "If I don't clean the kitchen floor again everyone will know how dirty I am."

Some people have repetitive thoughts but do not engage in repetitive action. Survivors may cope with their anxiety and memories of the abuse by repeatedly doing something. While they are busy cleaning, counting or checking they are distracted from thinking about their past and tend to feel less anxious. Cleaning is a common obsession for Survivors. When Survivors feel dirty inside they often try to make up for this by trying to keep their homes immaculately clean. They may spend many hours every day cleaning the house and be unable to leave a cup unwashed or a speck of dirt on the carpet.

I have huge fights with my husband if he leaves anything on the floor. I always take my vacuum cleaner up to bed with me. Sometimes I have to vacuum the whole house at four in the morning. *Pam*

Some Survivors also wash their bodies over and over again in an attempt to feel clean. Fiona was sexually and physically abused as a child. She felt dirty and was often nervous and afraid; she coped with these feelings by cleaning her bedroom.

When I was a child I used to scrub my bedroom at all times of the day. I felt dirty so I'd take up the carpet and scrub the floor and even the walls. I was always cleaning. I'd even get up in the night and start sweeping my bedroom. *Fiona*

This way of dealing with her feelings continued when she was an adult.

When I grew up and got my own house I was obsessed with cleaning. I'd start at seven in the morning and still be at it at midnight. If I didn't half-kill myself cleaning, I felt bad and dirty, so it was like a ritual—I cleaned to make myself feel better. *Fiona*

The more anxious a person with an obsession problem feels the more they clean, count or check. Doing these things brings temporary relief from anxiety followed by a feeling of even greater anxiety. When a Survivor is anxious because she feels out of control or in danger these repetitive thoughts and actions can be reassuring. They may also be a superstitious or childlike way of trying to escape danger.

Fiona was in danger of sexual and physical violence throughout her childhood. As an adult she still saw danger around her all the time and believed any happiness she had would be taken from her just as in her childhood. When she was under stress Fiona had obsessional thoughts about her daughter and husband being killed; she tried to escape her fears by cleaning her house until it was spotless.

I feel as if Amy and Andrew are going to be taken away from me. Every minute I'm with them seems to be the last. I can't enjoy them. I get flashes of them gone. The thoughts are different every day. One day it's Amy getting killed on her bike or being knocked down, the next it's they are both going to get killed in the car and another day it's the house is going to burn down. Everything around me feels dangerous. My obsession with cleaning the house is back and it has taken over this last week. *Fiona*

Coping with anxiety and fears

Feeling afraid increases your feelings of powerlessness; overcoming your fears will help you feel more in control of your life. If you experienced a great deal of fear in your childhood, as an adult, you may still feel tense and anxious. Trying not to think about your abuse can increase your anxiety. Working through your feelings about your childhood abuse will help you to reduce your anxiety. The fears a Survivor experiences as an adult are often related to her fears as a child and to the situations in which she was abused.

If you have a phobia or intense fear of certain situations, objects, people or animals, think about whether there is any link between the phobia and your abuse. Is there a connection between whatever frightens you now and your abuser, where the abuse occurred, what happened during the abuse or the threats the abuser used? Understanding the link between your specific fear and where it originates can help you to reduce the fear.

You may realize that you are afraid of bathrooms because you were abused in a bathroom or you are phobic about knives because you were threatened with knives as a child. Some fears may have no obvious link with the abuse, yet the stress caused by the abuse probably played an important part in creating and maintaining the fear. After attending a Survivors' group and working through her problems Kate realized that her fear of men was linked to her abuse.

I can handle men much better now. So much so that I recently took driving lessons with a male instructor and really enjoyed learning to drive. *Kate*

You have learned to feel anxious and afraid through your bad experiences. You can also learn how to reduce the bad feelings and live a normal life without all the fears. Anxious people are often afraid they are going to lose control. You can overcome this fear by learning to gain self-control in situations that are usually frightening.

The suggestions in the rest of this chapter can help you to reduce your symptoms of anxiety. It may also help you to read one of the books suggested at the end of this chapter or to go to an anxiety management or relaxation class. Learning to control your general anxiety will help reduce your fears and obsessions.

If you are very anxious or have a phobia or obsession that is disrupting your life ask your doctor to refer you for expert help. You do not need to tell your doctor about the sexual abuse. Look at the list of anxiety symptoms in Table 5 and check any that you experience. In the following section we suggest ways in which you can learn to deal with the three parts of anxiety.

Physical symptoms

You can begin to control the physical symptoms of anxiety by learning how to relax, learning how to breathe correctly and by exercising.

When people are afraid they tend to tense up their muscles and this can cause headaches, chest pains, stiffness, or pain in almost any part of the body. If you are anxious you are probably tensing up more and more as the day goes on. You need to find a way of relaxing your muscles. It will help to learn a relaxation exercise like the kind taught in prenatal classes or at the end of a yoga class.

Your doctor might know of a relaxation class near you, and some hospitals, womens' centers and adult-education centers run classes. Remember, you learned to be tense so you need to learn how to relax and let go of your tension again. Practice a relaxation exercise every day at first. When you feel generally less tense you need only do the relaxation exercise three or four times a week and when you are feeling particularly stressed. When people have been tense for a long time they sometimes feel strange when they begin to relax. Persevere and you will eventually become familiar and comfortable with the feeling of being relaxed.

For some people gardening, running, knitting, yoga, meditation or cooking can be relaxing. Breathing exercises are also very good ways of relaxing. It is important that you choose a way of relaxing that suits you and try to relax completely every day. When you can relax you can learn to notice the first signs of tension and then let go and relax right away before the tension builds up. Learning to relax will also help you sleep better.

Controlling your breathing
When we are afraid, a natural reaction is to breathe very fast or to gasp in air (hyperventilation). We breathe in oxygen and breathe

out carbon dioxide and the bloodstream usually contains a balance between carbon dioxide and oxygen. Hyperventilation occurs when someone breathes too fast and so breathes out too much carbon dioxide, creating an imbalance of oxygen and carbon dioxide in the blood. Many of the physical symptoms of anxiety are due to hyperventilation. Unfortunately hyperventilating also makes you feel short of breath so you try to breathe even faster, creating a greater imbalance in your blood.

When you feel yourself becoming afraid try to breathe very slowly and smoothly. Try closing your mouth and breathing through your nose. It's hard to breathe fast through your nose. Some people find it helps to breathe in and out of a paper bag. Hold the bag tightly around your mouth and nose, breathe out into the bag and then breathe the same air back in.

By doing this you breathe back in the carbon dioxide you have just breathed out, thus correcting the balance of oxygen and carbon dioxide in your blood. Overbreathing like this can become a habit so that people breathe too fast, or sigh a lot, even when they are not afraid. Practice breathing slowly and gently and become more aware of your breathing.

Exercising

Your body increases the production of stress hormones when you are afraid. Residues of these stress hormones left in your body can leave you feeling restless and unable to sleep; exercise can help eliminate them from your bloodstream. Exercise has also been shown to change people's mood and help them to feel better. Regular exercise can help you to overcome some of the physical effects of your anxiety and fears.

Challenging negative thoughts

Feeling afraid usually begins with negative thoughts about what is happening, what is about to happen, or what other people are thinking. A vicious circle begins with negative thoughts producing physical symptoms of fear which lead to more negative thoughts and so on. The fear may build up until you feel out of control. You can break this vicious circle if you learn to talk yourself through your fear by challenging your usual negative thoughts with more realistic thoughts.

Here is an example of the thoughts of an anxious Survivor

who feels very nervous about going into a local store alone. On the left are her usual negative thoughts and on the right are more realistic ways of thinking.

Negative thoughts	Realistic thoughts
Everyone is staring at me. They know there's something wrong with me. They think I'm dirty. My heart's beating too fast. Oh no, it's starting again. I'm going to have one of my spells. I must get out of here before I pass out.	The people are not staring at me, they are just looking around. No one can see what I'm feeling. My heart is beating faster because I'm nervous. It won't do me any harm. I've had these strange feelings before and they always pass. They don't hurt me. If anyone did notice what was happening to me they would just think I felt ill or something. No one knows I've been abused. I'm not going to pass out—I never have before. I'll just breathe slowly to calm myself down and I'll be alright. I'll buy the bread and go home for a cup of coffee.

Your negative thoughts make you feel more afraid. You may not realize you are having these negative thoughts and feel that the fear just descends upon you. By becoming aware of your negative thoughts and arguing against them you can reduce your fear. Write down the thoughts you have when you feel afraid and then try to challenge these thoughts by writing down more realistic thoughts. This will not be easy at first but it is a skill you can learn and with practice you will reduce your negative thoughts and your anxiety. (Chapter 10, Depression and Low Self-Esteem, contains more examples of how to challenge negative thoughts.)

No escaping

A very common response to fear is to run away, or to want to run away. Escaping from frightening situations may make you feel better immediately but it can make you more anxious in the long run. Fear and panic die down in time but if you escape then you do not learn that your fear would have died down anyway. You begin to believe that you are afraid of the situation itself when it is your negative thoughts in that situation that trigger the fear. When you go into that situation again you are more likely to run away because you escaped last time and felt better. This may happen in more and more places until eventually there are few places where you feel comfortable.

This is how agoraphobia develops. Other phobias develop in a similar way. The key rule is DO NOT ESCAPE when you are feeling afraid or are having a panic attack. Try to stay in the situation until your fear dies down. Find a quiet corner or sit down somewhere, but try to stick it out. If you feel you have to leave then do this slowly. Wait until you feel calmer and then return to the situation. Leave if you want to after your fear has died down. Remember, panic attacks are very unpleasant but they are not harmful. These instructions only apply to situations where you are afraid but you are not in any real danger. Of course, if you are in a situation where you may be attacked then you must leave for your own safety.

Facing up to your fears

Once you have been frightened in a situation you may avoid going into that situation again and this will cause your fear to get worse. The next important rule is DO NOT AVOID. To defeat your fears you need to face up to them. You can create and work through a program to help you overcome your fears.

The first step is to find out exactly what situations trigger your fears. You need to be as specific as possible. It may be going out alone that frightens you. It may be only supermarkets that frighten you or only supermarkets when they are very busy. Try to define clearly exactly which situations increase your fear, including where it happens, when it happens and what people are around (or not around) when it happens.

Draw up a list of situations where you get frightened starting with a situation where you experience only a little fear (i.e., going into a store when it's empty) and finishing with your most-feared situation (i.e., going into a crowded supermarket alone on a busy Saturday afternoon). You may find it easier to to do on your own, or you may want someone with you when you first start practicing, but aim to try it on your own when you can. Try to include as many steps as possible between the least- and most-frightening situations.

Start by attempting the situation on your list which frightens you the least. Learn to control your fear by not escaping, trying to relax, slowing your breathing and talking yourself through it by challenging your negative thoughts. Practice this every day.

When you can cope with the least-difficult situation then move down your list and try the next task. Relax, breathe slowly, control your negative thoughts and step-by-step face up to your feared situations.

Taking control of panic attacks

I have to be strict with myself and know that even when I panic now it doesn't mean it's the end of the world. I try to stay where I am, breathe slowly and concentrate on telling myself, "I can do it, I am sure to succeed." I find this helps. *Polly*

Panic attacks are intense waves of anxiety. To control them you need to deal with the three parts of anxiety in the ways described above:

- *Physical symptoms*. Try to relax, breathe slowly and smoothly.
- *Behaviors*. Stay where you are. Do not escape.
- *Negative thoughts*. Think realistic thoughts, i.e., "It's only a panic attack, it will soon pass, I won't pass out or go crazy. I've had them before and they are not very nice but nothing terrible happened."

When you have a panic attack you may also experience a feeling of dread as if something awful is going to happen. In fact the panic attack itself is the awful thing—nothing worse is going to happen. Just try to let the attack wash over you, don't fight it.

Coping with nightmares

Whenever I had a flashback or a nightmare I would write it down and this really helped. *Polly*

Nightmares are a way for your subconscious fears and memories to come to the surface. The best way to deal with them is to write them down in detail afterward so they cannot stay at the back of your mind as a subconscious fear. Remembering the abuse and working on your feelings about it will help you conquer your fears, and the nightmares will subside.

A note on medication

You may be taking tranquilizers or anti-depressants to help you with your anxiety. These drugs can help in the short term by suppressing your symptoms, but in the long term you need to face up to your fears to defeat them. The techniques described here may help you control your anxiety symptoms without taking any pills. DO NOT STOP TAKING ANY PILLS SUDDENLY—this can be very dangerous. If you want to reduce the amount of pills you are taking, discuss this with your doctor first.

Summary

The experience of childhood sexual abuse and the associated feelings of fear and dread often result in the adult Survivor feeling anxious and sometimes also suffering from specific fears, phobias or obsessions. You will probably find your anxiety will decrease as you work through your feelings about the abuse. You may also need to work on the symptoms themselves. To overcome your anxiety it is necessary to face up to your fears and work on your physical symptoms, negative thoughts and behaviors. You have learned to be anxious and fearful because of your childhood experiences. You can learn to overcome your fears and take control of your own life again.

Suggestions

- If your symptoms of fear or anxiety are disrupting your life see your doctor and discuss the problem with him or her. Ask for a referral to someone who can help with anxiety management or relaxation.
- Try following the steps in the Coping with Anxiety section.
- Practice some form of relaxation every day.

Further reading

Beckfield, Denise. *Master Your Panic.* Impact Publishers, 1994.
Marks, Isaac M. *Living with Fear.* McGraw-Hill, Inc., 1980.
Weekes, Claire. *Hope & Help for Your Nerves.* NAL/Dutton, 1990.
Weekes, Claire. *Peace from Nervous Suffering.* NAL/Dutton, 1990.
Resource Groups
A.I.M. (Agoraphobics In Motion). 1729 Crooks, Royal Oak, MI 48067-1306. (313) 547-0400.
Phobics Anonymous. P.O. Box 1180, Palm Springs, CA 92263. (619) 322-COPE.
Anxiety Disorders Association of America. 6000 Executive Blvd. #513, Rockville, MD 20852-3801. (301) 231-9350 or (900)-737-3400.

10

Depression and
Low Self-Esteem

How I wish I had sought help long before I did. I can remember feeling
isolated, guilty and having little self-esteem for as far back as I can
remember. I had no idea that my grim view of life and low opinion of
myself were linked to my sexual abuse. *Joanne*

SURVIVORS OFTEN HAVE A LOW OPINION OF THEMSELVES
and lack self-confidence and self-esteem. They may feel worthless, useless and unlovable. Many Survivors put on a front and
present themselves as capable, cheerful and confident, while
feeling miserable inside. Survivors may be so overwhelmed by
their low opinion of themselves and lack of confidence that they
suffer bouts of depression. Depression immobilizes people,
making them unable to act positively or find pleasure in things.
This in turn further undermines self-confidence and starts a
vicious circle of decreasing self-esteem and increasing depression. This chapter looks at low self-esteem and depression, the
links between them and what can be done to overcome them.

Low self-esteem

If children have a loving and supportive environment they
develop self-confidence and self-esteem as they grow up. They
learn:

- to trust their own judgment
- to feel safe in the world
- that they can be liked for themselves
- that they can make their own decisions
- that they are valuable
- that they deserve to be treated with love and respect

Children learn these things if they are around others who love and protect them and yet allow them the freedom to develop in their own way and to make mistakes. When these children become adults they are less likely to become depressed because their happy childhoods have given them confidence and made them feel positive about themselves.

What happens to a child who has been sexually abused? She might learn:

- not to trust her own judgment (the person she trusted betrayed her)
- to feel the world is a dangerous place where trusted people take advantage of her and use her for their own ends
- that she is only liked when she does what the abuser wants her to do; that she is not accepted for herself
- that she is controlled by other people and cannot decide for herself who can touch her body
- that she is not valued for herself and that she is treated as if her feelings don't matter
- that she deserves to be abused and to have her wishes disregarded

Such experiences have the effect of undermining the child's self-confidence and self-esteem, making her more likely to feel bad about herself and suffer from depression as an adult. Lucy and Jocelyn describe how they felt about themselves as children:

After the nightmare of being raped and sexually attacked by my uncle and dad I lost my self-esteem. I felt shy and had no self-confidence. I was frightened and I hated myself. I felt I could never please my mom and dad and always felt second-best. *Lucy*

My self-confidence was very low, I thought everyone was better than me. I couldn't think of anything I was good at. I could think of dozens of things I was bad at. I was nervous, frightened, always tense and I

Table 6—Depressed thoughts, feelings and behavior

Depressed thoughts include thoughts about being:	and thoughts about:	Depressed behavior includes:
punished	death	crying a lot or being
useless	illness	unable to cry
unable to control	accidents	withdrawing and
situations or alter	catastrophes	avoiding people
them	life being pointless	eating less than usual
disliked	**Depressed feelings include feelings of:**	staying in bed
worthless and	sadness	drinking alcohol,
unlovable	failure	over-eating or taking
a failure	guilt	drugs
a destructive person	self-hatred	doing very little
always used and	anger	not being able to
abused	dissatisfaction	sleep or waking up
ugly and repulsive	worry	early
fat	being out of control	being unable to make
	being overwhelmed	decisions or do
	helplessness	simple tasks
	numbness	

always had a tummy ache. I never said what I wanted, what I would like. I didn't think anyone was interested or really wanted to know. I didn't know who I was, what I wanted, and I felt I had no voice. I was letting events and other people carry me along. I was not in control. I was on a conveyor belt and I couldn't get off. *Jocelyn*

Like Lucy and Jocelyn, many Survivors give up, feeling inferior and lacking in self-confidence. They may feel so worthless and unacceptable that they put on a front to other people and never allow their real feelings and thoughts to be known.

Survivors may strive for the approval and love they feel unworthy of by always taking care of and trying to please others. Many Survivors seek approval to feel acceptable and think any form of rejection is devastating proof that they are unacceptable and unlovable.

Lack of self-confidence and self-esteem can lead to problems such as:

• not being able to say no to people
• not being able to ask for things
• always putting other people's needs first
• not being spontaneous
• not being able to make decisions

- waiting to see what happens rather than making a choice
- acting passively
- staying in bad relationships
- letting people take advantage
- feeling guilty
- feeling obliged to do things
- a feeling of having no choice or control
- hiding real feelings
- not being able to express opinions
- feeling let down by people
- compulsively caring for other people at one's own expense

When children are sexually abused they usually cannot fight back or stop the abuse. They are powerless and learn to passively accept the abuse, remain silent, and keep their feelings to themselves. The child learns that the abuser's feelings and needs are more important than her own. Her opinions and feelings don't count; she has no rights. She learns to be passive. Many Survivors give up, continuing to keep their feelings of anger and distress inside and passively accepting abuse from other people.

I was so used to being used. I didn't know I had a right to free choice about how I wanted to live my life, so I married an abusive man when I was 17. In many ways he was like my brother (the abuser), he abused me verbally, battered me and intimidated me by breaking up the furniture. His threats to kill me became almost a routine. I accepted my fate without rebellion for many years. I did not like my husband, yet if I had to describe my feelings during all those abusive years the only word that comes to my mind is numb. I was really passive. *Ingrid*

Survivors who always put other people's feelings and needs before their own and never stand up for themselves are likely to be used and abused again as adults. They may also be prone to occasional aggressive outbursts when the bottled-up feelings can no longer be held back and often then hate themselves and feel guilty, frightened and out of control. Passive behavior can make people feel more helpless and worthless and makes them more likely to become depressed.

Depression

Depression can be a very disturbing and frightening experience. People often feel that depression descends upon them from nowhere and feel powerless to understand or change how they are feeling. It can cause physical changes such as tiredness and loss of appetite but depression is not primarily a physical problem. Depression is rooted in a person's past experiences; her thoughts and feelings about herself and the world; and the ways she has learned to cope. Depression can be broken down into three parts: depressed feelings, depressed thoughts, and depressed behavior (see Table 6).

Depressed thoughts and feelings

Children who have been sexually abused often believe that they are worthless, inferior, unacceptable or unlovable. They believe these things because of the way they have been treated and sometimes because the abuser, or someone else, has told them this directly. By the time these children become adults they have already had years of practice in thinking negatively about themselves and often about the world in general. These negative or depressed thoughts become habits, automatic ways of thinking which Survivors may not even be conscious of, and which lead to depressed feelings.

Some Survivors have suffered from bouts of depression since childhood. Others may become depressed as adults because an upset, such as not getting promoted, reactivates their negative thoughts about themselves.

Depressed behavior

Depressed thoughts and feelings cause physical changes in people's bodies and affect their behavior. Some people feel constantly tired or lethargic when they are depressed. Others feel agitated and unable to sleep or eat. Some people are unable to cry when they are depressed and others become very tearful.

People also change their behavior when they are depressed to cope with their bad feelings. Drinking, over-eating, sleeping, taking drugs and self-injury are all ways of trying to blot-out negative feelings and thoughts. Depressed people tend to withdraw and avoid other people because they feel so worthless and unacceptable. They may attempt suicide to escape from their painful feelings or because they feel so helpless and hopeless about the future.

These types of behavior tend to make the negative thoughts and feelings worse. A drinking or eating binge temporarily blots-out bad feelings but then leads to feelings of guilt, self-hatred and hopelessness. Depressed behavior makes people more likely to have negative thoughts and feelings and this in turn makes them more likely to behave in a depressed way. Unless this vicious circle is broken the depression becomes worse and worse.

Overcoming depression and low self-esteem

Reading through this book and working on your thoughts and feelings about your abuse will help you build up your self-esteem and feel less depressed. You will begin to feel more self-confident and worthwhile as you start to feel less guilty and ashamed and stop blaming yourself for being abused. As you begin to feel better about yourself your depression will be easier to overcome. Talking to other people, especially other Survivors, or seeing a therapist can also be helpful.

When you feel depressed it is often extremely difficult to believe that you will ever feel any differently. Nothing seems to help and other people's suggestions can seem impossible to carry out. Feeling so hopeless and beyond help is part of being depressed. Fiona has now overcome her depression but can remember how hopeless she previously felt.

I can't put into words how much I hurt. The darkness, the emptiness and the feeling of hopelessness were unbearable. I never thought I'd get through it and even when it did start to lift I was frightened of going back there. As I write this and remember the pain I can't stop the tears but there is no fear because I know now I'll never be like that again. *Fiona*

Try to remember that people can and do overcome depression. Below we suggest ways of tackling your depressed behavior and thoughts and becoming more assertive. Take things one step at a time. Don't expect too much too soon. Try to be pleased and reward yourself for any positive changes you make, however small. Don't be tough on yourself if you don't change as quickly as you would like.

Changing depressed behavior

Depressed behavior is not only a reaction to depression, it also causes the depression to worsen. You can start to break the vicious circle of depression by making some changes in your behavior. It may be hard to get started if you're feeling hopeless. Take it one step at a time. Set yourself easy tasks you can achieve and feel good about. Work on some of the points below:

- Get up at a reasonable time rather than staying in bed and then feeling guilty. Reward yourself for getting up and start the day with some positive thoughts (see the section on affirmations).
- Exercise. Exercise helps people feel better both physically and mentally. Try walking, gardening, yoga or swimming.
- Try to eat regular meals even if you have little appetite. Choose good, healthy food to give you energy to tackle your problems. If you are overeating read chapter 11 on Eating Problems and do the exercises suggested there. Overeating is often a way of covering up bad feelings and seeking comfort.
- Do one thing every day that you enjoy, i.e., have a bath, listen to music. If you can't think of anything that you find enjoyable at the moment do something that you used to enjoy.
- Try to make some contact with people again. Avoiding people only increases thoughts that you are lonely and unlovable. Being with friends can help you begin to think and feel more positively—there are things to enjoy in life; people do like you; you are not alone.

Changing your behavior is only the first step towards overcoming depression. It is also important to work on changing your negative thoughts.

Challenging negative thoughts

Depression may seem to come out of the blue but it is brought on and maintained by negative thoughts. Negative thoughts affect your mood. Trying to recognize your negative thoughts and then challenging them by questioning whether these thoughts are realistic, helps you to reduce your feelings of depression. Negative thoughts happen automatically and can be difficult to identify so you will need to persevere with the exercise below. Before attempting this exercise read through the instructions and the examples.

Exercise

Draw a line down the middle of a piece of paper and head one side *negative thoughts* and the other side *realistic thoughts.* Notice what negative thoughts are running through your head, particularly if you suddenly begin to feel worse. Write the thoughts under the heading negative thoughts. Write them exactly as they go through your head in the first person and present tense (i.e., "I'm stupid."). Remember that it is the thoughts, not the feelings that you are trying to recognize. For example, don't write: "I was sitting feeling depressed and thinking about the future." Write the exact thoughts, for example: "I'll never feel any better, I'm going to be miserable for the rest of my life. There's no point in living."

Next ask yourself, are these thoughts really true? Is there another way of seeing the situation, or of explaining what has happened, or of seeing yourself? Write down these alternative, more realistic, thoughts. The negative thoughts may seem realistic to you at the moment because you are depressed. Try to be objective and look at the evidence for and against your negative thoughts. If you cannot think of any more realistic thoughts ask someone to help you.

Keep a paper and pen handy and write down your negative thoughts whenever they occur. Be sure to write the thoughts down rather than trying to do this exercise in your head. This exercise needs to be done regularly over a period of time. Negative thinking builds up over years and it takes time to break the habit completely but you may begin to feel a bit better very quickly.

Aim to write down your negative thoughts in simple statements as in the example below.

Negative thoughts	Realistic thoughts
I deserve to be abused.	No one deserves to be abused. I deserve to be treated with love and respect like any other human being.
I am a complete failure.	I am not a complete failure. I have survived being abused and brought up my children.

I am useless.

I am not useless. I sometimes
make mistakes like everyone else.

I will never feel any better.

Feeling better takes time and
effort. I have made the first step
by reading this book and facing
my problems. The Survivors in
this book have helped
themselves and so can I.

Every time Fiona felt depressed she stayed in bed. This gave
her more opportunity to slip into thinking negatively about
herself and her future. These thoughts happened automatically.
She wasn't even aware of all the negative thoughts which were
running through her head and making her feel even worse.
Fiona decided to challenge her negative thoughts to help lift her
depression. For the first time Fiona began to see that there were
alternative ways of seeing herself and her situation.

Negative thoughts

Realistic thoughts

I caused my parents and
others to treat me the way
they did by being disruptive.
It was all my fault.

No, it wasn't my fault. I
learned to behave like that.
I wasn't born disruptive.
Circumstances and situations
made me like that. I was
crying out for help. I had
bottled-up my anger,
frustration, fear and disgust
about my neglect and abuse. I
need not fear anything. I will
handle whatever life dishes
out. I am going to enjoy life
now and get stronger so I can
use my experience to help
others which I know I can do.

I'm dirty and my house
always looks dirty.

I am not dirty. I am as good
as anyone else. My house is
not perfectly clean the way I
wish it could be, like the ones
on TV. No one can be
that clean if there are people
and pets living in it comfortably.
My house is clean and tidy, a lot
cleaner than some and not as spotless as others but then it is not a

	show house. It is a home where people live and are comfortable.
I'm not as good as other people.	I'm just as good as the next person, if not better. I'm a very caring person who loves her family. I haven't done a bad job in raising Amy, keeping a home and getting educated even though I've had a hard life and suffered abuse. I am going to try to like myself.

Over the weeks Fiona began to see that her negative thoughts weren't realistic. She had gotten into the habit of thinking badly about herself because of how she'd been treated as a child. Fiona began to see that there were many good things about herself. She had survived abuse and had made a new life for herself and was trying to overcome her problems. She began to accept herself and feel more powerful.

Affirmations

Affirmations are positive statements about yourself. They help to remind you that you have good points and so increase your feelings of self-confidence and self-esteem. They also help by counteracting negative thoughts. Affirmations can help in overcoming depression and in stopping depression from developing.

Exercise

Write down three positive things about yourself. They could be things you like about yourself, or are good at, or are getting better at. If you can't think of anything yourself ask a friend to help you. Here are some examples:

- I am good at my job.
- I am courageous in facing my problems by reading this book.
- I am getting to like and accept myself more every day.
- I am a good listener.
- I am a great gardener.
- I like the way I keep on trying.

Say your positive statements every day before you get out of bed.

Assertiveness

Assertiveness training is a powerful way to increase self-esteem and can help in overcoming depression. It teaches that everyone has rights and that they can learn to think, feel and act positively by respecting their own rights and those of other people. Assertiveness training distinguishes four different types of behavior:

* *Assertive*—expressing feelings openly and honestly. Not allowing yourself to be used and put down, and not using or putting down anyone else.
* *Passive*—not saying how you feel. Putting other people's feelings and rights before your own. Putting yourself down ("I am stupid") and allowing other people to use you.
* *Aggressive*—putting your own feelings before anyone else's feelings. Using and putting down other people ("You are stupid"). Shouting and being physically aggressive.
* *Indirect*—trying to get your own way without appearing to do so. Putting down other people while appearing to be friendly on the surface. Lying, being sarcastic, "guilt-tripping" others, making excuses and being manipulative.

Most people behave in all these different ways at some point but they usually have one style of behavior which is more common than the others. Many Survivors behave passively most of the time, indirectly some of the time, and have occasional aggressive outbursts. Very few Survivors have learned how to be assertive.

There are now numerous assertiveness-training classes and some good books with exercises you can use to become more assertive: see end of this chapter for details. In the following account Katarina shows how assertiveness has helped her.

Since I went to an assertiveness-training class I have stopped accepting the blame and apologizing for everything that goes wrong in the lives of my family and other people. Before, I truly believed that everything was somehow my fault. Even if I was not directly involved, somehow I found a connection, a link that printed GUILT, BLAME, SHAME in capital letters in my mind. Now I realize I am not responsible for my family's happiness. I can love them and care for them, but ultimately they must create their own happiness. I cannot keep all unhappy experiences or problems from them.

As I refused to feel guilty anymore I understood that assertiveness is about how you value yourself. It is not right for me to treat other people better than I treat myself. I became more understanding, more forgiving and accepting of myself. I can see my faults and shortcomings but as I can accept them in others, I don't need to be perfect either.

Becoming more assertive has done something else for me. It has finally released me from this terrible need to put up the front of being "superwoman," the one who can cope with everything and anything without getting tired or stressed.

Too many people and things were eating away at my time and energy. There was not enough left for myself. So, I decided to change my life. I ignored the rooms with no wallpaper on their walls and I sat down in a chair and did nothing for an hour. It was the first time that I'd sat still without feeling guilty because there were other things to do. Then I made a list of my priorities and decided only to do the things that were really necessary or important to me.

The conscious decision to say "I don't have time for this" or "I feel tired" lifted enormous stress off me. I relaxed and found peace again. I have now gone back to doing some things that I gave up for a short while. But now I do it because I want to and not because I have to. This is the big difference in my life. *Katarina*

Fiona's coping methods

After suffering depression most of my childhood and adult life, at 29 I am now living. I know I have a long way to go but I no longer suffer depression like I did. I still get a little down, but who doesn't? I see life differently now. I'm interested in lots of things whereas before I used to think 'What's the point?' Now I am trying to make up for those lost years, enjoying life and getting as much out of it as I can. I am now able to love my family dearly and to accept love. *Fiona*

Fiona tackled her depression by changing her behavior (she made herself get up earlier, eat regularly and start seeing people again) and by challenging her negative thoughts. She realized she had gotten into the habit of thinking badly about herself and this made her feel depressed. Fiona went to an assertiveness-training group and began expressing her feelings. As she began to respect her own rights and feelings and those of other people her self-respect and self-confidence grew. She also worked on her memories and feelings about being sexually abused. As she began to see she wasn't to blame for the abuse she stopped feeling guilty and ashamed and began to feel more acceptable and worthwhile.

Fiona had felt helpless and hopeless about ever feeling any better but she overcame her depression. She started to feel better about herself, more hopeful about the future, and had renewed interest in life. Fiona regained her own strength and power, and you can too.

Suggestions

• Begin to change your depressed thoughts, feelings and behaviors by following the suggestions and exercises in the chapter.
• Read a book on assertiveness (see Further reading below).
• Attend a class on assertiveness or confidence building or form your own group with friends.

Further reading

Assertiveness and self-esteem
Alberti, Robert E.; Emmons, Michael L. *Your Perfect Right: A Guide to Assertive Living.* Impact Publishers, Inc., 1990.
Klein, Donald F.; Wender, Paul H. *Understanding Depression: A Complete Guide to Its Diagnosis, Course, & Treatment.* Oxford University Press, Inc., 1993.
Phelps, Stanlee; Austin, Nancy. *The Assertive Woman: A New Look.* Impact Publishers, 1987.
Smith, Manuel J. *When I Say No, I Feel Guilty.* Bantam Books, Inc., 1985.

Depression
Papolos, Demitri; Papolos, Janice. *Overcoming Depression: The Respected Reference for the Millions Who Suffer Depression & Manic Depression & for Their Families.* HarperCollins Publishers, Inc., 1992.
Preston, John. *You Can Beat Depression: A Guide to Recovery.* Impact Publishers, 1989.
Sanford, Linda Tschirhart; Mary Ellen Donovan. *Women and Self-Esteem: Understanding and Improving the Way We Think and Feel About Ourselves.* Penguin Books, 1986.

Resource groups
National Depressive & Manic-Depressive Association. 730 N. Franklin, #501, Chicago, IL 60610. (800) 82-NDMDA or (312) 642-0049.
Depressed Anonymous. 1013 Wagner Ave., Louisville, KY 40217. (502) 969-3359.
NOSAD (Nat'l Organization for Seasonal Affective Disorder). P.O. Box 451, Vienna, VA 22180. (301) 762-0768.

11

Eating Problems and Body Image

When I became a teenager I wanted to look pretty. I lost some weight, I looked like all the other girls. Yet when I looked in the mirror I only saw a fat girl, so ugly that I felt like apologizing every time someone had to look at me. I only saw myself with my brother's eyes. *Katarina*

MANY WOMEN IN OUR SOCIETY have a poor body image and are concerned about their weight, but Survivors of sexual abuse are even more likely to have problems in this area. Survivors are often left with a dislike or even a hatred of their own bodies, which usually focuses on their weight, size or shape. They may dislike all of their bodies or just certain parts like their stomachs, their genitals or hips. Many Survivors do not like to get undressed in public dressing rooms, do not like their partners to see them with no clothes on and often even avoid looking at their own bodies. It is not surprising that Survivors feel particularly bad about their bodies because during sexual abuse the body is invaded and treated without respect.

This dislike of the body often leads to attempts to change it by repeated dieting, usually interspersed with periods of breaking the diet and overeating. Survivors frequently turn to eating when they are upset or angry and find it difficult to eat in a normal way. Dieting and overeating can develop into a way of coping with their bad feelings about themselves and what has happened to them.

The difficulty was, how to get thin? I couldn't diet because I ate for comfort. I ate to stop thinking, to keep the fears at bay. So I kept on eating and simply vomited the food right back up. I ate when I felt bad about myself, then vomited. I gave in to sexual demands because I needed affection and reassurance. Then I'd feel bad about being promiscuous, so I'd eat. As the bulimia spiraled out of control I learned to feel guilty about that too. When I was sexually assaulted as an adult, I ate as a way of coping. I ate because I felt angry about the abuse, hating myself because I couldn't stop it from happening. I ate because I had no control over my body. I ate because I felt angry that other people felt they had a right to hit me, to abuse me. But most of all I ate because I was afraid I deserved the abuse. I vomited because I could not hold so much pain, so much fear, so much hate and so much anger within myself and I could find no other way of letting it out. *Shirley*

Some of these women end up with a much more serious problem by developing anorexia nervosa, bulimia or compulsive eating. Research studies on women with clinical eating disorders have found at least 50 percent had been sexually abused as children.

What is an eating problem?

Many women, and a growing number of young men, have problems centering around food and eating. A woman with an eating problem is overconcerned or preoccupied with her body size, weight and shape. She may weigh herself every day and feel her mood change according to the reading on the scales. She does not go out when she feels fat and feels life would be a lot better if she was a different shape or size.

This often leads to constant attempts to diet or to use other ways of trying to control and transform her body. Unfortunately when people try to follow a strict diet they often end up breaking the diet and overeating when they are under stress. Instead of eating when they are hungry, eating becomes a response to stress, bad feelings, or difficult events in their lives.

Eating can temporarily ease uncomfortable feelings. If people eat according to their own strict rules about what and when they can eat, instead of in response to their body signals, they can end up no longer knowing whether they are hungry or not. At times everyone eats in response to how they are feeling (agitated, lonely, upset) rather than because they are hungry, but for most people eating does not become their main way of dealing with bad feelings.

For some people, though, the problem develops into an eating disorder which can take over their lives and prevent them from dealing with the underlying causes of the problem. The main eating disorders are:

Compulsive eating—A compulsive eater is someone who eats in response to bad feelings or to avoid feeling anything at all. She may no longer even know when she is hungry or full. The compulsive eater is often, but not always, overweight. She frequently eats between meals and usually feels out of control when she does so. She has a low self-esteem and is preoccupied with her body size. She doesn't like to eat, or to eat much in public, and regularly tries to diet.

She is often afraid of being hungry and so eats when she isn't hungry to make sure she never experiences the feeling of hunger. Her inevitable failure at dieting makes her feel even more worthless and so she eats more to cope with this feeling. Many women, whether they have been sexually abused or not, are compulsive eaters.

Anorexia nervosa—At the other end of the scale the woman with anorexia nervosa generally eats very little at all. Anorexia nervosa is diagnosed when someone deliberately loses a quarter of her normal body weight, has a morbid fear of becoming fat and has hormonal changes including the loss of menstrual periods.

Half of the women with anorexia nervosa regularly lose control of their strict dieting and binge-eat large quantities of food. They then feel a need to get rid of the calories by self-induced vomiting, exercising, fasting, or by taking laxatives, diuretics or diet pills. Many young women go through a phase of restricting their food and losing weight but true anorexia nervosa is still quite rare.

Bulimia and bulimia nervosa—A much more prevalent problem is bulimia (binge-eating) or bulimia nervosa. Bulimia is very common but it is a secret problem. Most people who binge-eat are normal weight so, unlike anorexia nervosa, the problem is not visible to other people. Perhaps 10 percent of young women in their late teens or early twenties binge-eat, although for many it will be a passing phase. The majority of people who binge-eat are female but a growing number of young men also have this problem.

Bulimia is a disorder which includes phases of dieting, or restrained eating, followed by episodes of binge-eating very large quantities of food in a short amount of time. During a binge the food is not usually chewed or tasted but is quickly swallowed. This is accompanied by a feeling of being out of control. The foods most commonly eaten in a binge are those that people usually try to avoid eating when they are dieting such as chocolate, bread and other high-calorie foods. Binge-eating may temporarily lift their mood but afterwards they feel depressed and guilty about overeating and terrified of becoming fat and so they attempt to diet again.

Some women who diet and binge-eat use more drastic ways of preventing any weight gain after a binge. They may immediately make themselves vomit up all the food, or take large amounts of laxatives, diet pills or diuretics. These are all attempts to eliminate the extra calories and keep their weight down. For many this purging is also a self-punishment for losing control and overeating. This dieting/binging/purging cycle is called *bulimia nervosa.*

Even if you do not have a serious eating disorder you may, like many women, feel uncomfortable with your own body and the way you eat. If you are unhappy about your eating habits then the ideas and exercises in this chapter may help you understand more about why you eat or why you restrict your eating. Over time they may help you develop a more normal relationship with your body and your food intake. If your eating problem is disrupting your life or you feel unable to take control of your eating (or non-eating) then seek some outside help. Talk with your doctor for advice.

Eating problems—the background context

As a teenager I learned that being thin, looking acceptable on the outside, gained me approval and praise. It gave me some self-esteem, although not enough for me to get rid of the fear that I was a bad or unworthy person, so I had to try harder, get thinner, achieve more. *Shirley*

In western society the media is influential in setting up an image of the ideal woman as young, slim and sexually attractive.

I was afraid of being regarded as fat, because I felt that fat women have little status in our society, are viewed as failures, are the butt of senseless jokes and are not seen as individuals. *Shirley*

Women in our society are expected to take daily responsibility for providing food—planning meals, shopping, preparing, cooking and presenting meals. The pressures on women to be slim, dynamic, sexually attractive and to be a plump, motherly, homemaker lead to conflicts about their body image and their role in life. This results in most women feeling dissatisfied with their bodies and regularly putting themselves on diets regardless of whether they are overweight or not.

Dieting is rarely successful in the long term and certainly doesn't change the size and shape of the particular body parts which cause concern. Dieting can leave women feeling that they are failures—they can't even take control of their own eating and body size. This leads them to dislike themselves and their bodies even more.

Societal pressure leads to many women dieting on and off throughout their lives, but only some of them go on to develop eating problems. Whether a person develops an eating problem may be the result of further individual pressures such as the eating habits of their families, their own weight history and history of dieting, pressure to diet from peers and how they have learned to cope with their emotions. Women have low status in our society and often feel powerless in the outside world.

When they have problems, they may turn inward and try to control their own bodies instead of dealing with the external situation. Childhood abuse leaves the victim feeling very bad about herself and her body. Many women block-off their feelings about themselves and the memories of the abuse by becoming preoccupied with their body fat and dieting, and thus develop an eating problem. The books suggested under further reading at the end of this chapter will help you to look more closely at why women develop this preoccupation with food and body shape.

Sexual abuse and eating problems—issues in common

At least half of the women who have eating disorders have been sexually abused as children. What are the links between sexual abuse and the development of eating problems?

Body Image

Eating problems usually develop in people who already have a poor body image and a history of dieting. When people are sexually abused they learn to detest their own bodies. They associate their bodies with the physical and/or emotional pain and the shame of what has been done to them. The poor body image of Survivors makes them more likely to begin dieting and so develop an eating problem.

Swallowing feelings

After I became aware of the connection of my eating problem with the fact that I had been sexually abused as a child, I realized that at all the times in my life when I was under stress and felt unsafe and unsure of the future I ate more and put on weight. This fact became especially clear to me after my daughter told me she had been sexually abused by a neighbor some years earlier. During that first week, while I was trying to get help for her and also trying to cope with the memories of my own abuse and the pain I felt, I ate food almost non-stop. I felt very frightened, fearing that she would grow up with the same problems I had, and also fearing that I could not cope. I felt threatened. I so much wanted to be protected from all the pain, I wanted to feel safe. So I ate and I put on four pounds in that one week. *Katarina*

Survivors are left with many traumatic memories and bad feelings about themselves. We all know how easy it is to reach for food when we feel bad. It doesn't take away the bad feelings but it does push them down—we swallow our bad feelings and may briefly feel better. Overeating can be useful at first by blanking-out bad feelings and bringing a sense of relief. The bad feelings about the abuse are still there but they become buried deep inside. Instead Survivors are left feeling bad about breaking their diets and they feel out of control, stupid, guilty and fat.

This leaves them with bad feelings about themselves instead of anger at their abusers or sadness about their childhood. They often feel so bad about themselves that they reach out for more food to help them swallow their feelings. Eating to avoid bad feelings can become such a habit that people start to binge in response to any bad feeling or minor difficulty. Many women with eating disorders end up feeling completely numb and out of touch with their feelings.

On the other hand some Survivors have feelings of guilt and shame but cannot remember anything about the abuse. Women who suffer from bulimia cannot cope with having unfilled time ahead of them. They often binge-eat to distract themselves and fill the time to keep away unwanted memories, thoughts and feelings.

Guilt

Although the responsibility for sexual abuse always lies with the abuser, the victims nearly always feel guilty and blame themselves. Survivors sometimes harm themselves as a form of self-punishment for being so bad. The physical pain may also help by blocking-off the emotional distress. Dieting itself can be a form of self-deprivation and self-punishment. Women who are dieting feel greedy and guilty when they overeat because they have broken their diet.

It may be easier to cope with the guilt about overeating rather than the guilt about the abuse. Unfortunately this leaves Survivors feeling worse about themselves while the real problem remains unresolved. Women who deliberately vomit, take laxatives, diuretics, or diet pills are attempting to lose weight by getting rid of the calories, but these are also powerful ways of punishing themselves to help cope with the feelings of guilt.

Shame

The abuse changed my life from a very early age. I was ashamed of my body and frightened that people would be able to tell what was happening just by looking at my body. *Kate*

Many Survivors feel great shame because of what has happened to them, whether they feel guilty or not. For some dieting is a way of purifying the body and attempting to make the body perfect rather than dirty or shameful. The extreme form of this is in anorexia nervosa where women are often striving to be perfect in body and mind.

Women who suffer from bulimia nervosa and deliberately vomit after eating feel great shame and disgust at their own behavior. Vomiting and feeling this self-disgust may be safer ways for them to express their feelings of disgust about the abuse. People who were forced to have oral sex often vomit after overeating, perhaps repeating what happened to them as a child when they vomited, or wanted to vomit, after oral sex.

Secrecy

Common to all the eating problems is the need to eat in secret. People with eating problems will not eat in public or will eat very little in front of other people. Their eating is mostly done in secret and may involve secret episodes of vomiting. Women with bulimia nervosa are usually so ashamed of their binging and vomiting that they go to great lengths to make sure no one finds out about it. Bulimia has been called the *secret disorder*. Sexual abuse and eating behaviors share this theme of secrecy. Sexual abuse always occurs in secret and may be kept secret for many years.

Feelings of loss of control

Sexual abuse is forced onto children by the power and authority an adult or older child has over them. Children may also feel powerless to resist because of threats or actual physical violence from the abuser, or because they feel very confused about what is happening to them. When people are feeling powerless and out of control the one thing they can control is their own body. Small children who are being abused often overeat, refuse to eat, or wet or soil themselves (see chapter 6).

These are body functions that they alone can control and which adults cannot take control of. If feelings of powerlessness and loss of control develop as the child grows up, the body may again become a means of regaining some control.

Some people try to control and change their bodies by dieting and exercising. While dieting is an attempt to feel in control, the feelings of powerlessness are also expressed through losing control in binging and overeating. Unfortunately the feelings of powerlessness increase when their dieting doesn't work or when they lose control and binge.

Eating for protection

Women who overeat often experience conflict in their feelings about being overweight. On a conscious level they usually hate the idea of being fat and desperately want to become slim. However, when they explore their underlying feelings they often find, to their great surprise, that they are actually terrified of being thin. Some women believe that being fat makes them unattractive to men and therefore prevents any unwanted sexual advances.

For others being fat makes them feel physically stronger while being thin makes them feel vulnerable. A woman may feel that when she is overweight she has more presence, power and identity because she is seen as a person rather than as a woman. Being overweight can therefore be very useful for a Survivor who does not want to be seen as sexually attractive or who feels vulnerable and powerless because of the sexual abuse.

The underlying reasons for overeating vary for each individual but being fat often has a protective function. This is why some people find they can lose weight fairly easily at first but then as they lose weight their hidden fears begin to surface and they start overeating again.

Concern about their bodies and eating becomes an obvious and initially useful way for Survivors to deal with their bad feelings. Through dieting, binging and purging, Survivors can express many of their feelings relating to their body image, guilt and shame. Usually, though, they end up with bad feelings about themselves instead of about the underlying problem (the sexual abuse). To overcome an eating problem you need to start uncovering these bad feelings, accepting and expressing them.

Overcoming the problem

During the last few months I have again had a few times when I was under great stress but I have learned so much. I have learned that there is a lot more strength in me than I thought, and that no matter how difficult a situation may seem, somehow time dilutes the pain and solutions can and will be found. Instead of running away from my problems and feelings by eating I must face them and deal with them.

I had a few days lately which were really difficult to cope with. But suddenly, as the problems had been solved I realized that I ate normally during those times. No more eating non-stop, no more putting on weight. I don't need this protection anymore. I can only think that this is because I feel strong enough to cope with anything the future will bring and don't want to run away anymore. Nowadays I eat anything I want to and I am gradually losing weight. The irony of the situation is that now I like my body and losing weight is totally unimportant to me.
Katarina

To overcome an eating problem you have to find ways of allowing the emotional issues to surface again and find more useful ways of coping with them. It is also important to look at eating and dieting behavior because bad habits of weight control can also lead to the development and maintenance of eating problems. If you have an established eating problem or have difficulty in regaining control of your eating you will benefit from getting some professional help.

Dieting

An eating problem rarely develops without a history of dieting. People put themselves on diets in order to lose weight (often when they are not even overweight to start with), but strict dieting rarely helps anyone lose weight in the long term. In fact repeated dieting slows down the metabolic rate (the speed at which the body burns up calories). After returning to normal eating, the rate of weight-gain is faster–and so people who diet often end up fatter than before. *Dieting Makes You Fat* by Geoffrey Cannon argues strongly that strict dieting does not lead to permanent weight loss.

When a person is dieting she is trying to control her body. She tries to ignore the signals telling her she is hungry and that her body needs food. This self-starvation makes her pre-occupied with food and leaves her feeling deprived. If she breaks her diet by eating something "bad" (meaning high-calorie) she then feels she has lost control. This usually leads to binge-eating or overeating.

Dieting not only makes people fatter but also causes binge-eating or overeating. The first step in overcoming an eating problem is to stop dieting forever. This doesn't mean you cannot try to lose weight. A more practical way of losing weight is described later in the chapter.

Exploring your feelings about your body size

Women with eating problems use eating and concern about their body shape as a way to cope with their feelings. To stabilize your weight at a reasonable level and develop a healthy relationship with your body and food you need to find out what feelings you are hiding under your fat and find more useful ways of coping with them. *Fat is a Feminist Issue* by Susie Orbach is an excellent book which explores these ideas and makes practical suggestions. In this and the follow-up, *Fat is a Feminist Issue II*, exercises are described to help you to explore the feelings you associate with your own body, food and eating.

Most women have a fear of becoming fat or fatter. Exploring

your feelings about your weight often helps you see that being fat may also be useful in some way. It may make you feel protected and safe, or sexually unattractive. It is clearly very difficult for you to regain control of your eating or to lose weight if you have underlying fears about becoming slim.

Binge-eating

Binge-eating is usually triggered by an unpleasant event, stress, bad feelings or memories. Often the woman is feeling deprived of love, safety or comfort. She wants or feels something but doesn't know what this something is. She is invariably dieting and so she feels hungry and reaches out for food. Use your binge-eating, or eating when you are not hungry, to find out what you really want or what feelings you are avoiding.

Exercise

Next time you feel you are going to binge, try delaying the binge for ten minutes. If you find this difficult then try five minutes or one minute. Do something for yourself in this 10 minutes instead of binging—for example have a bath, read a magazine, phone a friend, go for a run. Think of things you enjoy doing that are free or cheap, last 10 to 20 minutes, and have nothing to do with food. Write these treats down. Instead of binging, give yourself one of your treats. Binge afterwards if you have to. The first step is to learn to delay the binge. Learning that you can delay a binge may also help you feel more in control.

Once you can delay your binges the next step is to use this delay to sit quietly, relax and think: What do I really want? What am I really feeling? This exercise is a way for you to find out what triggers a binge and to discover what you really want and feel.

If feelings like guilt, shame, etc. surface, you can work on them by using the ideas from the other chapters in this book. If you feel sad because you cannot get what you want immediately you may want to express this by crying. It is better to cry because you are sad than to eat because are sad.

Learn to eat whatever you want to if you really want it. Don't eat if you find that you are really feeling sad, angry or hurt rather than hungry. When you stop binging you may initially feel more depressed as your buried problems begin to surface but now you have the opportunity to deal with them directly instead of thinking about food and worrying about your weight. You may need to get professional help.

Purging
After binging many women learn to purge themselves by making themselves vomit up all the food they have eaten or by taking large quantities of laxatives, diuretics or diet pills. These are all attempts to get rid of the calories just consumed and therefore avoid becoming fat. All these ways of purging are physically very dangerous. There are many unpleasant and medically dangerous side effects of purging, including damage to the teeth and gums, throat hemorrhages and electrolyte disturbances (which can lead to epilepsy, kidney failure and other very serious problems). None of these methods of purging eliminate all the calories. Laxatives only stop a very small proportion of the calories from being absorbed. However many times you vomit you will still only prevent a portion of the calories from being absorbed.

Use the same technique to control your purging as you do to understand your binging, that is, delay and use the time to find out why you are doing it. Perhaps you will discover that purging (which is painful and dangerous) is a way of punishing yourself or of indirectly expressing your anger or other bad feelings.

Controlling my weight by vomiting was a way of coping with the hatred I felt towards myself, and it was a secret expression of the anger I felt inside myself but was too afraid to direct at the real causes of my anger. I could literally swallow my anger and pain by eating, then purge myself of it. *Shirley*

Most women who stop binging also stop purging. If you do not stop purging try to use the technique described above or seek professional help.

How to lose weight
If you feel you've explored and worked through your feelings about your weight and you are overweight, then you may want to try to lose some weight. It's very difficult to lose weight before you've dealt with any fears about being slim. The method below will not work unless you have overcome these fears. If you have been dieting on and off for years you may find it difficult to lose weight because your metabolism has slowed down.

- Stop dieting. Try to eat three meals a day, however small.
- Aim to lose one or two pounds a week maximum. If you lose more than this it will be water, not fat, that you are losing.
- One pound of fat is equivalent to 3,500 calories, so to lose one pound of fat per week you need to lose 3,500 calories per week (or 500 calories per day) from your usual calorie intake.
- Aim to cut 250 calories a day only off your normal eating. Try to do this by replacing fatty food and junk food with whole food. Junk food contains many calories but does not provide the nutrients your body needs so you very quickly become hungry again. Eating healthy foods will make you feel better as well as assisting you in controlling your weight.
- Burn off the other 250 calories a day by doing some exercise. Exercise not only burns off calories but can increase your metabolic rate so you burn off more calories whatever you are doing. If you try to lose weight without doing exercise then you will lose water and lean tissue (muscle) instead of the fat you want to lose.

Remember that strict dieting is very unlikely to help you lose weight and keep the weight off. You may actually end up heavier, feeling deprived and thinking about food much more. You will also be more likely to overeat when you do break your diet.

Body image
Most of my problems have gone. What has taken me longer is to accept that it is possible for a man to look at me without feeling repulsion. My poor body image and my eating problem have been with me for so long that they will take longer to leave me. *Katarina*

Disliking your body can distort your perception of your body so that it appears to you to be bigger and fatter than it actually is. You really can see yourself as fat when objectively you may be normal weight or even thin. It is possible to change your perception of your own body but it takes a lot of practice over a period of time. You've spent many years building up a distorted image so it will take time to see it accurately again. Try reading one of the recommended books and try out the exercises in them.

Exercise: Mirror work

When most women look in a full-length mirror they focus on the part of their bodies that they dislike the most, their stomachs, hips, breasts, etc. This distorts the way they see themselves. Try looking in a full-length mirror naked. What parts do you focus on? If you hate your thighs because you think they are too big then focusing on them makes them appear even bigger to you. Try to look at your whole body. Try not to judge it, just look at it. Try to accept and like yourself: "This is my body." Do this exercise twice a day when you are getting dressed and undressed.

Summary

Many women in our society dislike their own bodies and are preoccupied with food and their body image. Dieting is a way of trying to transform the body but it rarely leads to permanent weight loss and usually leaves women fatter than before and feeling even less in control of their lives. Some then go on to develop more serious problems such as compulsive eating, anorexia nervosa and bulimia.

At least 50 percent of women with eating problems have been sexually abused as children. Many Survivors develop difficulties around eating as a way of coping with their emotional problems. Both women with eating problems and Survivors of sexual abuse have feelings of dislike or disgust towards their own bodies. They also share feelings of guilt, shame, low self-worth and loss of control. Problems around eating may result in women experiencing a temporary relief from their distress about the abuse as their memories and bad feelings become buried. In the long term they lead to physical problems and a lowering of self-esteem.

To overcome an eating problem it is necessary to allow the memories and feelings to return to the surface so that they can be expressed and dealt with. One way of doing this is to explore what you are thinking and feeling when you reach out for food. It is also important to change your behaviors around food, such as restrained eating, binge-eating or purging. In order to do this it is important that you stop dieting. As you grow to understand and accept yourself you will probably find you can also learn to respect and accept your own body.

Sharing the pain with other women helped me to find better ways of coping. As the wounds caused by the abuse began to heal, as I began to see myself as a whole person, where the good in me began to feel as real as the bad things I had found in myself, I no longer saw myself as being fat. I am free of the bulimia because I am free of the abuse, free of the guilt, free of the hate, and I am free to find in myself the person that I want to be not the person I am afraid to be. *Shirley*

Exercises

1. Follow the suggestions and exercises described to help you to stop dieting and to overcome your eating and body-image problems.
2. Seek professional help if you have a serious eating problem or have difficulty in gaining control of your eating.
3. Don't deprive yourself (by dieting or ignoring your own feelings). Spend time on yourself and your own needs.

Further reading

Eating

Hall, Lindsey; Cohn, Leigh. *Bulimia: A Guide to Recovery*. Gürze Books, 1992.
Orbach, Susie. *Fat Is a Feminist Issue*. Berkley Publishing Group, 1982.
Orbach, Susie. *Fat Is a Feminist Issue II: The Anti-Diet Guide to Permanent Weight Loss*. Berkley Publishing Group, 1987.
Roth, Geneen. *Feeding the Hungry Heart: The Experience of Compulsive Eating*. NAL/Dutton, 1993.

Body Image

Freedman, Rita. *Bodylove: Learning to Like Our Looks & Ourselves*. HarperCollins Publishers, Inc., 1990.
Ussher, Jane. *The Psychology of the Female Body*. Routledge, 1989.

Resources groups

National Association of Anorexia Nervosa & Associated Disorders, Inc. (ANAD) P.O. Box 7, Highland Park, IL 60035. (708) 831-3438.
American Anorexia/Bulimia Association, Inc. 418 E. 76th St., New York, New York 10021. (212) 734-1114.
B.A.S.H. (Bulimia Anorexia Self-Help). P.O. Box 39903, St. Louis, MO 63138.
(ANRED) Anorexia Nervosa and Related Eating Disorders. P.O. Box 5102, Eugene, OR 97405. (503) 344-1144.
National Anorexic Aid Society, Inc. 1925 E. Dublin Granville Rd., Columbus, OH 43229-3517. (614) 436-1112.

12

Sex and Sexuality

Many survivors of childhood sexual abuse experience difficulties with sex and relationships as a result of their inappropriate and usually disturbing introduction to sexual matters. For children who are not sexually abused, sexuality is a developing process. Children gradually become aware of, and explore their own bodies, their own sexuality and their relationships with other people. Knowledge and experience develop slowly, giving the child time to adjust.

Sexual experiences should be associated with good feelings and with pleasure and relaxation. Even though teenagers often pressure each other about relationships they can still make their own choices about who they want to develop sexual relationships with and how far to go. The child who is sexually abused has no control over this process and is thus prevented from developing her knowledge and sexual experience at her own pace. We discussed the process of traumatic sexualization in chapter 3.

When children are sexually abused they are introduced to sexual acts which are not appropriate to their age or level of development. They may feel forced into submitting to sexual acts or doing things they don't want to do. Abusers often punish children who try to object to the abuse and give presents, money or affection for submission to sex.

Children learn that sex can be exchanged for rewards. The sexual abuse is often confusing, frightening or physically painful,

130

so sex becomes associated with negative feelings: fear, shame, tensions and dirtiness. The abuse may also be associated with good feelings, with affection, physical pleasure and orgasms. This can leave the child feeling even more confused.

He rubbed my clitoris with his finger until I had an orgasm. It was very confusing because while I liked the feelings it produced, I hated it because it was him who made it happen. My own body had now betrayed me. *Sandra*

Even if the abuse involves some good feelings the child has still been subjected to sexual experiences she hasn't chosen or that are too advanced for her age and with inappropriate people such as family members, adults or older children. The child does not have any control over the situation. She is not able to make choices about her sexual experiences nor to develop sexually at her own pace with her peers. Her experiences are very different from the child who has not been sexually abused. This process of traumatic sexualization leads to a variety of sexual problems in the adult Survivor.

Not all Survivors experience sexual problems but many women with sexual problems have been sexually abused. One study of a group of women seeking help for sexual difficulties found that 90 percent had been sexually abused as children.

This chapter looks at some of the sexual problems Survivors experience and suggests ways of understanding and overcoming these difficulties. The chapter is for people who are heterosexual or homosexual, and people with or without partners. It is for anyone who is interested in understanding more about their sexual feelings and learning to be more comfortable about sexual matters, as well as for people with specific sexual difficulties.

Ingrid, in her story below, describes the sexual difficulties she experienced as a result of being abused as a child.

Ingrid's story

I was sexually abused from around 1953 when I was four years old. In the years that followed as I grew into the age of harmless dates with boys I guessed that my feelings and attitudes were not the same as those of my friends. I had no way of relating to boys. My mother wanted to protect me and did not allow me to talk to or play with the boys in our neighborhood. The only boy I knew was my brother and he abused me. When my friends started to go out with boys and in giggles

Table 7—Sexual difficulties and responses to sexual abuse

Dislike or avoidance of:
 relationships
 physical contact
 sexual contact
 certain sexual activities
Dislike of touching or looking at oneself
Lack of physical pleasure in sex
Flashbacks
Inability to have an orgasm
Vaginismus (tightening spasms of the vaginal muscles)

Not being able to say no to sex
Having sex indiscriminately
Prostitution
Aggressive sexual behavior
Sexual pleasure linked to pain
Feeling guilty about sex
Feeling sex is dirty or disgusting
Confusion about sexual identity (male/female)

Confusion about sexual orientation (hetero-sexual/homosexual)
Lack of sexual knowledge
Sexualizing relationships and situations
Obsession with sex
Obsession with masturbating

and whispers talked about kissing in doorways, I did not understand them. As they talked I could almost feel my brother forcing his tongue down my throat and felt repulsion and disgust. My friends all seemed happy and excited. I felt an outsider.

By the time I was sexually involved with a man at the age of 16 I knew that my emotions were crippled, my feelings distorted. I looked at other girls and wondered why I could not be like them. I fell in love as totally as my friends, but when it came to kissing, touching and finally sex, I froze and lost all feelings. I felt numb, paralyzed, trapped. I agreed to sex more out of gratitude than desire and because I didn't know how to say no. He was the first man who wanted me, the first who did not get bored with me after two or three weeks because I was so quiet and he really seemed to like me. So when I became pregnant when I was 17, we got married.

At first I thought I was too young to like sex. I knew something was not right with the way I hated any physical contact. Maybe the problems would not have grown as large if he had been a more patient and understanding man. He knew about the abuse but did not care much. But sex was very important to him. It was never lovemaking, only sex. There was never any love-play involved. As I was cooking dinner, he pulled me away into the bedroom, with a wide grin pulled down my pants and had intercourse. At other times he came from behind when I was busy with something and suddenly masturbated all over me. But when I had time I was expected to be always ready and always willing to satisfy him. He wanted me to have an insatiable sexual appetite and initiate sex several times a day. To please him I tried to be like that but sometimes the disgust with my own behavior, the repulsion with the way he wanted sex was so great I would rather let him beat me. I felt sexually abused all through my marriage. The disgust I felt for my own abuser and what he did to me turned inward and I felt disgust with myself.

I hated it. I felt as if I was degrading myself. I felt dirty. I felt humiliated, especially when I tried my hardest to please him in bed and during intercourse he told me that all my friends and my brother's wife were better in bed than I was. I never learned what a loving touch could be like. He never stroked me, never caressed me, never tried to arouse me. My husband was abusive, unfaithful and humiliated me. Finally when he tried to persuade me to become a prostitute I had enough and left him. Maybe it was the sexual abuse that led me to get involved with him in the first place. Maybe it was because of the abuse that I stayed with him for seven years.

After my divorce I always had problems saying no. I did not want sex but I had been programmed from early childhood right through the years of marriage to be submissive so that I just could not refuse. I did not think anybody could like me for what I was, I imagined my only value was to be used. I went through a period of sleeping with a number of men. I couldn't say no and I was searching, without success, for some good feelings in sex, the way my friends felt, and the way it was portrayed, in gentle lovemaking scenes in films and books. I did not find it.

For years during my first marriage and after the divorce I kept wishing I could be a lesbian or a nun so I would never have to be touched by a man again. They seemed the only acceptable reasons to refuse sexual advances.

I met my second husband when I was 27. He was friendly to me and did not ask for sex. I was sure he would not physically or sexually abuse me. During my 14 years of marriage to him we rarely had sex and when we did I blocked-off any feelings of pleasure. Sometimes a touch felt nice, but as soon as I recognized it was pleasure I felt, it was like running into a brick wall. I consciously refused to enjoy any touch. Most of the time I could cope with the physical side of my marriage. But at times he behaved in a way that made me once again see myself as dirty. At times like those I could feel myself choking with disgust, as if somebody was strangling me and I could not breathe. All I wanted to do then was to run away, but I had not learned to say no or to express dislike for certain behavior. And so all too often as soon as my husband turned towards me I froze and inside me the abused child that was still present screamed with sheer terror. After a few years I learned to develop an asthma attack as soon as my husband followed me into the bedroom or as soon as I thought he wanted sex. I knew that I was bringing the attack on myself through my own will. A whole range of sudden symptoms like urticaria (hives) and hot flushes, etc. gave me time to delay and often stopped any attempt at intimacy. At first we used to joke that I was allergic to him, although I knew why I felt ill.

Until I married my second husband I had felt disgust with sex, in later years it turned into indifference. During therapy I gradually began to realize that I could allow myself to feel sexual pleasure without feeling disgusted and dirty. Now my sexual problems have gone and I regret bitterly the wasted years of being unable to enjoy intimacy when it was offered.

Sexual problems

Table 7 shows some of the physical and sexual difficulties which are often experienced by teenage and adult Survivors of sexual abuse. Survivors may experience different types of sexual problems at different times in their lives. Some of them are discussed below.

Avoiding physical contact and relationships
Some Survivors dislike all forms of physical contact and avoid any touch or closeness such as friendly hugs, handshakes or sitting next to someone. Many Survivors find the idea of sexual contact especially unpleasant, frightening or disturbing and may therefore avoid relationships. This often happens when the Survivor is a teenager:

When my girlfriends at school were experimenting with boys I shied away. *Jocelyn*

I didn't like boyfriends or being on my own with men. I used to spend a lot of time in my bedroom on my own. *Polly*

Avoiding relationships often adds to a teenage Survivor's feelings of isolation and of being different from other people. Anita recalls being teased at school for not having boyfriends and being sexually inexperienced. These problems may gradually disappear as a teenage Survivor reaches adulthood and manages to form relationships and deal with physical contact. Some Survivors choose to avoid men and develop sexual relationships with women. However, some Survivors carry the fear of physical contact into adulthood and avoid relationships altogether.

Indiscriminate sex
In contrast, many Survivors report that they have gone through a phase of having indiscriminate sex with many different people. This may start at an early age or follow a period of avoiding

relationships and physical contact.

Jocelyn shied away from boys as a young teenager but went through a period of indiscriminate sexual activity with many men in her late teens and early 20s.

When I did eventually sleep with someone I became promiscuous. Sex didn't really mean anything. My feelings didn't enter into it. I was living a role. *Jocelyn*

Like Jocelyn, many Survivors have learned as children to separate their feelings from their sexual activities. As adults sex may become a meaningless activity. Many Survivors feel that it doesn't matter what happens to them or their bodies anymore. As a teenager having sex with men and staying out at night may also be a way of avoiding going home to the abuser.

Many Survivors feel unable to say no to sex or feel that they have no choice and no control over their bodies.

I'm afraid of saying no to sexual advances. Often I initiate them in order to be in control of the situation and then end up getting a bad reputation. *Paula*

Sexually abused children learn that they cannot say no to sex; they have no choice. Children often also believe that they were responsible for the sexual abuse because they think they caused the abuser to become sexually excited. As adults, Survivors may still believe that they are responsible for other people becoming sexually aroused and therefore feel they must satisfy them.

I have been in situations where, when I look back, I could have said no to sex but I have felt unable to say no. I often felt that I have led the other person on in some way. I did not realize that men should be in control of their own bodies. I did not want to be a cock-teaser. My step-father called me a bitch in heat when I was 13 because I was out with a few friends who just happened to be boys. Perhaps I believed him. *Jane*

Survivors who find little pleasure in sex or experience sexual problems may try to find a solution to these problems by having sex with many men. For some Survivors sex is an attempt to get close to someone and receive some comfort. Often women end up feeling dissatisfied or even more lonely, disgusted and ashamed.

I was desperate for someone to like me, desperate for some feeling of tenderness, caring, comfort and closeness. I remember days when I stood at the window, alone in my apartment, looking out and waiting. I was so lonely that I would have taken anybody, and I mean anybody, as lover or friend, just to know someone cared. I would have sold my soul to the devil for somebody to put his arms around me with genuine feelings of liking me. There were a few men I only knew one evening before we had sex. I searched for love and closeness, but the morning after when I woke up the only feeling I had was of desperation, shame, guilt and a terrible emptiness. After a few months of searching for friendship and love I withdrew. I did not go out anymore and so did not get into contact with men anymore who were interested only in satisfying their sexual desire. The few moments of tenderness and holding was not worth the loneliness and the bad feelings afterwards. *Katarina*

For some Survivors indiscriminate and unsatisfactory sex becomes a pattern they continue throughout their adult life. Many Survivors, however, opt for one-on-one relationships or revert to avoiding relationships. They often feel ashamed of what they describe as their promiscuous phase. Fiona has come to understand that picking up men was a reaction to her loneliness and fear and is now able to accept herself without judgment:

I felt lonely most of my childhood but when I got to 17 and my mother left home I was extremely lonely. I'd go with men at night who I met in bars and night clubs. I never intended to have sex with them, I just wanted to be with someone. I hated going home alone. The house was so empty, everywhere so empty. I was looking desperately for someone to care. When I did find a man who cared for me I rejected him. I couldn't accept love so I just got hurt time after time with the ones who just wanted one thing. I'd sleep most of the day till it was time to go to the bar. Some nights I'd sit at the edge of our yard hoping to find someone to talk to.

The feelings as I sat there was as if I was chained to that place and I was crying out for someone to come and take me away. It was a big empty dark world out there, but I'd pray every night that someone (Mr. Right) would come for me and I could love him and he'd love me. Some nights if I'd been to a night club and hadn't found someone I'd walk home alone feeling so desperate. Then my desperation would turn to anger. I would want to cry but couldn't. My throat would feel so tight, I could hardly swallow so I would get angrier, and try harder to cry but couldn't. I would think of throwing myself under a car but I didn't have the guts. I'd finally get home, pig myself with food, smoke a cigarette and sleep the clock around.

On the other hand if I did find someone it usually ended up with them having sex with me. To them I was just another screw. I'd go home, usually the next day, feeling more depressed, and cry and feel ashamed. I'd usually fall in love with that kind (well, I thought it was love) and end up feeling hurt and used when they didn't speak to me the next time I saw them. There seemed to be no hope for me.

I'm free now, and with writing this for the first time I've realized that. I realize how bad I felt growing up and I can see how I've carried a lot of emotions and hurt into my adult life. I also know now that I wasn't a whore at 17. I was an empty, lonely, frightened young girl who had never loved or been loved. The nearest to love I got was being sexually abused time and time again, but now I'm learning to love. *Fiona*

Survivors who go through periods of having sex with many people may see sex as a meaningless activity or be desperately trying to seek some affection and closeness or feel unable to say no to sex.

Avoiding or disliking sex
Many Survivors dislike sex or find it disgusting or boring. Survivors who have chosen homosexual relationships may feel the same way. Survivors often marry or live with someone as adults but they may still dislike sex and try to avoid it whenever possible. Some Survivors marry but do not consummate their marriages. Others marry men who aren't particularly interested in sex and make few sexual demands.

Ingrid chose a sexually undemanding man as her second husband. Many Survivors find excuses for not having sex or bring on physical symptoms to avoid sex: Anita avoided sex throughout her pregnancy; Ingrid developed rashes and had asthma attacks. However, many Survivors do have sex, even though they dislike it or don't get pleasure from it. Sometimes this is done for their partner's sake or because they feel they have no choice. Married women may feel it is their duty as a wife to have sex however much they dislike it.

My first husband didn't understand why I had never played the field, so to speak. My first sexual experience, besides my father, was my first husband and then I never relaxed. I was always uptight and ended up crying most times. That marriage ended in divorce. *Pam*

Some Survivors lie passively and let their partner have sex with them without participating. Often they are repeating what happened when they were being abused.

Dislike of sex is usually a result of the bad feelings the Survivor has associated with sex. Feelings of fear, tension, guilt and shame can prevent Survivors from experiencing any sexual pleasure. Guilt about having sex or getting pleasure from it can cause Survivors to block-out good feelings during sex or touching, leaving them feeling dissatisfied or disgusted.

For some Survivors there is no pleasure in sex, for others the pleasurable feelings may come and go.

Turn offs

During sexual activity Survivors may suddenly turn-off sexually or feel frightened, angry or disgusted. This often happens because something (a word, a smell, a certain type of touch, or sexual position) has triggered memories of the abuse. This is not always a conscious process; they may simply feel bad without realizing why. Survivors often dislike certain sexual activities which happened during the abuse (i.e., oral sex) and may feel such behavior is perverted and disgusting. Some Survivors recognize that their feelings are connected with the abuse and that they are being reminded of the past.

A lot of the things my husband does to me would be considered natural behavior, but to me they are sickening memories of my childhood abuse. *Gail*

Others may not yet have made the link between their childhood abuse and adult feelings. Triggers that can cause Survivors to turn-off or start to feel bad include:

- words: breasts, father
- phrases: "I love you," "You like this, don't you?"
- smells: tobacco, alcohol, aftershave, engine oil
- touches: stroking the face, grabbing the legs
- positions: i.e., woman on top, man on top
- behaviors: oral sex, masturbation
- clothes: silk, jeans, dressing gown
- others: pubic hair, false teeth, glazed eyes

Flashbacks

During flashbacks the Survivor experiences a vivid memory of the abuse, so vivid that she feels she is reliving the abuse. She may feel she is a child again and see her partner as the abuser. This can be a terrifying experience. Some Survivors hit their partners during flashbacks believing them to be the abuser. Flashbacks commonly occur during sex but they can occur in any situation which reminds the Survivor of the abuse.

The triggers, listed above, which cause Survivors to turn-off or feel bad during sex, can also cause flashbacks to occur. Smells in particular can be powerful triggers for flashbacks. However, anything can trigger a flashback. What causes a flashback to occur for an individual Survivor will depend on her experiences and her memories of the abuse.

I have flashbacks. My husband once said he liked something I was doing to him and to keep on doing it. I felt sick, these words triggered something—the abuser was making me do something to him because he enjoyed it. *Jocelyn*

Partners may have no idea what is happening during a flashback. They may also have little understanding of why Survivors suddenly turn-off during sex or start to feel bad. This can cause major difficulties in relationships and leave both the Survivor and her partner feeling confused, frightened, upset, angry or rejected.

Lack of sexual knowledge

Survivors may have had many sexual experiences from a very early age but still have little sexual knowledge or understanding. They may have been too young to understand what was happening during the abuse or they may have closed their minds to what was happening. Children who have been sexually abused often do not show the usual curiosity about sexual matters or experiment like other children and teenagers. They may avoid sex education, and books, articles, TV programs or teenage talk about sex.

When my teenage friends talked about sex I either pretended I was in a hurry, or I deliberately concentrated on something different, so as not to hear anything they said. As an adult woman I wanted no knowledge of sex. It was disgusting, repulsive, humiliating. I knew all I needed to know for my purposes, that was how to bring the man to a climax as quickly as possible to get it over and done with. I wanted no further knowledge of sex. *Katarina*

Subjects that are met with embarrassed giggles by many children can be traumatic reminders of abuse for an abused child.

This situation leaves many Survivors in ignorance of basic knowledge about the make-up of men's and women's bodies, sexual behavior, contraception, pregnancy and childbirth.

Many adult Survivors continue to avoid matters concerning sex or bodies and may avoid looking at their own bodies.

I was in my early 20s when I looked at my vagina for the first time. I did not know what it was supposed to look like, but felt sure it was deformed somehow. I immediately made an appointment with my gynecologist who assured me I was perfectly normal. *Katarina*

Lack of knowledge about sex means that Survivors often do not know what would be considered normal or abnormal sexual behavior and do not know how to tackle problems which may arise.

Preoccupation with sex or with particular sexual practices

Some Survivors appear to be preoccupied with sex. They tell sexual jokes, bring sex into every conversation and see sex in all sorts of situations. For some Survivors this is a conscious front put on to cover up their own ignorance, insecurity and anxiety about sexual matters. Others become preoccupied by sex because so much of their childhood experience has been connected with sexual matters and this is how they have learned to view the world.

Some Survivors feel compelled to keep having sex or to masturbate again and again. This may be a sign of distress or a way of distracting themselves from thoughts and feelings about the abuse. Survivors may find themselves only able to gain pleasure from particular sexual practices, for example using certain objects, being tied up, having pain inflicted on them or inflicting pain. This usually reflects what has happened during their abuse. In this way adult Survivors act out their abuse through their own sexual behavior.

Prostitution

Sexual abuse can leave women feeling that it doesn't matter what happens to their bodies and seeing sex as something that can be exchanged for money or goods. Survivors may therefore see prostitution as a means of supporting themselves. Research studies have found that many prostitutes were sexually abused as children. Prostitution may be one of the few ways to get money for teenagers who have run away from home to escape the abuse or for Survivors who have lost out on their education, have small children to support or are in abusive relationships. Some Survivors feel that prostitution is a way of taking back control and getting even by making men pay for services they were forced to give as a child.

Overcoming the problems

You may find yourself becoming less negative about sex as you work your way through this book and begin to feel less guilty and ashamed about what has happened. Try to keep in mind that it isn't sex that's painful and frightening, but being abused. Your body was assaulted and your feelings were disregarded. Sexual feelings can be pleasurable, and sexual experiences alone, or with a partner, can be loving and enjoyable.

As I begin to love myself and my body I have also discovered that to have sex with someone I love deeply is the highest expression of joy, a celebration of being alive. My hunger for knowledge about my own body and that of my partner is insatiable. A whole new world is opening up for me. Now a kiss can move the earth and a touch takes away all gravity and makes me feel as if I can fly. *Ingrid*

Sexual problems can't be dealt with in isolation. Sexual problems are closely bound up with people's physical and emotional state of health, their relationship with their partner, feelings of self-worth, body image, sexual knowledge, and the ideas they have about what sex should and shouldn't involve.

Physical and emotional health
When people are anxious and depressed they often lose their interest and enjoyment in sex. If you're feeling distressed it may be better to work through some of the other chapters in this book or seek help with your emotional problems before tackling your sexual problems directly. It's difficult to enjoy sex if you are depressed, anxious, angry or tense. Give yourself time to feel better emotionally before dealing with this area.

The same applies to physical health. Physical injury, illness, poor health or tiredness can all lead to disinterest in, or aversion to sex. Taking medication could also affect your interest in sex.

Wait until you are feeling more physically healthy before tackling your sexual difficulties.

Relationships

Sexual problems are often associated with tension, anger, misunderstanding and lack of communication between partners. There is little hope of having a good sexual relationship with a partner if your relationship in general is not very good. It may be that you are angry with your partner for something he or she has done or not done. Maybe you feel hurt, neglected or just bored. These problems need to be dealt with first before you can deal with the sexual problems.

Talking about how you are feeling with your partner instead of bottling-up bad feelings is a good start. Assertiveness Training can help you with this (see chapter 10). Change becomes possible once you start to communicate more openly.

You may have chosen a partner that you do not feel sexually attracted to because he/she seemed safe and undemanding or because you accepted the first person who wanted you. You may feel so indebted to your partner for being with you that you feel you need to pay him or her back with sex.

Sex can become a focus for many other problems. Sometimes sex turns into a power struggle between partners: not having sex or having sex can become a way of punishing the other person or a way of taking control. You may need to get outside help to sort out problems in your relationship. A third party can often see more clearly what is going on than partners can themselves. Counseling can help partners understand each other better and strengthen their relationship. It can also give people the courage to leave relationships which aren't good for them. Survivors may be more likely to become involved in abusive relationships as adults as we discussed in chapter 3, and as some of the Survivors stories in this book have already illustrated.

No partner

You may not have a partner at the moment or have never had a partner. Don't be upset by our references to relationships or partners, these exercises are for you too. Having time and space free from a relationship can be useful for exploring your sexuality, expanding your knowledge and understanding, and feeling more comfortable with your body. If you wish to form a relationship but have been held back by your fear, anxiety or anger working through these exercises can help you begin to understand these feelings and become more relaxed and open to other people.

Exercise

Write down all the things which you feel are holding you back from having a relationship with someone else. Include any fears and anxieties about being close to someone and trusting them, and about the sexual side of a relationship.

Myths and messages

The first step in exploring your own sexuality and overcoming sexual problems is to understand what ideas you have learned about sexual feelings and behavior and where these ideas have come from. We learn about sex directly from what other people say to us or from what we read and see. We also learn about sex indirectly through the messages we receive in what people say or don't say, or in what they do or don't do. For example, a child who has her hand slapped when she is touching her genitals might feel she is doing something wrong and shameful. This is one message she has received about her sexual behavior.

The exercise below helps you to find out what messages you received about sex and to discover the thoughts and feelings about sex and your own sexuality which you have grown up with. Before doing this exercise read through all the instructions and the example.

Exercise: Messages about sex

Relax and let your mind reflect back over your childhood and teenage years. Think about the messages you received about sex. Write down the name of the first person who comes to mind who gave you a message about sex. Then write down what that message was. Next write down the name of another person and the message they gave you. Continue doing this until you can't think of any more. You might name an individual person or a group of people. You will have received some message about sex from your abuser. Put this message on your list if you can. If you find it too distressing to think about, leave the abuser out of this exercise for the moment.

Example: Polly's messages about sex.

Person	Message
Mother	Never spoke about sex, changed the TV channel when bed scenes came on. The message I got was sex is shameful and embarrassing.
School teacher	In Sex Education we learned about rabbits, sperm, eggs and conception. The message I got was that sex was a cold and clinical subject dealing with biology, not feelings.
Abuser	Raped me. The message I got was that sex is something that's done to me. I have no control or right to refuse it. How I feel sexually doesn't matter.
Boyfriend	Said I was cold and not very romantic. I got the message that I was sexually inadequate, that something was wrong with me.

Exercise: Challenging the myths and negative messages

Look at your list of messages about sex. Try to challenge any negative messages or thoughts about sex by writing the negative thoughts down on one side of a piece of paper and more reasonable or positive responses to these thoughts down the other.

Negative thoughts	Reasonable thoughts
I have no control over sex or right to refuse it.	It's my body. I have a right to say no to sex.
Sex is embarrassing and shameful.	Sex is natural. Some people are embarrassed about it but it doesn't have to be that way. I can learn to feel more relaxed about the subject.
Sex is dirty.	What's dirty about it? It's natural.

Notice which negative messages are influencing your feelings, thoughts and behavior now. Learning to challenge these negative thoughts is the first step towards a more positive attitude.

Learning about your body and sex

Having knowledge about how your body works and about sex is important in overcoming sexual difficulties. Fear thrives on ignorance. Fight your fear with knowledge and by learning to love and accept your body.

- Do the body image exercises recommended in chapter 11. Learn to accept all your body including the parts you may have avoided looking at and especially the sexual parts.
- Find some books or brochures to read with good clear information about your body and sexuality. Challenge the myths you have learned with some facts. Challenge the negative messages with positive information. Your local Family Planning Clinic and Health Department will probably have helpful free brochures.

The Survivors group has also changed me. Now I cannot learn enough about the way it feels in body and mind when making love with someone special and so I have read a few books on sex. To say they were an eye-opener is an understatement. The effect they had on me was enormous. I always thought there was me, the one who doesn't really know how to behave or what to feel and there is man—the mystery, the enigma. The first book I read, *Making Love,* turned out to be a book for men with sexual problems. In my ignorance I thought a man was always ready, willing and able to have sex and orgasm after orgasm.

As I read I understood that men are not all that different from women. They worry about the size of their penis as we do about the size or shape of our breasts. I had put men and sex on a pedestal to look up to and be in awe of. Now I understand that they have the same fears, worries and insecurities about their bodies and performance during sex. How could I ever hope to enjoy the relaxation needed for good sex if I pull in my stomach to make it look flatter? Or worry whether he has noticed a stretch mark or would he notice my thighs are too fat when he gives me oral sex? How many men worried about whether they were good enough for me when we had sex while I was nervous about whether I was touching and moving in the right way? The books I read made me feel an equal to the man. I realize how important communication is in lovemaking and how essential it is to feel relaxed in body and mind. *Katarina*

Learning to communicate

Learning to communicate more openly about sex and your feelings is essential in resolving sexual difficulties. Many people do
not know what words to use for the sexual parts of men's and
women's bodies and for sexual activities, and this makes it hard
to talk about sex. Some words may seem too crude and others
too clinical.

Exercise

Write down all the words you can think of to describe the female
genitals (vagina, pussy, cunt); the male genitals (penis, cock) and
sexual intercourse (fuck, make love, screw). Choose the words
you want to use and say the words loudly until you feel comfortable with them. If you have a partner say the words loudly with
your partner until it becomes easy. It's hard to talk about sex if
you don't have any words to use.

Follow your feelings

You have a right to say yes or no to being touched by another
person or to having sex with them. It is your body and your
choice. As a child you may have been unable to say no to being
touched or to sex and you may still feel that you do not have a
choice. Many Survivors think that they must touch or have sex
with another person even when they don't want to because:

- the other person wants to
- the other person is sexually excited
- it's their duty (i.e., to a husband)
- they've already responded to the kisses and the hugs
- other people's feelings are more important than their own
- the other person has been nice to them
- the other person will be bad tempered/upset/aggressive if they
  don't

These thoughts may have been learned from being abused.
Jane learned to give in to sex to avoid her stepfather's anger. You
don't have to have sex, touch someone else or be touched
unless you want to and choose to. This is your right whatever the
circumstances. However, you may not feel able to exercise this
right if you are afraid of the consequences, feel guilty or are

being threatened or overpowered.

Many Survivors feel anxious about sex because they begin to feel powerless, out of control and physically invaded again. Ultimately it can only be damaging to your own sexual feelings or relationship to have sex with someone when you don't want to. Learning to make a choice about what you do, and do not do, based on your feelings is a way of treating yourself and the other person with respect. It also helps you feel more in control of your own body and your own life.

While you are trying to deal with your feelings about being sexually abused you may find you do not want to have sex or any physical contact at all. Follow what you are feeling. Listen to your body. If you feel uncomfortable with someone then you probably do not want any physical or sexual contact. This is your right. If you have a partner explain how you are feeling and ask him/her to respect your wishes. These feelings do not have to last forever. Reassure your partner that this is part of the healing process. Many sexual problems arise because people do not speak about what they are really feeling, or act on those feelings; instead they pretend to their partner, or do what they think their partner wants them to do.

Learning to relax

Learning to relax is essential for dealing with sexual difficulties. Tension prevents the experience of sexual feelings and pleasure. You may have learned from the abuse to tense your body automatically when you are in any sexual situation and when you begin to have sexual feelings. Learn to relax in non-sexual situations to begin with. Learn to notice the difference between feeling relaxed and feeling tense. Notice where you hold tension in your body and what causes that tension to start. Next start to apply these techniques to sexual situations. Try to relax, notice where in your body you are holding any tension and what caused the tension to start. Many Survivors discover that they automatically tense their bodies as soon as their partner hugs or kisses them, or as soon as they begin to feel aroused.

Touching yourself

Survivors often feel uncomfortable about their own bodies and try to avoid thinking about them, looking at them, or touching them. They may have negative feelings about their bodies because this was the focus of the abuse. Learning to touch your-self is a way of exploring and overcoming these negative feelings and learning to love and accept your own body. Read through the exercise below before attempting it. Be aware that it might bring up negative feelings and recognize and accept these feel-ings. Discovering what sorts of touches bring up bad feelings can be helpful.

Exercise

This exercise does not have to be done in one sitting. Do it a little at a time and stop when you want to or if you feel very dis-tressed. Come back to the exercise when you feel ready.

Make some time when you can be on your own and feel relaxed. Find somewhere comfortable to lie or sit and then slowly begin to explore your own body by touching and stroking it or maybe gently massaging it with oil. Start with a part of your body which feels safe, maybe your face, feet or hands. Try differ-ent types of touching; gentle, firm, tickling, slow and fast. Notice your feelings as you are doing this and what feels good and what doesn't feel good.

Move to another safe part of your body and repeat this process. Gradually, work through all the parts of your body in this way. Leave your breasts and genitals, or any areas that you feel anxious about until last. Only attempt these areas when you feel ready and when you can relax and feel comfortable and safe.

As you are doing this exercise be aware of what gives you pleasure. Notice if you begin to feel tense or anxious with any type of touching or any part of your body. Does this remind you of anything that happened when you were abused? Notice any disturbing thoughts, images, feelings or memories that come up and write them down as soon as you can.

This exercise can help you learn about your own body and feelings and so understand and appreciate your own sexuality. This is a basic foundation for learning to feel comfortable with masturbation or a sexual relationship with another person.

Giving and receiving touches

When you have completed the exercise on touching yourself you can then go on to repeat a similar exercise with your partner (if you have one). The exercise is aimed to help you feel safe and comfortable with touching your partner and being touched. It also helps partners to communicate about what feels good or bad.

Exercise

The exercise below is in two parts and may take a number of sessions over a few weeks or months to complete. You must go at your own pace and not try to rush through the exercise. Before beginning this exercise make a pact with your partner that you will not have sexual intercourse or genital contact during the exercise sessions. You may feel safer and more relaxed when you know that touching will not lead to sex.

Find a time when you and your partner won't be disturbed and choose a warm and comfortable place to do this exercise. Find a way to relax together perhaps by doing a relaxation exercise or listening to music but avoid using alcohol or drugs. Ask your partner to touch the part of your body that feels the most comfortable and safe to you (your hands, arms, feet). Relax and simply accept the touches. Ask your partner to vary the speed and firmness of the touches and tell him or her what feels good and what doesn't. Repeat this exercise for different parts of your body. Take your time and gradually work towards the parts of your body that you have felt less comfortable with your partner touching. Only ask your partner to touch these parts of your body when you feel safe and ready for this.

Reverse the roles and become the person who gives the touches while your partner relaxes. Start with the part of your partner's body that you feel most safe and comfortable with. Tell your partner how you are feeling as you are touching him or her. Repeat this exercise for different parts of your partner's body, gradually working towards the parts you feel most uneasy about This part of the exercise is for you to look at your thoughts and feelings about touching someone else. Some Survivors have more difficulty in touching their partner than in being touched themselves. However, you might also want to ask your partner to tell you how she/he feels about the different types of touching you are giving.

Throughout these exercises notice how you are feeling. If you begin to feel anxious, tense or uncomfortable stop or ask your partner to stop. Relax and let any feelings, thoughts or memories come to the surface. Write them down and discuss as much as you want to with your partner. Go back to that area of the body or that type of touch only when you feel more comfortable about it.

This exercise enables Survivors to gradually work through any negative feelings about being touched or touching in a safe and relaxed atmosphere. It also helps partners to start to communicate about what feels pleasurable and what doesn't. Often partners have never done this and may have guessed incorrectly what the other person likes or dislikes. Learning to communicate openly in this way can help to break down anger, resentment and hurt which may have built up in the relationship.

Dealing with flashbacks

Flashbacks can be very distressing and frightening to Survivors and confusing to a partner when they happen during sex. If your partner doesn't already know what happens when you get a flashback explain it to him or her as soon as possible. When a flashback happens stop whatever you are doing and tell your partner that you are having a flashback. Then ask your partner to help you follow the four steps below. You can also follow these steps when you have a flashback and are on your own.

- Remind yourself how old you are, where you are and who you are with. Look around the room and name the objects in the room. Keep reminding yourself that you aren't a child with the abuser but an adult who is safe (I am 27; I have my own home in St. Louis; I am with my husband Mike; I can see my closet, my hairbrush, my shoes; the abuser is not here; I am safe).
- Find out what triggered the flashback—a word, a phrase, a smell, a touch, a certain type of sex or a certain sexual position. Tell your partner.
- If you were having sex and want to continue, do so. If you feel bad, and don't want to, don't.
- Write down the memory you had in the flashbacks as soon as you are able to do so. Flashbacks have the power to frighten you when you try to push the memories away. Keep writing down your flashbacks. They will stop eventually.

Summary

Many Survivors of sexual abuse experience sexual difficulties as teenagers and adults. This is a result of the process of traumatic sexualization that the Survivor experienced as a child. The sexual difficulties and responses range from a preoccupation with sex and sexual matters to fear and avoidance of sex and relationships. Survivors often find that their sexual difficulties and responses vary at different times of their life.

Overcoming sexual difficulties begins with working on feelings of guilt and shame about the sexual abuse. It also involves allowing yourself time to understand, explore, and develop your sexual knowledge and experience in a way that has been denied to you as a child. Difficulties with sex and sexuality are part of a bigger problem and cannot be tackled in isolation.

Dealing with sexual difficulties involves looking at emotional and physical health; relationship problems; myths and negative attitudes to sex; knowledge and understanding about bodies and sexual matters; and ways of communicating about sex. You can learn to understand and feel more positive about your body and about physical and sexual closeness. You can learn to feel in control, to relax and to enjoy sexual experiences on your own or with a partner.

Suggestions

- To explore your sexual feelings and overcome any difficulties follow the suggestions and exercises described in the chapter.
- Read some of the books listed under Further reading.

Further reading

Barbach, Lonnie G. *For Each Other: Sharing Sexual Intimacy.* NAL/Dutton, 1984.
Comfort, Alex. *The New Joy of Sex: A Gourmet Guide to Lovemaking for the Nineties.* Pocket Books, 1992.
Covington, Stephaine. *Awakening Your Sexuality: A Guide for Recovering Women.* HarperCollins Publishers, Inc., 1991.
Maltz, Wendy. *Sexual Healing Journey: A Guide for Survivors of Sexual Abuse.* HarperCollins Publishers, Inc., 1991.

Resource groups

Sex and Love Addicts Anonymous. P.O. Box 119, New Town Branch, Boston, MA 02258. (617) 332-1845.
National Council on Sexual Addiction. P.O. Box 3306, Boulder, CO 80307, (303) 494-5550.
Codependents of Sex Addicts. P.O. Box 14537, Minneapolis, MN 55414. (612) 537-6904.

13

Children

SURVIVORS SOMETIMES FIND THAT they have difficulties in relating to children. They may find they have no feelings for their children, cannot touch them or feel angry and hostile towards them. Other Survivors feel anxious and fearful for children and over-protect them or feel out of control and unable to cope. This chapter discusses the links between being sexually abused as a child and having problems with children as an adult and then looks at some of the problems in more detail and suggests ways of overcoming them.

Fiona's story

Fiona's story illustrates many of the difficulties that Survivors experience with children.

As I carried my baby I was frightened I would not be able to love it. When Amy was born I overprotected her. I wouldn't let her out of my sight nor let anyone do anything for her. She was mine, the first human I could love. I had a terrible fear of losing her and this made me depressed. I worried about her all the time and I was afraid to leave her with people in case she was abused.

I decided she wasn't going to be like me. She had to be perfectly clean and tidy and so had the house she lived in. This became an obsession with me. Even her hair had to be perfect. I'd blow-dry it every morning. I'd buy clothes for her and then wouldn't let her wear them in case they got dirty. I washed her if she got the least bit dirty.

I cared too much about what other people thought about me and

Amy. I chastised her when I thought other people would think that was the right thing to do. I got to the stage where I didn't know what was wrong and what was right. If I spanked her in front of others for doing something naughty then afterwards I felt that they thought I was a bad mother. If I didn't spank her I felt that they would talk about her and wouldn't like her.

I wanted so much for everyone to like her but often I convinced myself they didn't so I would push her away. My moods were always changing. I used to explode at her then feel that I was wicked and a bad parent. I would get so depressed. Even though I have never physically abused her I was always afraid: "What if I explode next time and hurt her?" So I would avoid chastising her and she would only have to cry and she got her own way. I tried so hard to be a perfect mother but the pressure would get too much and I would erupt again and then sink into a depression.

I'd have wrapped her up in cotton if I could. If other children teased her it would really hurt. I'd imagine Amy to be feeling like I felt as a child, "No one likes me." I used to get so mixed up, and confused my own emotions with Amy's. It was hard to cuddle my child because I never knew what was wrong or right. I'd feel guilty and afraid people might think I was abusing her. Because of all these obsessions my daughter became very clingy towards me. Again I imagined she felt like I did as a child so I wouldn't want to leave her. I believed she couldn't bear to be without me. I'd get irritable and angry when she'd cry for me.

I dreaded her starting to school even when she was a baby. What would I do without her? I'd get so depressed and worry about her. I was always living in the future. I avoided playing with her and was afraid to enjoy her company because I knew she would go to school one day.

I was tormented with the thought that she was lonely the way I had been. I thought of having another child as company for her but I knew I couldn't cope with another one. I felt really guilty and so sorry for her that I spoiled her to make up for it.

As time goes on I am beginning to get better and my obsessions are slowly going. I no longer chastise her for other people's sake but for what I think is right or wrong. I cuddle my daughter without fear. I know I would never hurt her. Now she is seven and I can explain my outbursts to her, telling her that it isn't her fault. I am working on all the other problems which are smaller now. She has been affected by all this but with time and care I know I can make it right. We have a very special relationship. She isn't clingy. I know she can survive without me being there to protect her all the time. I enjoy the freedom when she is at school and she enjoys school. I am learning to be assertive with her and to realize she is not me. She never will suffer abuse and pain the way I did. She is a happy little girl.

Sexual abuse and problems with children:
making the connections

Below we discuss three consequences of being sexually abused that can lead to problems with children: being reminded of the abuse, feeling very needy, and the lack of a good model of parenting. Making the connections between their present problems with children and their own past sexual abuse is the first step for Survivors in trying to understand and change their relationships with children.

Being reminded of the abuse

Something very surprising happened to me a few days ago. I went to buy my daughter some shoes and while she looked through the shelves, I sat on a low seat. A man came in with a little girl holding his hand. She was about two. They stood next to me and I was at eye-level with the child. We looked at each other, holding each other's eyes. Her eyes looked old, knowing. I wondered if she was being abused, and thought, maybe not now, maybe in two years. I was four when I was abused. I saw myself in the child. I looked at her eyes and cried. I did not sob, but my tears flowed relentlessly. *Katarina*

Survivors often try to bury their painful memories and feelings about their abuse. When Survivors are with children this way of coping can break down because they are reminded of their own childhood and abuse. This causes Survivors to have difficulties with children.

Forgotten memories and feelings about sexual abuse are brought back particularly by children who in some way remind the Survivor of herself as a child: children of the same age the Survivor was when the abuse started; children who look and act like the Survivor as a child; or children who have been sexually abused. Survivors who give birth to baby girls are often reminded of their own vulnerability as a child and of their own abuse. Giving birth to a boy can also be a reminder of the abuse, a reminder that some boys grow up to be abusers. Survivors may be disturbed and reminded of their abuse by seeing a baby boy's erection, a small child masturbating, or signs of a child's developing sexuality.

Ingrid was reminded of her abuse and experienced intense feelings of fear when her son reached the age her abuser was when the abuse started.

Although I could feel love for my daughters, I felt mainly indifference towards my son. But when he grew into a teenager, the age my abuser was when he abused me and threatened me, I began to fear him. *Ingrid*

Survivors neediness

Survivors were often very needy children because they weren't protected or understood and didn't have their feelings taken care of. Adult Survivors, who are still very needy themselves, are often unable to meet their children's needs or attempt to compensate for their own neediness by trying to give the children everything they didn't have themselves. Both reactions can cause problems in relating to children. Survivors may find they do not have the emotional or physical energy to meet their children's demands and to give the care and attention that is needed.

For Survivors who are having to cope with their own feelings and difficulties a child's demands can feel overwhelming. They may emotionally withdraw from their children or be unable to provide a happy and stimulating atmosphere. Some Survivors find even the physical demands of feeding, dressing and washing a child are more than they can cope with.

Problems are also caused by Survivors trying to compensate for their own neediness through their children. Fiona had never been clean as a child so she tried to keep Amy absolutely clean all the time. Fiona had often felt lonely as a child so she spoiled Amy when she thought Amy felt lonely. Fiona's compensation didn't help Amy because Fiona wasn't responding to Amy's feelings or needs but to her own childhood feelings. She was trying, through Amy, to make right the things that were wrong for her as a child.

Lack of a good parenting model

People usually learn the basic ideas of parenting from their own parents' behavior. Survivors who have been sexually abused by parents, and sometimes physically and emotionally abused as well, may find they have difficulty in parenting because they have never learned basic skills that others take for granted.

Survivors may feel so anxious about how to be a good parent that they feel paralyzed by uncertainty or try to copy others. Survivors may sometimes repeat their parents' poor behavior (for example, by not listening to a child or threatening the child

Table 8—Difficulties with children

Excessive fears for children's safety	Physically abusing children	Not being able to say no to children
Over-protecting children	Emotionally abusing children	Feeling helpless and out of control with children
Inappropriately protecting children	Verbally abusing children	Not feeling love for your own children
Rejecting children	Sexually abusing children	Excessively washing children
Anger and hostility towards children	Over-indulging children	Unable to cope with the child being upset/hurt/angry
Not being able to show affection and love to children	Not being able to assert your own needs with children	Confusing own feelings with the child's
Not being able to touch children		

with being put into a home) without realizing the effect they are having on the child. More commonly Survivors are so desperate not to repeat the abusive parenting they suffered that they go to the opposite extreme, allowing children to do anything they want to, avoiding physical contact with them and never saying no to the children.

Problems with children

Table 8 lists some of the problems Survivors experience with children. Below we discuss some of the main problems in more detail.

No feelings

Some Survivors find that they do not feel love for their children or are unable to give the emotional care and support a child needs. Below Ingrid describes her lack of feeling for her son.

My son was born and when I saw him for the first time I felt nothing. No joy, but no resentment either. "Well," I thought, "maybe mother-love comes later." I tried to be the kind of mother I had seen in others, but the mother-love never came. I did like him most of the time but equally felt no need to have him close to me. I had no understanding of the needs of a child.

I fed him, clothed him and gave him material things, but I did not nurture him emotionally. I had nothing to guide me and no emotions to give. I never hit him but I never showed him love either. I was glad when my son stopped coming to me looking for love and affection.

Sometimes I felt sorry for him and tried to pull myself together and play with him or read him a story. But within minutes I felt as if something inside me was screaming to get away from him. I felt imprisoned and crowded. I knew that I had to share myself with him, give him part of myself, but there was so little left. So much had been taken away from me by abuse, humiliation and hurt. There was a small part of me in which I had made my little haven of peace by blocking out emotions and feelings. I felt this little part would now be invaded by this child and I would be forced to acknowledge feelings of some kind. *Ingrid*

Ingrid was unable to love her son because she had tried to forget about her abuse and had buried her feelings. In burying her bad feelings she had also buried her ability to love and feel happy and close to someone. Ingrid felt threatened by her son and felt that if she opened herself up and started loving him she might also open up her feelings about her abuse. She was also very needy and felt she had so little left of herself that her son might take it all away. Ingrid had not been given the emotional care she had needed as a child and didn't have the parenting skills to cope with her son.

Like Ingrid, Survivors may be unable to feel anything for their children or simply not know how to give emotional care and love if they have never experienced this themselves. The child who does not receive the love he or she needs may become over-anxious and clingy, angry and badly behaved, or cutoff and emotionally withdrawn.

Avoiding touch

I still remember the relief I felt when my six-year-old son asked me not to hold his hand in the street anymore, because he was a big boy now. From that day onwards I used that excuse not to touch him physically. I think the last time I kissed him was when he was about five or six years old. *Ingrid*

Some Survivors avoid physical contact with their children. They may avoid hugging, kissing or holding hands with the child and refuse to bathe the child or have the child sit on their knee. When Survivors are very needy themselves, or are emotionally distressed, a child wanting to be hugged and kissed can feel like another demand that they feel unable to meet. Survivors who are withdrawn or depressed may find it hard to express physical affection and Survivors who have no feelings for their children or feel hostile towards them may not want to.

Physical contact between a Survivor, as an adult, and a child may bring back memories and feelings about the abuse. In pushing the child away the Survivor is pushing away these memories and feelings. Survivors who sometimes physically reject children may at other times be able to show love and affection and overcompensate at these times by pulling the child towards them and hugging and loving them profusely. This seesaw between physical rejection and compensating over-loving can be very confusing and hurtful to a child.

Survivors may also be unsure about what kind of touching is right for a parent or adult to give a child. Is it normal to hug, kiss or stroke a child or is it abuse? Is it normal to bathe a child, or be in bed with a child, or hold a child when the parent is naked, or is it abuse? Survivors who have been abused by their own parents are more likely to have these worries and may feel so frightened of abusing that they stop touching their children altogether.

It is natural to play with your baby but it felt wrong to me, like I was interfering with her. I couldn't cuddle her without feeling bad about it. I loved Lynn very much and she needed to know that but I just couldn't show her. So Lynn was isolated in her own little world. She was also always putting her arms around strangers. Now I find Lynn either won't leave me alone or doesn't come near me at all. *Sally*

Survivors may also avoid physical contact with children because they fear other people might think they are abusing their children. They may have heard that people who have been sexually abused become abusers and so fear they will start abusing their children. Most Survivors, however, feel strongly about wanting to protect children and do not want sexual contact with them.

Children can be distressed by parents avoiding touching, cuddling and kissing. They may feel anxious or angry or become clingy or withdrawn.

Anger and rejection

There I was, finally I had a baby. All mine, all I'd ever wanted, a baby. "Congratulations, it's a boy!" Why was I crying? I'd got my wish come true but I wanted a girl.

I was just so happy at first to have a baby that I soon got over it being a boy. Two years later I was in the middle of a nervous breakdown. I hated my two-year-old son. I couldn't stand the sight of him. I hated men of all descriptions. I felt that they were full of demands especially my son as he couldn't do anything himself. "I want my breakfast now, mom, please" is a pretty normal request in anybody's eyes, but the "I want" syndrome grated on my brain. Everybody always seemed to be wanting, but nobody said "What do you want? How do you feel? What do you want to do?" or even, "Thank you."

As I became more depressed I couldn't bring myself to do anything but the essentials like give my son breakfast, dinner, etc. I couldn't love him, cuddle him, play with him, be interested in any way in him or spend time with him. I didn't even want to be in the same room with him for any length of time. This lasted until my husband pointed out that I was being an awful mother to my son and he would grow up hating me.

One day my son had done something wrong (hardly surprising since he spent all day, everyday, playing alone in his bedroom, out of my sight) and I went to town on him and couldn't stop spanking him. If my husband hadn't come home when he did I would have probably spanked my son so much that it would have been classed as physical abuse. I sat on the stairs in my husband's arms shouting and screaming, "I swore I'd never beat my kids like my father beat me."

My husband made me realize I needed help. I went to a group for adults who were sexually abused as children. Talking to other women and mothers I found out I wasn't the only one who felt this way or treated their children this way. I realized the reason I hated my son so much was the fact that he was a boy, and I was frightened of him becoming an abuser. I'd just never understood this before. *Pam*

Pam was trying to meet the demands of a two-year-old child when she had not sorted out her feelings about her sexual abuse and was in great need of care and support herself. As with Ingrid, Pam's own neediness interfered with her ability to meet her child's needs and she felt angry and resentful about his demands. Pam saw her son as a potential abuser and was angry at him for reminding her of her abuse.

Underneath her depression Pam hid a huge well of anger about her own childhood, her abuse and the abuser. These buried feelings of anger were beginning to surface and Pam was directing them at her son. Children are always easy targets for anger and hostility. They are smaller and less powerful than an adult and usually forgive their parents' outbursts. Survivors may vent feelings on children that they are too frightened to express elsewhere—anger is expressed at a small son but not at the abuser. Some Survivors are angry and hostile towards their children because they do not know how else to keep control. This may have been the only form of discipline they saw from their own parents. Many Survivors want to love and care for their children but don't know how to overcome their bad feelings or change their behavior.

Anger and rejection towards a child can lead to the child having problems such as bed-wetting, temper tantrums, running away, sullen or clingy behavior. The Survivor may find herself unable to cope with these problems and feel even more anger and resentment towards the child.

Overprotecting

Many Survivors find themselves overprotecting their children because they are frightened that their children will also be sexually abused. This may involve keeping the child in the house, not allowing him/her to do normal childhood things, shouting at the child for showing physical affection, making sure the child keeps her body well covered at all times, not allowing the child to play with other children or to go on trips. A Survivor may not react in the same way with all her children. Some Survivors overprotect girls but not boys. Survivors are particularly likely to overprotect any child who reminds them of themselves as children.

Sally's eldest daughter Lynn looks and acts very much like Sally did as a child. Sally feels Lynn is a vulnerable child who is destined to be abused.

I was very protective with Lynn and still am at times. No one is allowed to come near her, I am always so afraid that she is in danger from others. *Sally*

She acts much more strictly with Lynn than with her younger daughter and gets extremely angry if Lynn hugs or kisses Sally's male friends.

Ingrid had been abused by her brother and because of this tried to protect her daughters from males in the family.

I have to be very careful not to destroy my family life. The suspicion I hold against my son and my husband whenever they get close to my daughters is tearing me apart. If my son suggests a game of chess in his room with his sister I have to force myself not to interfere because I see the abuser getting me into the bedroom under a pretense. Because of the abuse I have destroyed any beginnings of a normal brother/sister relationship because I tried to separate them whenever possible. For the first years I did not realize what I was doing. When I did realize, I forced myself to stop, not always with success. If one of my daughters sits on my husband's lap I have to look the other way because I cannot bear to watch what it might lead to (or would have led to had it been me and my abuser). Often I have to go out of the room. While I was watching and worrying about my own family my youngest daughter was sexually abused by a neighbor. She did not tell me until three years after the abuse. *Ingrid*

Ingrid was being reminded of her own abuse. She was responding to her own feelings of vulnerability and fear about being abused rather than usefully and realistically protecting her children. She didn't concern herself with the danger from people outside the family because this hadn't been her experience. This kind of protection—seeing danger for specific children only or from a specific type of person is inappropriate and does not guarantee children's safety.

Louise was enraged when her daughter Rebecca showed her panties while doing a somersault at a party. Rebecca was spanked and sent home. Louise still blamed herself for being abused and felt she'd provoked it by not keeping her body properly covered up. She was frightened by Rebecca's behavior and spanked her because she did not want her to be abused and did not know how else to protect her.

I know children have always done somersaults and that my reaction to Rebecca showing her panties was extreme. I try to hide it, but I live in constant fear of her exposing herself and perhaps creating the conditions that caused me to be abused as a child. *Louise*

Louise's attempt to protect Rebecca was inappropriate. Rebecca wasn't putting herself at danger by showing her panties; people don't suddenly abuse because they see a child's panties.

Children are vulnerable and need to be protected in appropriate ways. Survivors, however, often overprotect their children in ways that are restrictive and stifling and which can cause problems for and with the child. Inappropriate protection may leave the child feeling confused or ashamed and doesn't help to keep her safe from abuse.

No control

Elizabeth didn't like to say no to her children and spoil their fun. She let them do whatever they wanted to do. They were always climbing on her, pulling at her, demanding her attention and asking for candy and presents. Elizabeth became worn-out and her children became more and more unruly. Every so often Elizabeth's patience snapped and she shouted and screamed at her children and then felt terribly guilty. She'd cry and tell her children she was sorry over and over again and buy them candy to make up. Elizabeth felt helpless and out of control.

Elizabeth had been physically and sexually abused as a child by her father. She had grown up feeling frightened and lacking in self-confidence and did not want her own children to be like this. She was so frightened of treating her own children badly that she didn't put any restrictions on them at all. Elizabeth was trying to make up for the abuse she had suffered as a child through her own children. She had also never experienced parents treating children firmly but fairly and she didn't know how to be assertive.

Like Elizabeth, many Survivors are so anxious to make their children's childhood different from their own that they allow their own feelings and needs to be trampled on. As children Survivors were deprived of their rights when they were being abused. As adults Survivors may not know how to assert themselves or may feel they have no right to do so.

I was totally unable to assert myself with my children. It was very difficult for me to ask them to help with any housework. Sometimes I forced myself to ask meekly if one of them would be kind enough to wash the dishes or vacuum. It was very, very difficult for me and I could only do it after apologizing profusely. If they refused, I gave up and ended up doing it myself, biting back the tears of humiliation about being treated like a maid. *Katarina*

Survivors often find it hard to trust other people and lack friendships and close relationships. Survivors sometimes feel that the only people they can trust and love completely are their own children and are very anxious not to jeopardize these relationships. They may be fearful of making any demands on their children, saying no to them, or putting any limits on what they can do, in case they lose their children's love.

Like Elizabeth and Katarina, many Survivors feel out of control with their children or worn down by continually meeting their demands. Problems will arise between Survivors and their children if Survivors do not teach their children the difference between acceptable and unacceptable behavior.

Deprived of children

Sexual abuse can result in some women being unable to have children because they have been physically damaged by sexually transmitted diseases, forced sexual intercourse, sexual torture or insertion of objects in their vaginas. This can leave them infertile, prone to miscarriages or in need of hysterectomies. Sexual abuse also causes emotional damage which may make Survivors decide not to have children because they think they won't be able to cope, or because they fear passing on their problems to their own children.

Some Survivors are deprived of having children because of their fears of men and sexual intercourse. Being deprived of children in these ways can be a further cause of grief and anger to Survivors and can cause feelings of resentment and jealousy towards mothers and their children. Some Survivors who do have children are unable to cope with taking care of them because of the emotional problems they are suffering themselves or because of difficulties with the child.

They may have to allow other people to take over caring for the child temporarily or permanently, or have the child taken into a home or foster family. Survivors may miss out on stages of their children's lives, and feel guilty for not being able to cope or not being a good mother. Having children taken into another's care or losing custody of children can feel like a further punishment or abuse.

Sexually abused children

Ingrid had been sexually abused as a child and recently discovered that her daughter, Rosie aged eight, had also been abused a few years previously.

When my youngest daughter told me she had been sexually abused I developed eczema on both my legs within hours. I started scratching it until it bled and in the days that followed opened the wounds again and again. I did not know if I could cope. Would I be strong enough, not only for myself but also for her? I felt ashamed of myself and my lack of self-control. I realized what I was doing but I could not stop. Scratching my eczema had been my only way of coping with my suffering as a child. I was coping in the same way again. *Ingrid*

Rosie's abuse brought back disturbing memories and feelings for Ingrid, but because Ingrid had attended a Survivors group she could cope and was able to support Rosie without blaming her.

Fiona also discovered that her daughter Amy had been sexually abused by two neighborhood boys.

The day I found out what had been happening must have been the worst day of my life. At the time I was still in therapy myself and I was very sensitive to it all. I kept calm although I wanted to scream at her. I was loving and supporting although at that time I disliked her and my overwhelming instinct and desire was to run away, to get away from her. The whole situation had brought up things I didn't want to cope with. I saw my daughter the way I saw myself all those years ago. She was dirty, ruined and no good. She was like a damaged toy. I couldn't handle this. I'd protected her and worked hard all those years to make sure my daughter wouldn't be like me. *Fiona*

Fiona felt the same disgust for Amy that she felt for herself but she was at least able to outwardly support and accept Amy. In therapy Fiona worked through her own feelings about herself and stopped blaming Amy when she stopped blaming herself.

Now 18 months later Amy and I talk openly about it all. I now trust her and know she would tell me if anything ever happened again. I am learning that what happened to me many years ago wasn't my fault just like it wasn't Amy's fault. It seemed like the end of the world when Amy told me. I never believed I could love her or that things would be normal between us again. Now I have dealt with my worst fear and the whole situation has helped bring up things about myself and by dealing with them I am a stronger person. *Fiona*

Survivors who discover their own child has been abused have to deal with their feelings about both their child's abuse and their memories and feelings about their own abuse. Survivors who are teachers, nurses, social workers or work with children in any way are also likely to come in contact with sexually abused children and may have difficulties in dealing with this situation.

The Survivor may feel angry and hostile towards sexually abused children for reminding her of her own abuse or for disclosing the abuse when the Survivor herself has kept silent. The Survivor may also block-off the child's abuse, or feel powerless to protect the child and consequently do nothing.

Survivors who still blame themselves for being abused may also blame abused children. A Survivor's reaction to an abused child is often mixed up with her feelings about her own abuse.

Dealing with a sexually abused child can be traumatic for a Survivor who has not worked through her own sexual abuse. A Survivor who has helped and healed herself is in a position to help and support an abused child with strength and confidence.

Overcoming the problems

Working through this book, getting therapy and talking to other people about your sexual abuse will generally help you feel better and improve your relationships with children. Below we discuss ways in which you can work on overcoming your problems with children by remembering the abuse, dealing with your own neediness and learning to be a more confident parent.

Remembering the abuse

Trying to forget the abuse is a coping strategy which doesn't always work and makes you vulnerable to being suddenly reminded of your abuse and childhood feelings. Children may remind you of your own abuse and this can cause problems unless you are willing to face your memories and feelings by allowing them to surface and dealing with them.

Exercise

When you are with children try to observe your own thoughts and feelings. Notice if they remind you of yourself or of your abuse. Take note of any strong feelings (anger, distress, fear) that you have when you are with children. As soon as you can, write down your observations and any childhood memories and feelings that have surfaced.

Observing your own feelings, memories, and behavior, and writing them down will help you sort out which feelings are about your own childhood and abuse and which are about the children you are with. Getting therapy for yourself individually or in a group, or talking to other Survivors can also help this process.

Survivor's neediness

Many Survivors hate who they were as children. Try to understand and accept the child that you were at the time when you were being sexually abused. You cannot change what happened to her but it is possible to find this needy child within yourself and to understand and care for her in the same way that you might care for any child who is feeling frightened, vulnerable or distressed. With this care the needy child can mature into a strong and independent adult. Without this care part of you will remain frozen as a needy child who feels frightened and alone. Penny Parkes' book *Rescuing the Inner Child* (see Further reading at end of chapter) explains these ideas in detail and is well worth reading. Below we suggest two exercises to help you contact and accept your inner child.

Exercise 1: Photograph

Find a photograph of yourself at the age you were being abused. Try to recall what you were like and what you did and felt. Try to remember what feelings you had that you weren't able to express, and the times you were misunderstood and not cared for. What kind of love and care did you want that you weren't getting? Keep this photograph with you and everytime you look at it try to accept the child you were.

Exercise 2: Letter to and from the inner child

Write a letter to this inner child from the adult you are now, allowing yourself to express all the feelings you have towards her both good and bad. Write your letter in simple language, the sort of language a child could understand. Next write a reply from this child to yourself as you are now. Write about how you felt and what you needed that you didn't get. Continue writing letters to and from the inner child until the adult part of yourself is able to support and accept the inner child and the inner child feels comforted.

This exercise may be much harder to do than it appears, especially for Survivors who hate or fear their inner child. You may find yourself feeling upset or disturbed as you begin to experience the pain of your childhood. Take your time. You may need to write a series of letters over a number of weeks or months.

Ingrid's letter was written at a time when she had begun to love and support her inner child.

My dearest Ingrid,

I am sorry you had to wait such a long time on your own, confused and lonely. I did not know you were there and when I first saw you in my mind a few weeks ago, still waiting, still crying, I was frightened and needed to think for a while before making contact with you. Please don't feel sad anymore. I am here now, strong enough for both of us. Let me explain to you about what happened. I can still sense your confusion.

As I write now I am looking at a photo of you. You are in a park with mother and your brother, Hank. I picked this photo out because it showed me clearly the difference in size, and consequently power, between you and Hank. It is obvious that you couldn't have stopped him from abusing you. Try to remember this. It will help you to stop blaming yourself.

Sometimes you cried during the abuse. You were so young then that you did not know what he was doing but you felt disgusted. What he tried to do with you was something too advanced for your age, something adults do and then it is OK; it is not disgusting when it happens between loving adults. Please, don't be ashamed that you allowed him to touch you and kiss you. You were so eager to be liked by everyone that you were willing to do just about anything in return. Please don't feel bad about this. You have done nothing wrong. Maybe it will help you if you understand why your need to please was so great.

Mother tried to kill herself when you were two. Father wanted to divorce her. She refused and he stayed but hardly talked to any of the family after that. Mother was so involved in her own problems that she could not see your problems and only took care of your physical needs. Every member of the family was so wrapped up in their own problems that they couldn't give you the love and attention you so desperately needed. It was not because you were not nice enough, it was simply because they needed all their strength to cope with themselves. You thought if you were nicer, more giving and the best at school, they would love you and notice you. You obeyed every wish they had and tried your hardest to please them.

Dearest child, I am on your side, and I will always be standing by you. Nobody has the right to abuse another person, no matter what has happened to them. Hank had no right to do that to you. What you must understand is that the abuse happened because of something in him that made him want to abuse you, not because of anything you did or said. It was his fault the abuse started, his fault it continued and his responsibility alone. You were only abused because you had to share his bedroom. If another child had been sleeping in that room, that other child would have been abused

I have learned that it is never too late to change. Just because you have been alone and lonely for almost 40 years, it does not mean you have to stay like that. When I first saw you as the distressed child still within me, I saw you with your arms outstretched, tears streaming down your face and so much in need of love that I cried. I felt bad because you were so unhappy, and because I had neglected you. All we can do now is make a new beginning.

Promise me that you will tell me whenever something frightens or worries you and I will promise you to listen. I will be there for you whenever you need me. You are safe now, and I will make sure that nobody ever hurts you again. Put your hand in mine and come with me. I am your best friend and the one person who will never leave you. I love you, my child. You will never be alone again. *Ingrid*

Writing the letters to and from the inner child and keeping the photograph of yourself as a child with you will help you to accept and care for yourself as a child. Once your own inner child feels supported and cared for you will be better prepared to offer the same support and care to children you are with.

Confident parenting

You may already have good parenting skills but lack self-confidence. No parent or child is perfect. Tantrums, bed-wetting and arguments about eating or bedtime are common at certain ages and don't necessarily mean you lack skills as a parent. Survivors often begin to feel more confident about their parenting skills once they start to talk with other parents and share their anxieties, problems and different coping methods.

Reading a book on child care (see Further reading), attending a parenting skills class or talking to someone who is skilled with children such as a visiting nurse or teacher can also be useful. Don't be afraid to ask for help or to share your anxieties with others. It is only concerned parents who do this. You can also build up your parenting skills and become more confident by learning to be assertive with your children and discovering useful ways to protect them. We discuss this below.

Assertiveness

Building up self-esteem and self-confidence and learning to behave more assertively can help you feel stronger and more in control of yourself and your children. It can also help you deal more fairly and equally with children. What children feel and want is important but what you feel and want is important too. Children need to be taught to respect other people's rights as well as their own. Look back at the section on assertiveness in chapter 10.

Children are always trying to test the limits of what they are allowed to do. If you never say no or allow children to do anything and then suddenly become very angry and restrictive they feel confused. Try using a five-stage system to signal to a child that they are pushing the limits with their behavior. Start with a simple request and if the child does not do as you ask, become firmer at each stage.

Example of five-stage system
1. (Firm voice at normal level) "Please don't touch that. It could easily break. Come and look at this." (Offer an alternative toy.)
2. (Firm voice, frown and point at the object) "I have told you before don't touch that. Come here."
3. (Raising voice) "No! Don't touch." (Softer voice, smiling) "Come and look at this."
4. (Keeping voice raised) "No! Don't touch that. If you try to do that again you will have to go to your bedroom for five minutes." (Or "I will take you home," "You will not go swimming this afternoon," etc.)
5. Carry out what you said you would do at stage 4.

At stage 4 make sure that what you say you will do is not too harsh or out of proportion to the child's bad behavior, and that you are prepared to carry it out. Your child will begin to learn when she is going too far and stop before stage 5. This system also helps you know what to do next. You can use this method to ask the child to do something or to stop doing something. If the child is endangering herself you will need to take immediate action.

Not being firm and never saying no is exhausting. It will not help children learn how to deal with other people nor will it make them love and respect you. Adults and children respect and like other people who behave assertively rather than allowing themselves to be walked on. Finding the right balance between what you need and what the child needs will benefit you both. Children are likely to grow up feeling self-confident and cared for if they are treated fairly, consistently and with love.

Protecting children appropriately
Feeling constantly fearful that your children might be abused comes from feelings of fear and vulnerability resulting from your own abuse. It is therefore important to sort out your own feel-

ings first and then work together with your children to help protect them from abuse. However, you should take immediate action to keep children away from anyone who has abused a child. Chapter 17 looks at how to protect children from sexual abuse and suggests a number of guidelines. There are many books which deal with protecting children which you might find helpful to read (see the Further reading list in chapter 17).

Survivors may have heard that people who have been sexually abused become abusers. This is not correct. Most people who have been sexually abused never abuse children. It is true that some abusers have been sexually abused themselves as children but there are many more victims than abusers

Hugging, kissing, stroking and bathing a child are all normal expressions of love and care if they are given and received in that spirit. The same actions can be abusive if they are done for the adult's benefit and are inappropriate or unwanted by the child. People who are touching children in this way or are having sexual fantasies about children need to get help now by talking to a counselor or phoning a help line (see Useful Addresses).

Learning new and more appropriate ways to protect children can help increase your confidence and remind you that it is not the child's behavior, dress or words which provoke abuse. It can also help you to feel better about giving your children the affection and love they need.

Getting help for your children

I got a social worker and Sarah started a day-nursery full time. The people there would often say that she just sat in a corner playing with a doll. How did I feel about that? I had created this baby and I could not give her what she needed. I felt so bad about it all. Now Sarah is a lot better. She is able to mix with children and play. With the help we have received, Sarah and I now have a pretty good mother-and-daughter relationship. *Sally*

If your problems with your children have been going on for a long time, especially if you have been angry with and rejecting them, your children may have developed their own problems and require help. If your child is showing disturbed behavior or is withdrawn and unhappy get help for her/him now (see Useful Addresses). This does not mean you have failed as a parent. It is an acknowledgement of your own problems and a responsible and caring way to help your child.

Summary

Survivors often have many problems with children because of the ways they have been affected by being sexually abused. As Fiona's story shows these problems can be overcome with the right sort of help. Working on your memories and feelings about your own sexual abuse, and on your neediness, will allow you to begin to relate to children in their own right rather than as reminders of yourself as a child. Learning new parenting skills will also help you become a better and more confident parent. After attending a Survivors group Pam had a very different attitude towards her son.

I am now aware that my son is a person in his own right and is influenced by his parents, including me. Now I can love my son for the first time and it's wonderful. The things I've missed out on are unbelievable. I wish I'd sought help earlier. It's super to be able to cuddle him, climb into bed with him to read him a bedtime story and to do these things because I love him, not because of a sense of duty. The only thing I can't do yet, because he is a boy, is bathe him, but this is a small problem compared to how I was before. At least he knows I love him and he loves me. *Pam*

It is possible to make things better for you and your children. Keep working on it and don't give up hope.

Suggestions

- Being sexually abused can affect the way you relate to your own children. Write down any ways you think your abuse may have affected the way you feel about, or behave towards, your children. Look at Table 8 and check any of the difficulties with children that apply to you.
- You can help yourself to overcome your difficulties with children by learning to become a more confident parent, and by dealing with your memories and feelings about the abuse and your own neediness. Follow the suggestions and do the exercises described in the chapter.
- Read one of the books on protecting children from sexual abuse, listed under Further Reading in chapter 17. Talk to your children about how to keep themselves safe.

Further reading

Allen, Juliet V. *What Do I Do When . . . ? A Handbook for Parents and Other Beleaguered Adults.* Impact Publishers, 1983.

Guhl, Beverly; Fontenelle, Don H. *Purrfect Parenting.* Fisher Books, 1987.

Guhl, Beverly. *Teenage Years: A Parent's Survival Guide.* Fisher Books, 1989.

McBride, Angela B. *Enjoy a Good Life with Your Teenager.* Fisher Books, 1989.

Parks, Penny. *Rescuing the "Inner Child": Therapy for Adults Sexually Abused as Children.* International Specialized Book Services, 1993.

14

Mothers

SURVIVORS OF SEXUAL ABUSE often have difficulties in their relationships with their mothers. Mothers are supposed to love, support and protect their children. They are expected to prevent bad things from happening to their children and always be there to listen and to make things better. The child who has been sexually abused did not have this help and protection. She may not have been listened to and her mother may not have been there when she needed her. Mothers do sometimes sexually abuse their children but more often the mother is not abusing and is potentially in a position to help and support the abused child. In this chapter we look at the way in which sexual abuse can affect a Survivor's relationship with her mother or person in a similar care-giving role.

Difficulties between mothers and Survivors are not inevitable. The mother may realize that her child is being sexually abused and support and protect her. The mother-child relationship can be strengthened if the child can share her feelings with her mother and feel loved and supported. Unfortunately this rarely happens. Mothers usually do not know that their children are being sexually abused because sexual abuse happens in secret and is kept secret. Sometimes mothers do know or suspect that their child is being sexually abused but do not stop the abuse or protect the child. Mothers may be unable to cope with their own feelings of anger or distress about the abuse of their child. There are many ways in which sexual abuse can damage rather than strengthen the relationship between the child or adult Survivor and her mother.

Survivors' feelings toward their mothers are often a confused mixture of anger, love, hatred, pity, resentment and a desire to protect them. Some of the difficulties Survivors experience in their relationships with their mothers are discussed in more detail below Exercises are suggested to help understand and come to terms with the feelings and overcome these difficulties.

Difficulties with mothers

Feeling protective
As a child I felt that telling would make my mom more unhappy and she'd feel guilty. I felt very protective toward my mom. *Jane*

Few children tell their mothers that they are being sexually abused. They are frightened of the consequences of telling—of being blamed, disbelieved or punished. Many sexually abused children also fear the distress and pain their mothers might feel if they knew what was happening. Abusers often keep children silent by telling them that their mothers would be upset if they knew. Children therefore tolerate great pain themselves to protect their mothers from suffering. The child finds herself protecting her mother rather than being protected by her.

As I got older I didn't want my mom to be upset. How could I hurt her by telling her what had happened? I feel really sorry for her because her life has been so unhappy. I wouldn't like her to feel upset because she didn't protect me. I love her and wish I could change her life for her. *Kate*

The child may feel especially protective if the abuser is her mother's partner.

The secrecy can create a barrier between mother and daughter and cause difficulties in the relationship. The mother cannot understand why her child is distressed or why she is behaving differently and the child cannot tell. Many Survivors describe having a close relationship with their mother until the abuse started. New stepfathers are sometimes jealous of the mother's relationship with her child; abusing the child can have the added benefit for him of destroying this close relationship.

The secrecy frequently continues into adulthood. Survivors

who have overcome many of their difficulties and speak openly about their abuse may still insist that their mothers must never know. They find it hard to break the habit of protecting their mothers and may protect her feelings at the expense of their own. Survivors are often trying to give their mothers the care and protection they would like to have had themselves as a child. Underlying this caring and giving, however, is often a great well of neediness. The Survivor may feel a sense of grief and anger that as a child she never really experienced the feeling of being mothered and of being dependent and secure and that now as an adult she does not have a close, confiding and trusting mother-daughter relationship.

Katarina decided it was better to believe that her mother would have protected her if she'd known rather than tell her and risk a different reaction.

I could not tell my mother about the abuse. I was frightened what her reactions would be. As long as she didn't know I could cling to the thought she would have protected me. She was a very strong believer in family unity. What if she had not completely separated me from my brother (the abuser)? He would have carried out his threats without doubt and she was too gullible to think bad of her own son. I would have lost that last ray of hope—the complete trust in my mother. *Katarina*

Katarina was not only protecting her mother by not telling, she was also protecting her own hope that if her mother had known she would have given her all the love and protection she needed.

For adult Survivors, protecting their mother can create practical problems and add further strain to the relationship. Survivors may find themselves caught up in a web of lies in an attempt to explain why they are avoiding the abuser or why they are receiving counseling. If the abuser lives with her mother the Survivor may visit infrequently and keep her children away to protect them. Mothers who do not know about the abuse and do not understand why this is happening usually feel hurt and rejected by this behavior.

I finally decided I never wanted to see my abuser again so if I knew my brother was visiting my mother, I would leave before he arrived or didn't go in the first place. I stopped going to her birthday parties or for Christmas dinners. She felt very hurt by this and often asked me why. I told her it was because I didn't like my brother but when asked for the reason I remained silent. She asked my brother. He told her he didn't know what I could have against him, he hadn't done anything wrong. She was very hurt by my behavior but I thought she would feel even more hurt if she knew the truth. She could blame me for being stubborn; if she had known the truth she would have blamed herself. *Katarina*

Survivors may jeopardize their relationships with their mothers to protect them from knowing about the abuse.

Feeling neglected
Survivors often feel angry, upset or resentful about their mother's failure to notice that they were being sexually abused. Mothers are expected to be sensitive to their children's feelings and needs and to know what is happening to them. When a child's distress is not noticed, the child may feel let down and neglected even if she has consciously tried to hide the abuse from her mother and put on a cheerful front.

Jane felt let down by her mother's failure to make time for her and really listen and find out what was wrong.

I was abused by my stepfather from about seven to 17. My mother's marriage to my father had been a violent one and that's why she divorced him. My mother worked hard studying to become a teacher. When she married my stepfather we moved to Wakefield. I don't think she suspected that he was abusing me and my sister Lizzie. If we had nightmares or tantrums she thought we were disturbed because of our court-ordered visits with our real father. The more I look back over my childhood the more I realize how inattentive she was. I used to think she threw herself into her work (teaching) because she was unhappy at home, in her marriage. I didn't feel that my mother was there for me. With hindsight I can understand why, but at the time it made me feel that I was not worth being taken care of. *Jane*

Many Survivors feel angry with their mothers for not noticing the abuse. Katarina feels her mother should have realized that she was being abused.

I was four or five when my brother ejaculated between my closed legs. His semen wet my nightclothes and the sheet. I was blamed for wetting the bed. As an adult now I feel a mixture of anger and contempt for my mother for not noticing the difference between semen and urine when she changed my nightclothes and sheet. *Katarina*

If the abuse remains secret and these feelings from child-hood are not resolved, adult Survivors may continue to feel let down and uncared for in the relationships with their mothers whatever their mothers do. They continue to hope silently that their mothers will notice their distress and voluntarily offer the care and support they crave. When this doesn't happen Survivors may be overwhelmed with anger and distress and emotionally withdraw from their mothers in an attempt to protect themselves and to punish their mothers.

Feeling abandoned and badly treated

In some cases mothers are aware that abuse is happening and take no action to stop it. They accuse the child of lying, or turn a blind eye to it and allow the child to continue to be abused.

When I finally told my mom about being abused by my dad and by her boyfriend she said I had made it all up. As far back as I can remember my mom would try to convince me that things I knew to be true were lies, and in the end I would just believe her. At one point I tried to convince myself that perhaps I had dreamed it all. I know she knew about it though, even before I said anything, because I can remember hearing her and her boyfriend arguing about it. *Sally*

Some mothers support and stay with abusive partners even if this means losing custody of their child or destroying their relationship with the adult Survivor. As an adult, Joanne told her mother she had been abused by her stepfather, Ken, and was blamed and abandoned by her. Her mother chose to stay with Ken even though he had just been released from prison for abusing his natural daughter.

I felt hurt at my mother's decision to side with my stepfather and abandon my family and me for him. *Joanne*

Even if the mother stops the abuse or leaves the abuser she may still be angry at the Survivor or blame her for what has happened. Some mothers are openly hostile and treat the Survivor badly. Others are cold and distant and take advantage of the Survivor's feelings of guilt.

The adult Survivor may feel angry and resentful toward her mother for abandoning her and treating her badly. She may find ways to get back at her mother or feel consumed with a rage she can't express. However, Survivors are often devastated by their mother's reactions and feel no anger, but an enormous sense of grief and loss.

I still feel very confused about my mother. Although I am the victim, I am the one who has lost my family. I don't speak to any of my family except my aunt. I don't know what hurts the most—the abuse or losing my family because of it. I have a husband, three super kids and a nice home, but I still wish I had a true mom and a grandma for my kids. *Sally*

They may try to gain their mother's love and understanding by doing things for her and always trying to please her.

I have always had a bad relationship with my mom. I have tried hundreds of times to make it better but the more I tried and the more I did for her the more she wanted. Thus the relationship was one-sided. On the few occasions she did anything to help me I never seemed to be able to show her enough thanks. *Sally*

Some Survivors continue to accept poor treatment from their mothers or to be abused and disregarded by them in the hope of one day gaining the love and acceptance they crave. Others, like Sally, may stop seeing their mothers but continue to feel abandoned and to grieve for the loss of the relationship.

Dealing with mother's distress about the abuse
There are really no words to describe my feeling when I understood that my daughters had been sexually abused. It was something like hearing of the death of someone you love—in fact something did die. There was pain and an overwhelming sense of loss and desperation. When that passed there was overwhelming anger. Anger against my husband for his treachery and against the girls for what seemed like deceit on their part because they had not told me. I was angry with God that such evil had overtaken us. I had a tremendous feeling of failure which crept into all my activities and sapped my self-confidence. I swung between thoughts of murder and suicide but ended up rejecting both. *Grace* (Jane's mother)

Mothers are often thrown into emotional turmoil when they find out that their daughter or son has been sexually abused. They may be overwhelmed with grief, anger, distress or with feelings of failure and helplessness. They may also suffer financial and practical problems if the disclosure results in a marriage breakup or a breadwinner going to prison.

Survivors can have great difficulty in coping with their mother's distress about the abuse and this may add to their own feelings of guilt.

My sister Lizzie and I finally decided to tell my mother about the abuse because we felt that it would help her understand the estranged relationship between her and Lizzie. When we told her I didn't doubt that she believed us but she was very upset, as I had always imagined she would be. I felt responsible for causing her that pain and distress. We didn't discuss our feelings or any details about the abuse with her. I really felt that she couldn't cope with it any more. *Jane*

Survivors often blame themselves for causing their mother's distress and other people may also blame them for telling about the abuse. Some mothers openly express their distress. A mother may look to her daughter for support, especially if the abuse has remained a secret between the two of them. But the Survivor may feel unable to cope with her mother's feelings as well as her own emotional pain. Mothers and Survivors thrown together in this situation often cannot help each other and may make each other's problems worse. Survivors may also feel that their mothers are so involved with their own distress that the Survivor's feelings and needs are being overlooked.

My mother would not be honest with me in discussions and always turned it around to discuss her own unhappy childhood. Perhaps this was her way of coping with her guilt feelings, but I began to feel strongly that I could no longer rationalize or cope with her feelings when I was trying to help myself. *Jane*

Survivors may find themselves in the familiar position of trying to protect, support and "mother" their own mothers and feel angry and resentful about this situation. Alternatively, both mother and daughter may avoid mentioning the sexual abuse or the abuser for fear of upsetting the other person. This creates a barrier in the relationship and may lead to misunderstandings and a lack of closeness in the relationship. Melanie thought she had ruined her parents' lives by disclosing the abuse. She didn't talk about the abuse again because she felt guilty and didn't want to hurt her mother.

Mom never knew exactly what did happen to me. I could never really talk about it. I felt I had broken up my mom and dad as a normal husband and wife, as from that time on my mother didn't want anything to do with him on the sexual side of the marriage. What happened to me turned her off. She blamed my dad as he was nearby when it was happening. *Melanie*

Melanie's mother, however, felt guilty for not protecting her daughter. She thought Melanie blamed her and so she avoided mentioning the abuse. The relationship became more and more strained and they both became extremely sensitive to any criticism from each other.

Dealing with the difficulties

Below we look at ways in which you can begin to explore and understand your feelings toward your mother and consider what changes you might make in your relationship. Dealing with the general problems caused by your sexual abuse by working through this book and by talking to other Survivors or a counselor can also help. It is helpful to read this section and do the exercises even if your mother is dead or if you have no contact with her.

Exploring your feelings

The relationship between you and your mother may involve many complex and conflicting feelings. You may not have allowed yourself time to find out what you really feel about your mother. As an abused child you may have felt that your feelings didn't matter and that you had no right to express them. It is helpful to get in touch with these childhood feelings by doing the letter-writing exercise from the inner child (see chapter 13) before going on to the exercise below.

The exercise below helps you to explore your feelings toward your mother and express them in a safe way. You may be surprised by your feelings. Many Survivors think they feel only anger for their mothers but discover that underneath they yearn to be loved and accepted. Others find that the love and respect they feel toward their mothers masks strong feelings of anger and resentment.

Exercise: Letter to your mother

Write a letter to your mother (not to send) expressing all the feelings you have toward her and all the things you would never dare say. Below are three examples of letters written by Survivors in the Wakefield groups.

Joanne's letter
Dear Mother,

It's sad when you realize a mother and daughter relationship is over, even if it wasn't very good to begin with. I remember the letter you wrote to me after you heard that I was going to the police. "How could you do this to me?," you said. How could I cause you to be by yourself if he got convicted again? I'm afraid I was so full of anger at the time that we didn't get around to that.

I know that the day I brought the abuse out into the open with you was the final straw and after that we seemed to drift apart forever. You asked why we didn't visit with the children when Ken was in the house. I never said at the time that I could remember the time you came home early to find the doors locked while I was being abused, and the day I was trying to tell you what he was doing to me only to remember his threats and back down, afraid to finish the sentence. I never said I could remember the time you shoved a newspaper article under his nose on a case of incest and didn't do anything more when he just laughed off the suggestion and said you were being stupid. Why on earth didn't you protect me from his abuse? Indeed why didn't you protect yourself, me and my brothers from his cruelty and violence? I feel even more hurt that you didn't protect us now that I have children of my own. What kind of a mother were you?

I know you probably cannot understand why I am still so bitter at what Ken did to me. Perhaps you believe that because the abuse has ended I shouldn't still be affected by it. What a misconception that is. Though perhaps you could be excused for thinking that, as even I had no idea that the abuse was the cause of all my problems until I began meeting with the Survivors group.

Now I'm really glad that I have had the opportunity to air my feelings with you. They have haunted me for years. It does sound sad but it looks likely that my life will continue without you. How sad it is that we couldn't have a close relationship with one another as I believe every mother and child should have. But you have made your choice, mother, and decided to stand by the man who sexually abused his daughter and your own daughter. How can I ever come to grips with that!

Polly's letter
Dear Mom,

I am writing this down as I found it hard to say. I want to tell you how I feel and have felt over the years.

When I confronted you about granddad you said we had to understand that my grandma was a cold person and that my granddad was a sensitive warm person. This was your excuse for what he did to us. Well, I think that is garbage. If he needed sex that much then why didn't he find a prostitute or leave grandma? To abuse us children was wrong. I feel angry at you because you didn't protect us in spite of it happening to you when you were little. You say he put his hands down your pants but you told him not to and he stopped. Well, he did worse things to us. He made us have anal sex, oral sex, made us touch his penis and do other things.

Why is it that none of us could talk to you? You were so strict about anything to do with sex like switching the TV channels, never talking about periods or anything. Yet all those years you let that happen to all of us and not only from granddad but other men as well. I could scream at you sometimes.

I couldn't understand how you never noticed or did you just ignore it? You keep going on about how wonderful he is. Well, I don't want you to because it makes me feel sick. He was an old perverted bastard and I hate him. The way you just overlook everything makes me hate you as well. You have always blamed grandma for it all but you are blaming the wrong person. You are trying to put your guilt on everyone except yourself. You cannot go on burying your head in the sand.

Lorna's letter

Dear Mom,

I want to know why you didn't help me when Uncle Charlie was abusing me. Why didn't you know? Why didn't you stop him? There were lots of times I wanted to tell you what was going on but you never seemed to be there for long enough and anyway I didn't think you cared. Even when you thought I had run away you just punished me. Why didn't it occur to you that I was frightened? I know you thought I did not care about you as much as my brothers and sisters did. I did but I just didn't know how to let you know. There were times I hated you because you didn't help me. Sometimes I felt like screaming at you that I was there and I needed you as much as the others. It seemed that you did not care or you were too busy to notice, I don't know which.

Notice if you are directing all your anger for the abuse toward your mother and excusing the abuser. Mothers are not responsible for abuse committed by another person. Mothers who fail to listen to the child, to take action, or to stop the abuse are responsible for this, but the abuser is always responsible for the abuse. Many Survivors initially blame themselves for the abuse, then blame their mothers for not protecting them and then finally place the responsibility for the abuse with the abuser.

Exercise: Letter from your mother

If you have already written a letter to your mother you can now write a reply to that letter. Write a letter to yourself as if you were your mother at the time you were being abused.

Seeing the situation through your mother's eyes can help you understand that your mother may not have known about the abuse. Until very recently most mothers were not aware of the risk to their children of sexual abuse, especially from relatives or friends. If you were behaving badly or strangely the idea that you were being sexually abused would probably never have occurred to your mother.

Seeing the situation through your mother's eyes can also help you understand that she treated you the way she did because of her own circumstances—not because you were a bad or unlovable child. She may have been too busy to notice your distress or unable to cope with the circumstances she was in. She may have been afraid of losing her partner, her home, her family. She may have been depressed, anxious, angry or resentful about her own life. And she may have been sexually abused herself.

Mothers may cope with the suspicion that their child is being sexually abused by pushing it to the back of their minds, blocking it out and pretending it isn't happening. They may remain silent because they also fear the consequences of telling.

Whatever your mother's problems or circumstances she was still responsible if she neglected you, badly treated you or abandoned you. The aim of this letter-writing exercise is not to make excuses for your mother's behavior. It is to help you understand that you deserved love and protection. She behaved the way she did because this was her way of dealing with life and not because you were unlovable.

Lorna wondered if she hadn't been protected because her mother didn't care. However when she thought about the family circumstances at the time she was being abused she realized her mother was trying to cope with working night shifts, a husband who was always out drinking, and bringing up six children (one of whom was in the hospital). Lorna then wrote this reply to herself from her mother.

Dear Lorna,

    I could not help you when your Uncle Charlie was abusing you because I did not know what he was doing. I knew that you didn't like

him but you would not say why. I asked you lots of times but you just
pulled the blinds down on me. There were times I tried to talk to you
or listen but you were not interested. It's true that I punished you
when I thought you had run away but I did not know what else I could
do. You would not, or could not, talk to me. Your sister was in the hospital and I had four other children at home to take care of beside you.

There was not always the time that was needed for everyone. All
my children had been fairly happy, then you changed and became
moody and would not talk to me. It was really difficult. I knew you were
unhappy but I could not help you because I did not know how to. I also
had other responsibilities. I thought I had lost you but I did not know
what I had done wrong, or what I could do to help you.

Lorna realized that although her mother had failed to protect
her it was because of the family's circumstances and because her
mother did not know how to help—not because Lorna was
unlovable.

You may find yourself feeling less angry with your mother as
you begin to understand her situation more or cease to blame
her for things she wasn't responsible for. Or, you may find yourself feeling angry with her for the first time because you realize
you have been protecting your mother when she should have
been protecting you.

Making changes

Relationships between mothers and daughters are never perfect.
Many difficulties can arise that have nothing to do with sexual
abuse. Mothers are never able to live up to the image of an ideal
mother and children invariably feel hurt in some way by their
parents. It's realistic to accept that there may be some difficulties. You may never have the totally loving and supportive
mother you would really like. However, being frequently upset,
damaged or abused by your mother is not acceptable.

Many Survivors feel that they cannot assert themselves with
their mothers and feel themselves to be victims of their mother's
put-downs, constant demands, lack of support or insensitive
treatment. Like Sally's mother, your mother may have convinced
you that you are always in the wrong. Remember that as an
abused child you became accustomed to being treated badly,
without respect and as if your feelings and needs didn't matter.
You may have learned to put up with this type of behavior and
accepted it.

Survivors may also continue to accept bad treatment from their mothers because they feel:

- powerless to do anything else
- frightened of having an argument
- frightened of losing the relationship
- they deserve to be treated badly
- she's right, they are useless/no good/to blame for being abused
- they are in the wrong or being unreasonable
- they have to respect their mother and do as they are told
- they have to try to please her
- they are to blame for upsetting her/making her angry
- they are to blame for breaking up the family
- their own feelings are not as important as other people's

No one deserves to be treated badly. Both you and your mother are adults and could have an equal relationship where you respect your own and each other's rights. Accept that there may be difficulties, but don't accept being used and abused. Passively accepting bad treatment and trying desperately to please will not gain your mother's love, as Sally discovered. Ask yourself if this approach has worked so far?

Feeling less guilty and responsible for the abuse and for your mother's feelings can help you feel and behave differently. You may be able to make changes in the relationship with your mother by changing your behavior, discussing the problems and requesting that she make changes in her behavior. Talking openly and honestly is a good way to encourage someone else to do the same. Behaving assertively encourages other people to behave assertively in return and discourages abusive behavior. Working through the following exercises can be helpful even if you decide not to confront your mother face-to-face.

Exercise 1

Write a description of the relationship you have with your mother. Think about the way she treats you and the way you treat her. What do you like about the relationship? What do you dislike? Is the relationship with your mother good for you or are you being damaged and abused?

Exercise 2

Make a list of some of the things you would like to change with your mother starting with the easiest items first.

Example
1. I want to ask her to come to my house every two weeks instead of me always going to her house.
2. I want to say no to going to Sunday dinner every week.
3. I want to ask her not to give the children presents every time she sees them.
4. I want to tell her that I feel hurt and upset when she criticizes my appearance and ask her not to do it.
5. I want to tell her I don't want to hear about what a wonderful man her father (my abuser) was.

Pick out the easiest task from your list and write down how you might approach this assertively with your mother. Decide what you want to say and how you can say it assertively. Write down all the different ways in which your mother might react and how you could respond. Get a friend to pretend to be your mother and practice what you could say. Speak to your mother only if you want to and after you have done this practice and feel confident.

Talking to your mother about the abuse
You may want to tell your mother about the abuse or, if she already knows, to talk to her about it again. This can help the relationship by breaking the silence, clearing up any misunderstandings and allowing each of you to express your feelings.

However this may not be a helpful step to take. You need to use your own judgment and talk it over with a friend or a professional. Telling your mother is not an essential part of the healing process and you may decide you do not want to do this.

If you do decide to tell your mother, make sure you only do so after careful preparation and when you are quite sure that you know you are not to blame for what happened. Read the section in chapter 15 on confronting the abuser. The preparations you need to make before telling to your mother are very similar. Prepare yourself for all the different reactions your mother might have, for example being upset, angry, not believing you. Act out what might happen with someone else playing the part of your mother so you can rehearse your responses. If possible arrange for both your mother and yourself to have someone around to support you afterwards. Be prepared for the fact that things won't be better immediately but it may help in the long term.

If the abuse is already known to your mother, there may be more talking that needs to be done. Twenty years after Melanie had first told her mother about the abuse she brought up the subject again and they were able to clear up their misunderstandings and develop a better relationship.

Since the abuse the relationship between my mother and myself had been very strained. A while ago I did manage to talk to her about it. It seemed to help us both to form a closer-knit relationship. It was very hard to talk to her about it but afterward we seemed to communicate better. *Melanie*

Melanie realized she wasn't to blame for her mother's upset nor for the difficulties in the relationship between her parents. The Survivor is not responsible for her mother's distress. It is the abuser, by his actions, who is responsible for causing distress to the Survivor and to the Survivor's mother.

Since I received both one-on-one therapy and group therapy I don't feel responsible for the abuse anymore. My stepfather was responsible. This has also made me feel less responsible for my mother. *Jane*

The Survivor can encourage her mother to get help from a therapist or in a group for mothers of children who have been sexually abused. Jane encouraged her mother, Grace, to have individual therapy. Later Jane, her sister Lizzie, and Grace went for therapy together to try to sort out the difficulties they had in relating to each other.

By the time my mother, my sister and I met together my mother had had some one-on-one therapy and had had a chance to talk about her feelings in a more constructive situation. I felt that she had had time for reflection. She was less defensive than she had been previously about what my sister and I had to say and I think she really listened. The situation didn't allow her to use diversions as she had done previously. The psychologist was objective and could repeat what each of us was saying and allow us to clarify what we meant. Also because the psychologist was there I felt safe. *Jane*

Not seeing your mother

Sometimes it is not possible for Survivors to change their relationships with their mothers. A mother who supports the abuser or blames the Survivor for the abuse may demand that the Survivor retracts her disclosure or take the blame for the abuse. Survivors who are presented with these ultimatums or have tried to improve their relationship with their mothers and are still being put-down, damaged or abused, may decide that the only thing they can do is to stop seeing their mother. This might be a temporary or permanent solution to the problem.

Sally held onto the relationship with her mother for many years, trying to please her and win her love and support. Sally's mother continued to blame and disbelieve her, turned other family members against her, and tried to cause trouble between Sally and her husband. Sally eventually thought that holding onto the relationship, and the small hope that her mother would change, was not worth all the pain and grief it was causing.

I always wanted to be able to talk to my mom and tell her how I felt and even to have a good mother and daughter relationship. I know now that it will never be. I have not talked with my mom for over a year and now I feel free to spend my life with my husband and children. *Sally*

Although abandoning a relationship with your mother might be extremely painful it may be the right choice for you. You do not have to maintain a relationship with anyone just because they are a family member. Some Survivors choose to distance themselves from their mothers or stop seeing them while they are working through their own problems and resume the relationship when they feel stronger.

Summary

Survivors often have difficulties with their mothers because of the sexual abuse. They may feel neglected, abandoned or badly treated. They may also have a strong desire to protect their mothers from knowing about the abuse or feel responsible for the distress that disclosure can cause. Survivors' feelings toward their mothers may be a mixture of love, hate, resentment, pity, anger and disappointment.

Survivors can work on these problems by exploring and expressing their feelings and then trying to make changes in the relationship. In this way Survivors can sort out their feelings toward their mothers, refuse to accept bad treatment, regain their own power and move toward a better relationship.

Suggestion

• Follow the suggestions and exercises outlined in the chapter to help you understand your feelings toward your mother and make positive changes.

Further reading

Ashley, Sandi. *The Missing Voice: Writings by Mothers of Incest Victims.*
 Kendall / Hunt Publishing Company, 1992.
Friday, Nancy. *My Mother, My Self.* Dell Publishing Company, 1987.
Gundlach, Julie K. *My Mother Before Me: When Daughters Discover Mothers.*
 Barricade Books, Inc., 1992.
Secunda, Victoria. *When You and Your Mother Can't be Friends.* Delacorte Press, 1991.

15

Abusers

There were so many years during which I wanted you to like me and have the relationship of a big brother that some of my friends had and that I envied so much. I don't think you ever did like me. There were years in which I hated you so much I thought of ways to kill you everyday. Katarina

KATARINA, IN COMMON WITH MANY SURVIVORS, had conflicting feelings about her abuser. She wanted to have a normal loving brother-sister relationship with him but she also hated him for what he was doing to her. Children may have negative feelings towards their abusers because of the abuse but they may also have positive feelings, especially if the abusers are close relatives or friends.

In chapter 4 we looked at how abusers set up situations where they can manipulate and abuse children and at some of the reasons why they abuse. In this chapter we will look at the kinds of people who abuse children, the feelings Survivors have towards their abusers and ways in which these feelings can be explored and expressed.

What are abusers like?

What kinds of people abuse children? Here is a list of some of the characteristics Kate saw in her father:

Cunning, deceitful, a liar, gives the impression he's helpful and generous but this is only to cover the abuse that will follow or because he's afraid someone may tell. Disloyal—uses information told in confidence to suit him. Bad-tempered and violent. Puts others down to build himself up. Tries to make people feel sorry for him. Thinks his ideas are the only right ones. He's never wrong. If you disagree or have another idea you're wrong and shouted down. Selfish. *Kate*

To the outside world however, he was a respected businessman admired by many.

This monster robbed me of the first 30 years of my life. Yet no one outside the family suspected. Social workers liked him, educational welfare officers liked him, some teachers liked him, policemen liked him. But they didn't know his secret. *Kate*

Jane's stepfather (her abuser) was cruel and manipulative within the home but he gave a very different impression of himself to their neighbors. An abuser may be seen by outsiders as a good, kind, generous and respected member of the community, the kind of person who looks after others, not the kind of person who would abuse a child. This can be very difficult for children. It can confirm their feelings that they are to blame for the abuse and that no one will believe them if they try to tell.

Some abusers, like Joanne's, are violent and cruel.

My stepfather was a violent man and he would drink heavily every night at a neighborhood bar. He'd come home and beat my mother and us if we got in the way. I remember him hitting my mother so badly that she had to stay in the hospital for a week. He was mentally cruel towards us all too. On reflection I can see he was very immature and took great pleasure in cruelly teasing us. We weren't allowed indoors even when the weather was bad. My brothers and I would stand on the far side of the backyard fence and stare into the kitchen window because we were so cold. *Joanne*

Other abusers are quiet, kind and fun to be with. Very few abusers fit the stereotype of a dirty old man. Abusers may be young or old, male or female, rich or poor, kind or cruel, scruffy or smart, strong or frail. Abusers may be dominant men who rule their families with a rod of iron, weak ineffectual men, women who keep themselves to themselves, or friendly young men who are well liked in the neighborhood. In fact they are indistinguishable from any other parent, relative, neighbor or friend. Abusers may be laborers, elected officials, professors, unemployed, stockbrokers, housewives, bus drivers, teachers, clergy, or from any other occupation.

Although the majority of abusers are men there are some women who abuse children, both boys and girls. It is difficult for people to accept that women can and do abuse children, especially their own children. It is particularly difficult for victims, both male and female, to accept or disclose that they were abused by women, especially if it was their mother. A mother is supposed to nurture and protect her children and those children who are abused by their mother may feel they have suffered the greatest betrayal of all. Most research studies show two to four per cent of abusers are female, although some workers in the field of sexual abuse suspect the figures are higher than this because victims find it so difficult to talk about abuse by women. Women sexually abuse children by themselves or with a male abuser.

It is not possible to tell abusers from non-abusive people unless you know they are abusing. People of all classes, cultures, ages and personalities abuse.

Feelings towards the abuser

I lie awake at night and I can feel you groping me and I am physically sick. At the memory of your name I'm sick. I could stab you and think nothing of it. Torture wouldn't be sufficient punishment for you. I hope when you die you go to hell but even that's too good for you. I will never ever forgive you for what you've done. You deserve anything evil that comes your way. *Pam*

Pam's feelings towards her abuser (her father) are simple: she hates him. Kate too is angry at her abuser (her father) for the damage he has done to her and to his many other victims.

I feel anger that he robbed me of my childhood, kept me from developing my skills to the fullest extent and made me miss opportunities through lack of confidence. I will never, never be able to trust my abuser, even though he may stop abusing. I feel annoyed with him that he's been so disloyal to his wife and family and that he's damaged so many lives. I feel angry that so many people, male and female, have lost years out of their lives because of him. *Kate*

Kate also feels sorry for her abuser.

I pity the abuser, he now has to live with himself and at some stage in his life he surely will have to admit to himself the terrible things he's done and the harm he has caused others. I feel sorry because he must be a sad and lonely man—being an abuser made him miss out on a lot of important relationships in his life. *Kate*

Children are brought up to believe they should love their families and feel confused when parents, or people taking care of them, also abuse them. Children may love their fathers, brothers, mothers, uncles and find it hard to understand how someone they love can hurt them so much. When Sheila first came for therapy she talked about how much she loved her father even though he had physically and sexually abused her. She blamed herself for the abuse and felt no anger towards him. After she started to understand that he was responsible for the abuse she began to feel angry with him although she still loved him. This is what she wrote after his death:

Why did you have to leave me? I wish you knew what sort of a mess you had left behind. It's so unfair of you to have escaped the way you did. Believe it or not, there were times when I really loved you and other times when I hated you. I wish you could see the pain that I feel inside. I sometimes sit and think about the past and what you did to me and I feel so hurt and angry. I feel that you have destroyed me inside and that you have taken away part of my life.

When I was young I loved and trusted you, and you just used me. How could you do that to me? I will always remember when I was young how I followed you everywhere. You were like some kind of hero to me. I thought I was very special to you, but now when I think of those days I just want to cry because it hurts so much. I felt so guilty when I came up to the hospital to see you the first time you tried to commit suicide. I thought it was my fault because the night before I stood up to you and said no and ran away from you. So when you came home again I never said anything to you, even though you were hurting me and ruining my childhood, because I did not want you to leave me.

I wish things could have been different because I really did love you. *Sheila*

Abusers can be kind to children and take them on outings, give them treats they wouldn't normally get and pay them a lot of attention. They win the children's trust and affection. A child may therefore love the abuser and enjoy spending time with him but feel confused when the abuser behaves sexually towards her.

Maria was abused by her half-brother, Ian, and at times she hated him for the pain she felt because of the abuse. Yet he was her closest friend throughout her childhood and he had loved, protected and comforted her as well as abusing her.

How can I still love Ian and want to put my arms around him and tell him I still love him and forgive him and yet in the next breath want to tell him I hate him and want to beat the living daylights out of him? I'm so confused. *Maria*

It can be difficult for a Survivor to feel anger towards an abuser whom she also loves. Abusers can appear to be warm and caring people when they are not abusing. This can be very confusing for the child and strengthens the child's belief that she must have done something wrong for the abuser to act like this with her. She feels there must be something bad in her that brings out this uncharacteristic behavior in the abuser and this can make her turn her anger inward so that she hates herself and blames herself for the abuse. By blaming herself for the abuse she can keep on loving the abuser. In adulthood Survivors may continue to love their abusers despite the pain the abuser inflicted on them. Some Survivors are so terrified of their abusers that they see them, hear them, smell them or feel their touch when they are not there and even when they are dead.

Survivors experience all sorts of feelings towards their abusers including hate, love, fear, guilt, concern, disgust, affection, betrayal, pity and anger. Often they have a complex mixture of these feelings which can leave them feeling confused. The exercises following may help you understand and work through your feelings towards your abuser.

Working on your feelings about the abuser

Exploring your feelings towards your abuser and finding a way of expressing these feelings can help you break free of your confusion and pain. It can help to talk to a counselor or therapist about this. It may not help to talk to a friend or relative as many people get angry at the thought of child abuse and may expect you to feel anger towards your abuser. Polly feels nothing but hate towards her abuser (her grandfather) whereas her sister (who was also abused by him) still loves him. The sisters feel angry with each other because of this difference and cannot share their feelings or talk about the abuse. Polly believes her sister should also hate her grandfather. You cannot change your feelings because you or other people think you should. There is no right or wrong way to feel. It is important to begin by recognizing and accepting your feelings for your abuser, whatever they are, and to start to work from there.

In therapy Survivors begin to understand that their abusers were responsible for the abuse and that they manipulated the children into the abusive situation. They realize that it is the abuser who is to blame for the abuse and not themselves. For the first time, like Sheila and Maria, they begin to lose their anger at themselves and turn the anger towards their abusers.

As you work through your feelings you may find that you are also angry at the abuser you believed you loved; or that you love the abuser you thought you only hated; or that under your anger is grief at losing your childhood. The following exercises may help you to discover and release some of your feelings.

About 50 percent of the Wakefield Survivors have been sexually abused by more than one person. If you have had more than one abuser, apply the suggestions in this chapter to each of them.

Exercise 1: Talking to a pillow

This exercise can be a helpful way for you to explore your own feelings towards your abuser and to express them without having to consider his reaction.

Do this exercise when you are alone and feeling safe and want to work through your feelings about your abuser. Pick a pillow to represent your abuser. Sit on a chair and place the pillow on another chair opposite you at whatever feels the most comfortable distance. Imagine the pillow is your abuser and start to talk to him. Begin by telling him how he has damaged your life. You may feel many emotions rising in you. Accept them and express them to the abuser. Often talking isn't enough. If you get angry you may want to throw the pillow on the ground and punch it, stamp on it or kick it around the room. This is a helpful way for you to let your feelings out without hurting yourself or anyone else. In fact this technique is helpful whenever you get angry at someone.

Anger is only one of the feelings that may arise. You may feel upset, afraid, love, hate, pity, distaste, or any mixture of feelings. The aim of the exercise is to allow you to discover what you are feeling and express your feelings outwardly instead of holding them in or harming yourself. The idea of talking to a pillow may seem strange but many people have really benefited from venting their feelings in this way.

Exercise 2: Letters to your abuser

Writing a letter to your abuser without sending it is another way for you to explore and express your feelings. Allow yourself plenty of time and let yourself write whatever comes into your head. You may want to describe all the things the abuser did to you and how it made you feel at the time. You may want to tell him how the abuse affected your life as you grew older and how you feel towards him now. Writing can help you understand the full range of your feelings and give you an opportunity to get them off your chest.

Polly's grandfather had abused her and all her sisters. When she was a young adult Polly had written and mailed a letter to her grandfather about the abuse, but when her family found out they forced her to write again and retract what she had said. Polly felt betrayed yet again and was left feeling intensely angry. After she had been in a Survivors group Polly wanted to confront her grandfather again but he had long since died. She wrote another letter, this time for herself.

Dear Bastard,

Yes, Bastard—because you are this and many more names.

I confronted you before in a letter telling you I forgive you for everything you did to me. I was made to deny it for my grandma's sake in case she might have a heart attack or something.

I now know that you abused all my sisters and my mom. So it was not a matter of any of us leading you on. You were the guilty one and you did whatever you wanted to do to innocent children who could not defend themselves and you made them swear to secrecy.

Well, you dirty old pig, it's time you realized what you have done. We could have had you sent to prison for good because there are too many of us for the courts to say it is our imagination. So how does it make you feel to know you are hated intensely by your own grandchildren? Not once did you show any remorse by saying you were sorry although you had plenty of opportunities.

Now that you're dead the past has not died with you. I'm so glad you're dead because now I won't have to worry about other children being around a monster like you.

The abuse is not going to ruin my life because I'm fighting it and getting help. People like you are the ones who need help yet you're so sick you think you're normal. I would hate to be in your shoes because

I believe in God, whether you do or not, and you will find punishment for what you've done.

I hope you rot in hell.

Polly

After writing this letter Polly felt she had at last been able to express her true feelings and she began to feel less troubled by her anger.

Shirley wanted to vent her anger and tell the abuser how harmful his actions were and how the trauma can affect the child, the adolescent, the adult. Shirley didn't know where her abuser was so she couldn't tell him to his face. She wrote a letter instead.

Dear Abuser,

For many years I have hated you, and for many years I wanted to march in on you when your store was full of people and dump all my hatred upon you, to humiliate you as you humiliated me. I wanted to scream out the hurt you caused and show you that we, the children of abuse, grow up but we don't ever forget.

Have you any idea of the damage you have done? Did you really think it was such a harmless bit of fun to grope a small child's body ? Did you really think that you could do that and leave a child's mind and soul untouched? If there is any shred of human decency left in you, and if you truly understood the damage you inflicted, you would never do such a thing again. So I am going to tell you about the damage you have done to me.

You polluted my mind with things I knew nothing about, things no child should have to know. In violating me you caused me to feel ashamed and dirty, and that sense of feeling unclean never went away. I grew up both rejecting my body and yet desperately trying to control it. One of the greatest crimes you committed was that you caused me to doubt my self-worth. It was not I who was degraded, whose worth as a person was lessened. Now I can hold my head up knowing I did nothing wrong.

I felt guilty. You knew that children are told never to take candy from strangers, so you gave me candy after abusing me knowing I wouldn't refuse it. Knowing that in taking it I would be doing something I knew to be wrong, thus ensuring my silence and my guilt. Was that all I was worth to you, a candy bar? In giving me that you made me wrong so I could never tell anyone what you had done.

Are you so sure it has all been worth it? For a few minutes of sexual excitement, for a moment of power over a child, you inflicted so much harm, damaged my life and the lives of so many others. You will not be able to lay the blame on the child all your life. We, the abused, refuse to accept all the hurt, anguish and guilt you have tried to force upon us. We, the abused, can heal, we can find peace, we can be free; while you, the abuser, can never rest. You must always hide from yourself, from your guilt, from your shame; for if you knew their true measure they would surely overwhelm you.

I am on my way to freedom. Freedom from you, from all the pain, guilt, hatred and fear you inspired. I am free now to love a man without fearing him.
Shirley

Katarina wanted to tell her abuser, her brother, how he had damaged her life. She wanted to express her anger and her sadness at being unable to relate to him as a brother.

Brother,
I was asked to write to you and, thinking about it, I agree that it is a good thing to tell you what I think about you and what damage you have done to me.

You have been so smart; not only abusing my body but also making sure I would grow up with fear in my heart and no self-esteem. For 20 years after the abuse I still thought of myself as less worthy than other people. You made sure that if you were around I felt like a worm about to be stepped on. I wanted to see you dead but my fear of you made it impossible to attack you in any other way than in my mind. I was still helpless.

If only you had shown some form of remorse, treated me with kindness when we were growing up. Although I hated you there was a part in me that desperately wanted to forgive you, to be liked by you, to make a new start and become at last a brother and sister in the way I had seen in other families. Yet I know if I had told you what damage your abuse did to me you would have done no more than shrug your shoulders and say "So what?"
Katarina

In her letter Katarina went on to describe in detail how his abuse had affected her whole life and expressed her anger to him for this. Having talked about her abuse and worked through her feelings Katarina's feelings towards her brother have changed:

Of course I am still angry. But it is not the same kind of anger anymore that I used to feel. The kind of anger I feel now is anger at someone who has done me wrong, who knew it completely and did not care. It is the healthy kind of anger not the kind that sees no reason and is nothing but blind fury. If I see him in the street, when I go back to my hometown, I am now strong enough to look him in the eyes. *Katarina*

Confronting the abuser

Some Survivors feel they need to confront their abusers by talking face-to-face about the abuse and the effect it has had on their lives. Many Survivors have come to terms with their abuse and learned to feel much better about themselves without confronting their abusers. Some Survivors have no contact with their abusers or their abusers may be dead. Do not feel you should confront your abuser. It is not an essential part of the healing process. Sorting out your own feelings towards the abuser is the important thing.

Most of you will not want to confront your abusers but it may still help you to treat this section as an exercise and work through the full preparation without doing the actual confrontation. It can help you to explore and express your feelings and it may also help you to release some of your fear and regain your own power. If you decide that you want to confront your abuser, IT IS VERY IMPORTANT THAT YOU DO NOT DO THIS UNTIL YOU ARE FULLY PREPARED.

In this section we will look at why Survivors want to confront their abusers, how you can prepare yourself for a confrontation, and at what happened when some of the Wakefield Survivors confronted their abusers.

Why confront the abuser?
Pam remembers how she talked to friends at work about her plans to confront her abuser.

One of my fellow workers said "You only want to confront your father to split him and your mother up, to teach them a lesson." I replied, nearly in tears, "No, that isn't the reason I want to confront him. I want to get over the anxieties I have about men in general. I look at men that I don't know and think of them as potential child abusers." *Pam*

Like Pam, some Survivors want to confront their abusers to overcome their fear of him and of men in general. Some Survivors decide to confront their abusers to protect other children, especially when they know he has already abused many victims.

I knew my father had abused a lot of other members of my family and I suspected he was still doing so. I could protect my own children from him but how could I protect everyone else? I asked my sister to come

with me to support me when I confronted him. Our aim was not to
hurt him but to stop him from hurting anyone else. He admitted he
had done some things to his daughters which he regretted but denied
abusing anyone else. He said the others just wanted to make trouble
and were out to get him. We told him we were watching him and that I
was not going to keep quiet if he continued abusing. *Kate*

There were other benefits for Kate from this confrontation:

I did not say all the things I wanted to say, but I was surprised to find
that I had passed the burden of guilt back to him, where it rightly
belongs. I felt strong. The power relationship between us changed after
this. He avoided me rather than me having to avoid him. *Kate*

Sexual abuse occurs in secret. The abuser gets the child to
comply by using some form of power (adult authority, physical
strength, threats), leaving the victim feeling powerless and controlled by the abuser. Often the victims feel they are under the
abuser's power for the rest of their lives. Confronting the abuser
can break the secret and take this power away from him.
Although Kate had primarily gone to confront her abuser to
protect other children she also found the power relationship
between them had reversed.

Some women still care about their abuser but find the relationship between them very difficult because of the long-held
secret. Discussing the abuse and facing up to it can clear the air.

I talked to my dad about the abuse for a couple of hours. I was aston-
ished at how we both talked as we hadn't talked to each other for years.
My last words to him were "I love you as a father but hate you for what
happened." *Lucy*

Survivors have many different reasons for wanting to confront their abusers. These include:

• to break the silence and with it the hold the abuser may still
  have over them
• to reverse the power relationship
• to rid themselves of the fear they still have inside—the fear an
  abused child has of her adult abuser
• to help them get over their own fears and anxieties about men
  in general
• to express their own anger and distress

- to get the abuser to acknowledge what he has done and to see the harm he has caused
- to clear the air and help resolve their feelings towards the abuser
- to protect other children from the abuser

Some of these aims probably won't be achieved. Abusers will rarely admit to the abuse so Survivors must be prepared for their reactions. If a Survivor hopes the abuser will acknowledge the harm he has done she is very likely to be disappointed.

How to confront your abuser

Your own feelings

It is important that you do not plan to confront your abuser until you have worked through your own feelings about the abuse. It is best to have some counseling first or to at least have read this book and talked to others about the abuse. You need to feel certain that the abuse was not your fault and the abuser was responsible for what happened. The abuser may accuse you of being a liar, say you are crazy or blame you for the abuse. You will end up feeling much worse if you have any doubt about what happened and who was responsible.

It is also important that you do not see the abuser if you are full of rage. The purpose is to talk to him, not to attack him physically. Attacking him could put you in physical danger and have legal consequences. It will also leave you feeling helpless and out of control again. Make sure you have first worked through the exercises in this chapter on expressing your feelings (talking to a pillow and writing letters).

Support

If you know of anyone else who has been abused by the same person ask them to confront the abuser with you. Go through all the preparations with them. If you have a partner or friend with you when you confront the abuser make sure they understand they are there for support only. It will not help you feel empowered again if another person takes over and confronts the abuser or deals with the abuser's reactions. If you are going to confront the abuser alone then have someone you trust in the next room. Afterwards you will probably need someone to talk to about how

you feel so make sure there will be someone available to support
you.

Exercise 3: What are you going to say?

You need to think carefully about exactly what you want to say to
your abuser and how you will say it. To do this you need to think
about why you want to confront him. Do you want to express
how you feel about the abuse? Do you want to tell the abuser
how he has damaged your life? Write down exactly why you are
going to confront your abuser, what you want to express and
how you are going to say it. It is helpful to talk this over in detail
with someone ahead of the actual meeting.

The abuser's response

Survivors expectations of what might happen can be very wrong.
They often think that the abuser will be hurt and upset if they
confront him, and assume he must feel dreadful about what he
has done. Abusers usually deny what they have done however
strong the evidence against them. This could be devastating if
you are not prepared for it but can still be useful if you have prepared yourself. You can still vent your anger, bring the abuse into
the open (thereby destroying the secret), and reverse the power
relationship.

   If the abuser admits to the abuse at all he will probably mini-
mize it; i.e., "Well, I did touch you but I was only tickling you."
He may try to blame or threaten you.

Exercise 4

Think about all the possible responses your abuser may have and
how you could reply to them. Here are some examples:

Abuser's reactions	Possible replies
Denying:	
I did not touch you.	Yes, you did. You had intercourse with me.
I don't know what you're talking about.	Yes, you do, you made me touch your penis.

You are a liar/mentally ill/ imagining it.	I am not a liar/mentally ill/ imagining it, you did touch my private parts.

Minimizing:

I was only tickling you.	You did not tickle me, you rubbed my genitals.
I was teaching you the facts of life.	You were not teaching me the facts of life, you sexually abused me.
I was only playing with you.	You were not only playing with me, you masturbated over me.

Blaming:

You enjoyed it.	You were responsible. You sexually abused me.
You kept taking your clothes off in front of me. You asked for it.	You were an adult and you sexually abused a child.

Threatening:

No one will speak to you again.	I am not to blame, you are responsible for the abuse.
I'll tell your parents what you've done.	You are responsible for the abuse, you are to blame.

Keep your replies simple. The abuser may try to overwhelm you by denying the abuse in many different ways. Do not be side-tracked, use the stuck-record technique and simply repeat your chosen reply over and over again.

What if the abuser cries?

A few abusers break down, cry and say they are sorry. Survivors may then feel pity for the abusers and regret hurting them. It is the abuser that hurt you; if he is upset it is because of what he has done. Remember that abusers manipulate their victims so they can sexually abuse them. The abuser may be crying because he is genuinely sorry or he may be crying to manipulate you into feeling sorry for him and therefore retracting what you have said.

He may also be crying for himself because he is frightened of other people knowing what he has done or of being prosecuted by the police.

Examples of how you can respond:

- "You are upset because of what you have done."
- "Don't expect me to comfort you, you abused me."
- "Well, you should be upset about this."

Practice
Practice with a friend or therapist. This is very important. Get a friend to pretend to be the abuser and act out the confrontation. Practice all the abuser's possible reactions, however unlikely or upsetting they are, and how you would respond. You will need to do this several times.

Plan in detail where, when and how you are going to confront the abuser. Choose a place where you feel comfortable and safe, your home or neutral territory. Some Survivors chose to confront their abusers in a public place with a friend nearby for added protection.

VERY IMPORTANT: Do not confront someone who may be violent, but still work through these exercises for your own benefit.

Pam's confrontation
Pam phoned her parents and told them to come over to see her that evening at 8.30 p.m.

We hadn't had contact for over two years. My immediate thought was—would I break down?

I had my husband make coffee to keep him out of the way—I had to do this alone. My mother sat beside my father in the family room so I told her to go sit in the dining room. I then confronted my father with exactly what he'd done to me. He'd raped me and sucked my body. I told him how this had affected me, particularly over the past two years when I had had a nervous breakdown. I told him that I became agoraphobic and I couldn't have a sexual relationship with my husband because all I saw was my father's face. I told him I hated him so much.

He sat there for approximately an hour and listened to me. I then told him I wanted to tell my mother in front of him to prove to her I wasn't lying. I'd actually told her about it at the time it first happened and many times since, but she'd dismissed me as a liar.

My father more or less made his admission of guilt by non-denial. But I was pleased because normally you can't talk to him without him blowing his top. He was completely devastated and I thought, "Well, now you can walk around with it on your conscience for the rest of your life."

I told them both they were lucky to be alive walking out of my house, because all I wanted to do was kick their teeth in or stab them both to death. I hated them so much. Their reaction was that they didn't blame me. *Pam*

Pam's father did not admit his guilt but he didn't deny it either. Pam had at last managed to express her anger and distress to her parents and this marked a turning point in her relationship with them and in her own feelings.

When they had gone I felt like I'd been carrying a heavy backpack and somebody had just taken it off me. I felt absolutely marvelous. I felt I'd really achieved something. All I ever wanted was a mom and dad who cared and loved me. Up to the present the change in them is unbelievable but for the better and I feel a lot better within myself. There is life after abuse and this is what it took for me to find that out. *Pam*

Pam's husband Brian, describes the change in her relationship with her parents after the confrontation.

The big turning point came when Pam decided to confront the abuser, her father. She got 24 years of anger off her chest in that many minutes. Now she is a changed woman, never to be intimidated by her parents again. In fact they are now a bit unnerved by her and at her beck and call. Since then there has been some form of family relationship. On my part it is toleration because they are Pam's parents. On her part—they are always her parents in the end. *Brian*

Claire and Joan's confrontation

Claire and Joan are sisters who were both abused by their brother-in-law Tony, the husband of their eldest sister. They decided to confront Tony because Joan was still feeling depressed and powerless at the end of her group therapy and because they were worried he might be abusing his own children. As Claire said:

I want to confront him, to show him how bad it is and to stop him if he's still doing it. I don't want him to think he has escaped. I want him to feel ashamed of what he did. *Claire*

They had several meetings to discuss what they thought might happen and to brief their husbands. In the meetings they also planned what they wanted to say and practiced assertive ways of dealing with all Tony's possible reactions. Claire and Joan originally thought Tony would admit what he had done and get upset. Without the meetings and practice they wouldn't have been prepared for what actually happened.

My younger sister Joan and I decided to confront our abuser, Tony, together. We were quite scared but we felt ready to go ahead with it. We both felt like we needed to do this and in a strange way I was looking forward to it.

The scene was set at Joan's house. Her husband left the house but while we waited for Tony to arrive we were wishing that he had stayed. Later we were very proud of ourselves for doing it alone. As we saw Tony walk up the sidewalk, Joan decided to calm herself by doing a few of the breathing exercises we had learned at group therapy.

Tony had no idea why we wanted to see him but we wasted no time. I was the first to speak and I told him that Joan and I were seeing a psychologist because of what he had done to us as children. Color drained from his face and I felt stronger. Very annoyed, he said, that he didn't know what we were talking about and that he'd never done anything to us. Joan had to spell it out and all the time he was denying it. He said he was only tickling us. By this time he was standing at the door and saying he was leaving. Joan suddenly became very strong and confident and continued to tell him how well we remembered where and when those awful things took place and he got very frightened and raised his voice.

He continued to trip himself up with his lies and as he kept changing his story he seemed to get smaller and smaller, weaker and weaker. We felt more sure of his guilt than ever now. We kept saying over again "Yes, you did it." He said we were both insane and he felt sorry for us. Then he used his last weapon when he said "I'll tell your mom and dad—what will they say about what you've done?"

Something clicked inside me—I had heard this before from him, all those years ago. Except this time instead of feeling guilty I felt more sure I was doing the right thing and said "Yes, what would they say to you, if they knew what you did to their children?"

We continued to surprise him by telling him we knew of two other women who had been his victims. We told him we could take him to court and that we were worried about his own daughters. He still denied everything and said he was going to get his wife, Rita (our sister). She arrived shortly, alone. He had told her what had been said and swore that he hadn't done anything.

When it was all over I felt sorry for my sister Rita. I wanted to put my arms around her but I couldn't because she still didn't say she believed us. I still felt we had done the right thing.

It was a big relief to know it was all over and I wouldn't have to do it again. I was full of confidence and thought we performed well. We couldn't have done it any better and we did it alone, without our men behind us. Now Tony knows how much he hurt us and spoiled Joan's life and now he's spoiled his own. It feels really great to put the guilt on him. It's changed my life.

I don't blush very much these days. Each day I get a little more confident and like myself better. I released a lot of anger on that day and now I feel much calmer. It's changing Joan's life too. The very next day she went swimming and instead of rushing into the water, so that no one could see her body, she sat there for a while and could look at people in the water and hold her head up high. She didn't feel ashamed anymore.

I don't feel like keeping it a secret anymore. In fact I want to tell all the family except mom and dad—not because of shame this time but to protect them from feeling they let us down by failing to protect us from this pathetic person. *Claire*

Their sister, Rita, soon believed them and Claire and Joan made sure his own children were safe by contacting Social Services (chapter 17 describes the procedures for protecting children). During the confrontations Tony seemed to grow smaller and weaker to the sisters while they felt themselves growing bigger and stronger. Claire and Joan had anticipated all of Tony's possible responses and practiced how they would reply so it didn't matter that he denied abusing them. What was important was that they were able to confront him and show him and themselves that they were no longer ashamed and were not responsible for the abuse. Joan got her power back and immediately began improving. Her depression lifted and she began to feel more confident every day.

Joanne's attempted prosecution

Joanne had spent her childhood in fear of her stepfather, Ken, who was physically violent as well as sexually abusive. As an adult she had told her mother and family what had happened to her but was shunned by them and still felt she carried the blame for the abuse. Joanne decided not to confront her stepfather directly as he was a violent man. However she still wanted Ken and her family to acknowledge that it was Ken, and not she, who was responsible for the abuse and so she went to the police and gave a statement. Unfortunately the case was never brought to court because of lack of supporting evidence. Joanne, however, was not disheartened by this because Ken was arrested and her accusation made public. She expressed her feelings by writing a letter without sending it.

Dear Ken,

Well, you are probably feeling very relieved at the moment after hearing that you're not going to be prosecuted after all, even though you sexually abused me for years. At the beginning of the Survivors group I would have been devastated if I'd have known that the case wouldn't go to court but now, much to my surprise, I don't feel bitter. I feel I've made my point to you. You now know how much I hate you and that if possible I would have seen you imprisoned once again. I felt a great deal of satisfaction when I heard that you'd had to have minor surgery for stomach pains due to the stress and worry you've been going through for the past ten months. This gave me pleasure to hear. At least you've suffered in some way after all the suffering you caused me and all those around you.

For all those years I was absolutely terrified of you. Well now I feel so proud and full of strength to have stood up to you. For the past year I've been the one who has had power over you. My actions have brought worry and fear to you. For years you told me that if I spoke about it "no one would ever want to have anything to do with me ever again." How it delights me when I know you now realize that I can discuss this terrible secret with others and with members of our family. How false those threats were but as a child these and other threats seemed very real. It hurts to realize how commonly these threats are made by you and your fellow abusers.

I thank my lucky stars daily that I've received help. I'm relieved to say that I sincerely feel as if I've been reborn at age 31. At least you haven't ruined my whole life. I'll never forgive you for what you've done to me and the way you messed up my life up until now with my husband and my own children. They have seen me during my periods of depression and sadness, though not any more. You can't hurt me any more. I'm finally rid of you. I don't feel I'll ever be able to forgive you, but I'm certainly on the way to forgetting about what you did and the problems you have caused. I am now moving ahead with my life and, perhaps more importantly, I'm aware that my life is now richer than yours.

Joanne

Joanne had anticipated all the things that could happen if she gave a statement to the police so that even though the case was dropped before it got to court, confronting her abuser in this way helped Joanne regain her own power. After the confrontation Joanne wrote:

He now knows he doesn't have a hold over me anymore. He can no longer frighten me with the threat that everyone will blame me and reject me if I tell about the abuse.

Summary

Abusers do not fit a stereotype. They can be men or women of any personality type, in any walk of life. The feelings Survivors have towards their abusers can be just as varied. They may have a conflicting mixture of feelings including hate, love, fear, guilt, concern, disgust, betrayal, pity and anger. The exercises suggested in this chapter can help Survivors to explore and understand their feelings towards their abusers; to express their feelings and so release some of their pain; and to regain their personal power.

Suggestions

- Explore your feelings towards your abusers using the exercises described in this chapter (talking to a cushion or writing a letter to the abusers, or by talking to a counselor or therapist.
- Use the "How to confront your abuser" section of this chapter as an exercise to help regain your power. If you decide you want to express your feelings face-to-face with your abuser read the suggestions and do the exercises described in the chapter. DO NOT confront your abuser without full preparation—it will only cause you more emotional distress. DO NOT confront an abuser who is likely to be violent.
- If you know or suspect that your abuser is currently abusing another child, protect the child by informing the child-protecttion agency or get some advice by contacting one of the telephone help-lines listed in Further Reading and Useful Addresses. Also see chapter 17 on Prevention.

16

Overcoming the Problems

Before I went for therapy I thought I would never feel strong enough to take charge of my own life. I wouldn't have believed it was possible for my life to change so much. Jane

YOU CAN LEARN TO FEEL BETTER about yourself and overcome the problems resulting from your sexual abuse. In this chapter we look at how Survivors can break free from their problems and regain their own power. Survivors describe what it was like being in a group that helped them and how they feel after individual or group therapy. Some of the quotations and information in this chapter derive from research conducted on the Wakefield Survivor groups by Sally Pinnell, Clinical Psychologist.

Getting help

We have seen how childhood sexual abuse results in adult Survivors feeling bad about themselves and experiencing problems in many areas of their lives. Some Survivors are only mildly affected by the abuse but others hate themselves and feel that their lives have been destroyed by the abuse.

How can you begin to break free from the effects of the abuse and take control of your own life? Reading this book and working through the exercises is a start. Talking to a trusted friend or family member may also help by breaking the secret and allowing you to feel accepted by someone who knows what has happened to you. For some Survivors this may be enough but others will need to get further help by seeking individual therapy or joining a Survivors group. Before you decide you do not need any further help, talk it over (in person or on a telephone help line) with someone who could offer help. You may find it difficult to seek help because you feel ashamed and worthless or think your problems are insignificant.

I was afraid I would be wasting the psychologist's time. I was not worthy of nice people wasting their valuable time on a disgusting person like me. *Eileen*

Feeling unworthy is one of the effects of being sexually abused. You deserve help.

If you are being abused in any way or have been abused no matter how long ago it happened, please tell someone and get some help. You owe it to yourself. *Joan*

There is a Useful Addresses section at the back of this book with suggestions of people or organizations you can contact. If the person you speak to doesn't believe you, or responds inappropriately, then keep on telling until someone does.

How can anything help?
I couldn't believe that just talking would help, it did, it does. I like myself, I did nothing wrong. *Jocelyn*

If you were sexually abused as a child then nothing can change that fact. What can change is the way you see yourself, the way you understand what happened during the abuse and the way you feel about yourself and others. Building up a relationship with someone who knows your background and problems (rather than someone who just knows the front that many Survivors hide behind) can help you overcome problems in trusting others. Understanding the events of your childhood as an adult will help you see that you were not to blame for the abuse, you were not guilty. In time the feelings of guilt, shame and self-blame will also change.

You can conquer problems relating to your sexual identity, your sexuality and your sexual behavior by working on your feelings about yourself. Your feelings of powerlessness will fade as you learn to face up to your fears, rather than avoiding them, and begin to take control of your own life, your own problems and your own feelings. Your own power will grow as you assert yourself in the world and discover who you really are without the burden of shame and fear. Reading this book, going for therapy or joining a group can help you overcome your problems.

Writing
I've found writing really helpful, once I started writing I couldn't stop. It really surprised me—I could write better than I could talk. *Claire*

Writing can help you to overcome your problems whether you are working on your problems alone or with the help of others. Survivors have found writing especially helpful in allowing them to remember their experiences, explore and express their feelings, face up to their fears and accept their experiences and themselves. In chapter 1 we suggested you do the written exercises at the end of each chapter. This can be difficult for some people but many Survivors find this is an important part of the healing process.

Some Survivors are too frightened of writing their thoughts down. They are frightened that someone else will see them or afraid that if they are written down on paper they will have to face up to the fact that the events really happened.

I found writing terrifying. I would scrawl things down but I couldn't look at them or else I would throw them away. *Colleen*

Many Survivors feel the need to throw away or destroy their writings at first. Keep a stamped addressed envelope ready and mail them to someone you trust (a therapist if you have one) as soon as you've written them. You can ask the person who receives the letters to read them or just hold onto them until you are ready to read them again or show them to someone else.

I always used to burn my writings but then I started mailing them to my therapist as soon as I'd written them. Mailing them still felt like I was getting rid of them again but then they arrived at her office and it was there in black and white—not hidden anymore. It was still my secret when I burned them so I was pleased when I could let my therapist read them. I felt so much better that it wasn't hidden. Everything before had to be a secret—no openness at all. *Lucy*

You may find it difficult to begin writing.

It's difficult to get started, you're thinking about who is going to see it, but once you start you don't know where to stop. One of the girls from an earlier group kept all her writings and says she can see how much she has improved. One girl says she writes down her thoughts when her mind is racing and it helps her to stop thinking about it. I'm going to try that at the times when I can't concentrate. *Claire*

Writing becomes a way of helping you to cope with your thoughts and feelings and a way of releasing all your secret fears and memories.

At first I tended not to think about things so they wouldn't hurt as much. Now I think things out and write them down, not push them down. It's best to deal with things. I'm really good at that now. *Claire*

Often writing helps the Survivors remember things they had forgotten.

So I started writing. It was really helpful. I could go back and remember. Once I started writing I couldn't stop. It wasn't just about the abuse it was about all my childhood. By writing it down I really could see why it wasn't my fault—why it happened and why I couldn't tell. That was the best part, it was a real help. *Mavis*

If you have not been able to do the written exercises at the end of the chapters, why not try again now?

Joining a survivors group

After I saw my therapist three or four times she suggested I join a group but I didn't want to go. The idea of being in a group of other women really frightened me. But I eventually said yes and it was the best thing I've ever done. *Jocelyn*

Not everyone would like to join a group or has the opportunity to join one. We have found that Survivors benefit a great deal from being in a group and overcome their problems much more quickly.

Fears about joining a group

I saw my therapist four times before I joined the group. I was terrified of being in a group. I didn't want to speak to anyone else about it. It was this secret between the psychologist and me and nobody else. I was frightened of the group and didn't think it would help but I would have given anything to go as I'd gotten so desperate. I don't know what

I expected. I was so afraid of anyone knowing what had happened to me. I was so ashamed of it. It was my secret. What would they think of me? I thought they would blame me for letting it happen. *Lucy*

Many people are nervous or extremely frightened at the thought of joining a group. Sexual abuse occurs in secret and the feelings of shame arise partly from keeping this secret. Widening the circle of people who know about the secret by joining a group can be very frightening. But feeling accepted by other people who know the secret can help reduce the feeling of shame.

I didn't want to go to the group at first because it would increase the number of people who knew what happened to me. My psychologist said she could talk to me about how other Survivors feel. But it would be different for me to talk to the women myself, to actually go into a room with other Survivors, who know I have been abused too and have the same feelings. I didn't know if I would get to the first group meeting until I actually got there. Walking into the room I realized everyone was in the same boat. I didn't feel threatened when I walked in but I didn't enjoy it. I felt I'd come this far and had to do it. *Jocelyn*

Survivors often fear that someone else in the group will know them or talk about them outside the group.

I am a professional woman and I had fears of joining a group in case someone from the group would recognize me and discuss me in public. Everyone would know what I had done. The group discussed confidentiality and the therapists asked every member present to respect each other. They said it was unlikely that anyone would discuss another group member in public because they had all suffered the same or similar experiences. This was very reassuring to me and put me at ease immediately. *Eileen*

Many women say they should not be part of a Survivors group because they feel phony. They think they shouldn't be in the group because they can't remember what happened during their abuse or they think their abuse was not as serious as every-one else's.

The first week at the group I knew I had been abused but not remem-bering much about it. I didn't know if it had really happened and that was my big fear. At first you feel everyone else is much worse off than you and then you put it into perspective and realize that whatever the form of the abuse it has affected each of us. *Jocelyn*

Many Survivors feel they are different from everyone else or that their abuse was different. In the group Survivors become aware that they share many feelings in common and that whatever has happened to them, it is just another form of abuse.

It may help you overcome your fears about joining a group if you can arrange to meet a Survivor who has already been in a group. You can talk together about what actually happens in the group and the more experienced group member may be able to support you in getting to the first meeting.

In the Wakefield groups there is no pressure to talk about what actually happened during the sexual abuse or who the abuser was. The initial emphasis is on how the abuse made the Survivors feel about themselves and how it affects their lives now.

We didn't give all the gory details of our abuse, we talked about the problems the abuse had left us with. I had forgotten so much about my own abuse but others in the group could remember and a lot of things they said prompted flashbacks and memories in me. *Jocelyn*

The group then moves on to understanding and expressing their feelings about the abuse and to working out ways of overcoming their current problems.

Sticking with it
In the first session the therapists explained how we were likely to feel worse during the first few weeks because discussing the abuse made it more of a reality. It was only by reliving the experiences that we could face up to our problems and overcome our bad feelings. This was very true. I soon began to feel the past feelings of shame and self-disgust and all the childhood experiences and emotions came flooding back to me. Having been pre-warned about this was very helpful. *Eileen*

You may get to the first meeting but want to drop out after a few weeks. It's certainly not easy being in a Survivors group or in individual therapy. All the bad memories and unpleasant feelings that you have been trying to push to the back of your mind come to the surface. You need to face them again so you can accept them, share them, release the pain and power of the memories and start the healing process.

During the time you are attending the group sessions you start thinking about your abuse all the time, even when you're eating or cooking you're still thinking about it. You wake up in the night thinking about it again and you feel you should just hide it and try to forget about it again. But you know you've got to get it out and deal with it, you can't hide it forever.

At first I thought, what have I done—I'm making things worse. I wished I'd never started. But now I realize I've got to get it out and face it and then maybe I can break free from it.

I went through a phase of feeling really angry that I could have been so different if I hadn't been abused. It's been a horrible year. There was a lot to be uncovered and it wasn't nice. It's been very hard but I've got it sorted out now. *Claire*

Here is what Pam's husband had to say:

Eventually Pam got help at a Survivors group, but it didn't all end there. The more she went to the group for a while the worse she became. For a few weeks there was no living with her. For two days after each group session, it was like living with a skunk with hemorrhoids. I still cringe at the thought of those days. It was worth it though. Pam is certainly a different person now as compared to the one who started going to the survivors group. She still has some hang-ups but she is much more assertive and capable in day-to-day life. *Brian*

There may be times when you want to give up and to blot it all out again. However, if you try to push your feelings down they will surface again or come out in other ways such as anxiety, depression or eating problems. Talk about your feelings and try to stick it out.

It got a lot worse. It seems so long ago now since I've had a bad episode. But there were times when things were getting the best of me. It was triggering memories that I brought home with me and were on my mind all the time. I was worse than before I went to the group. It seemed to last a long while but it was probably just three or four days. It was as if it was all fighting to come out and then it was all right. I phoned my psychologist and said I didn't know if it was worth it. But then I went back to the group and talked it through with them, and that really helped. But I couldn't have stopped halfway through. I knew if I got there the first week that I would stick it out to the end. *Jocelyn*

How the group helped

In the rest of this section we look at what Survivors found most helpful about being in a group.

Creating a safe environment

If I had to think of one thing that helped me in the group it would be honesty. I really believe throughout my life I haven't been honest with anybody and I felt in the group from the beginning that everyone wanted to be honest. We had all held a secret but it wasn't a secret in there. I could go in there and say anything, things I wouldn't have told anyone else, and I knew it was safe. *Jocelyn*

One of the most important things about a group is that it can create a safe environment where Survivors can talk freely without putting on a brave face. They can talk honestly about their inner-most fears and still feel respected and accepted by the other group members. This helps them to overcome the feelings of guilt and shame. They can also start to learn to trust others again.

When I was there in the room I started to feel better but then I had to go home and cope with the outside world. Even though it was difficult, hard work and distressing, I felt even more secure there than in individual work with the therapist. *Colleen*

The room was the first place that I knew I could go to and be safe. The first time in my life I would feel that safety, that security, that peace, for which I had always been yearning and searching. I could go there to be among people I knew would accept me for me, not my act, not my front. I could relax with people for the very first time in my life. I felt comfortable and at home. The room was my place of security and it gave me the courage to break free and be born again, totally free of my guilt. *Claire*

Sharing feelings and being accepted

Before I joined the group I tended not to think about things so they wouldn't hurt as much. Getting things out in the open was upsetting at the time but you need to do that to carry on and go further. You think it's going to hurt too much to get things out but it's worth it even if it's difficult. I didn't realize how badly it affected people, the women have done some awful things to themselves and I think I've gotten away very mildly. But it's nice to know the other people know what you're going through and what you're thinking about. You feel you can trust them because they've gone through it. *Claire*

In the group Survivors can share their feelings about them-selves and still feel accepted.

I always thought other people were judging me. In the group you talk to other people who know exactly how you feel and accept you. *Anita*

I've only felt like me again since joining the group and getting everything out and hearing others saying similar things. It's like looking in a mirror. There's a feeling in the group that other people are interested in what you've got to say. There wasn't an ulterior motive to what people were saying or doing. A couple in my group were very open and honest from the beginning which made it easier for me—we jelled quickly. I could never eat anything before the group and after the group I could never go straight home.

One day I went into the group and said it felt lighter in the room and it was, as if everyone had suddenly unburdened themselves. We seemed to find each week if you'd had a bad week then the others had had similar experiences. We went through a period where we all had a lot of nightmares or we were all angry at our mothers. We could relate to each other so well. *Jocelyn*

Talking to each other helps the Survivors let go of some of their bad feelings.

I feel better when I come out of a group meeting. When I arrive I feel tense and a bit nervous but once I've left the group and I'm walking down the street I feel great. You have a chance to say what you feel. It's a way of releasing it. You may have been bottling it up all week but when you get to the group you can talk about it. *Mavis*

The Survivors also learn to trust each other.

Most surprisingly the group became very close-knit and extremely supportive with each other even during the first few weeks. There was a feeling of trust and a strong bond began to build between us. This was extremely helpful as no one felt inhibited in discussing very deep and intimate problems. *Eileen*

They start to feel safe enough to allow their innermost feelings to surface and be expressed. Facing up to their feelings instead of blocking them off also helps them to feel less powerless and more in control.

As the group continued to meet I saw such a big change in me in the way I thought about myself. When things cropped up that I couldn't cope with they supported and helped me. They didn't tell me what to do, but they would give me ideas and we'd talk about it. I knew they were supporting me and I wasn't alone, whereas before I'd always been alone. *Lucy*

Making the connections

As long as I can remember I'd never liked myself, I was always moody, bad-tempered and angry. Since going to the group and letting my anger out I'm not like that anymore. I realized I was angry for a reason. *Jocelyn*

Survivors grow up thinking of themselves as bad, crazy or different from other people. As adults they may still believe these things about themselves and so feel worthless and depressed. They often do not connect their present feelings and problems with their earlier abuse. In the group they can see how the other group members have similar problems and begin to understand where their own problems come from.

I didn't know my shaking had anything to do with my abuse. *Mavis*

I kept telling myself I haven't been affected, I don't need to go to the group. But I'm glad I did because as the group has gone on I've realized the abuse affected me more than I thought. At first I told myself I was just going along for Joan's sake (my sister), but I'm getting a lot out of it for myself. I can see how it's affected me now. I thought if you were sexually abused it only affected you in a relationship with another man but it causes all sorts of problems. I'd never thought about that at all. *Claire*

My abuse happened when I was about seven. I couldn't remember a lot. I thought it hadn't affected me because I couldn't remember what actually happened and it didn't go on for very long. But since being in the group I can see that I was riddled with guilt. You don't realize how much it has affected you until you get into a group and then you can see. It messed up 23 years of my life. *Jocelyn*

Making friends

I couldn't wish for a better group. We're friends and see each other outside the group and phone each other if we've got a problem or are worried about each other. *Lucy*

Sharing their feelings and being accepted by people who knew about their sexual abuse helped the women to learn to trust each other and develop close friendships, often for the first time in their lives.

I used to feel there wasn't any point in living at all. It's hard to feel that people like you if you don't really like yourself. I'm surprised how well we all got along in the group.

It's been good to be able to get in touch with the group members between sessions even though we didn't at the beginning. *Colleen*

The girls in our group have become very close. When I come to the group I look forward to seeing all the other girls and finding out how they've been getting along. The girls from another group came to meet us. I noticed that they were very, very close, like they'd known each other for years, like sisters. *Claire*

The relationship between Survivors in a group is like that between men fighting a war in the trenches. They all have different personalities and different likes and dislikes. In the outside world they might never become friends, yet they have shared something that forms a bond. They have gone through hell together, fought side by side for every little victory one of them has achieved and picked each other up in their setbacks and defeats. The bond between men who have fought a war in the trenches will last long after peace has come for all of them. Similarly, the bond between Survivors is still there, long after each one of us has built a new life and has found peace with herself at last. *Ingrid*

Survivors often stay friends after the group has ended.

I'm talking about not going to the self-help group anymore but I do want to meet and keep in touch with the other women because we have shared so much. *Jocelyn*

Helping others

Being in a group with other people who have had similar experiences not only helps each woman understand her own problems but also allows her to help the other group members. Helping others, while respecting her own needs, can increase the Survivor's self-esteem and decrease her feelings of powerlessness.

It was definitely good for me to listen to other people and feel I could help. Giving support as well as receiving it gives you confidence and helps you realize things about your own situation. *Colleen*

It also helped being able to help the others. You can understand how they feel and talk about how you coped. Helping someone else made me feel better about myself. *Lucy*

Overcoming the problems

I've changed in so many ways I wouldn't have believed it. It would be nice if you could take a video at the beginning and end of the group to see the big difference in everybody because they've all changed so much. Other members of the group probably see you change a lot quicker than you do yourself. *Lucy*

How do the women feel after they have been in individual therapy or in a survivors group? How does it change them and their lives? Below we look at some of the changes in the Wakefield Survivors.

Breaking free of the guilt and shame

Sometimes I used to wonder if I would ever get over this feeling of guilt. Now I don't feel guilty about what happened—I can lay the blame at my stepfather's door. The group has been wonderful for me—I don't know what would have happened to me if I hadn't been referred to a Clinical Psychologist. *Jane*

Understanding how an abuser plans and sets up the situation where he can abuse helps Survivors put the responsibility for the abuse onto the abuser and in time break free from their own feelings of guilt.

Meeting others who were also sexually abused as children took away the terrible isolation. For the first time I talked to people who understood how I felt and why. When I listened to them I thought "They could not have stopped their abuser, why did I feel guilty all my life that I found no way to stop mine?" The shame and guilt began to leave after our first group meeting. *Katarina*

Sharing their experiences with others and being accepted allows Survivors to feel less ashamed and able to talk without shame about their abuse to their friends and family. I was so frightened of anybody else finding out. Now I feel like I want to tell more people. *Claire*

Some time soon I'll tell my mom. Before I really worried about anyone knowing but now the world could know as long as it helped them and helped me. *Lucy*

Along with the decrease in the feelings of guilt and shame comes an increase in self-esteem: the Survivors feel better about themselves as people and accept they have rights too.

I feel better about saying what I think. It doesn't matter so much how people see me. I feel more confident that I am doing the right thing. I hadn't realized how much time I spent trying to please people and ultimately not succeeding. I take more time now to stand back and assess situations rather than jumping in. *Jane*

Better relationships
I've got more confidence but I still have a way to go. I'm starting to get along with other people again. I'm going out a lot more I never used to go out at all while my husband was working away from home. *Mavis*

I'm more open with other people—I want to be friends now. *Jocelyn*

Therapy allows Survivors to feel better about themselves and overcome their lack of trust. This enables them to begin forming relationships with other people. As we saw earlier, Survivors who attended groups were also helped by forming close friendships within the group.

Before the group I was frightened of making relationships and I thought that anyone who looked at me would know what had happened to me. I thought I was such a terrible person. I didn't want to go out before. It's nice now to go out socially. *Lucy*

Survivors learn to trust their therapist or each other first, then they can begin to develop other relationships. After working on their feelings towards their abusers they can also improve their relationships with their sexual partners or begin to form new sexual relationships with people they can trust.

Lucy had been terrified of men but after the group she became engaged and is now married.

Overcoming sexual problems
For years I had sex promiscuously, trading sex for a moment's attention, for a hug even. This was followed by several years of total dislike of sex after the birth of my first child. I gradually learned to share my feelings, fears and needs with my husband, and to help him share his with me. As we learned to communicate within other safe areas of our relationship, to communicate with our hearts and minds, we were more able to communicate with our bodies. We learned to give each other privacy and to support one another. Gradually we could give one another the confidence we each needed to let ourselves be vulnerable. Sex can be about love and now for us it can be as free and liberated, as erotic or as close and comforting as we both want it to be. *Shirley*

Survivors often have sexual difficulties resulting from their earlier abuse. They can work on these problems with a therapist or in a group by learning to accept their bodies, to love and respect themselves and to trust and relate to other people. Survivors often do not know what is normal sexually and it can help to discuss this in a group and learn more about sex and sexuality. Learning to enjoy sexual intimacy may not happen early in therapy because it is important to deal with issues relating to self-esteem, body image, trust in others and communication with your partner (if you have one) first. As Shirley's account shows, it is possible to overcome any problems concerning sex and develop a close and loving sexual relationship.

Feeling powerful
Now I feel that I am in control. I know I still have weaknesses and I will continue to work on them. I am not a perfect person but I now understand that I also have talents and a lot to offer. I am so thankful to Jehovah God that he has brought and directed me through the right channel so at last I can feel like me and know who I am. *Kate*

Having no control about what happens during sexual abuse often leaves Survivors feeling powerless in their later lives and unsure who they are. During therapy Survivors learn to face up to their fears and overcome their feelings of powerlessness. Many return to work or start new jobs.

I quit my job after I had a panic attack in the lunch room. Before the group I didn't think I would ever be able to get another job. I don't know when the change started but near the end of the group sessions I got a job working at a bar. The first time I tensed up and began shaking but the owner said I did well. I enjoy it now, I feel better about myself since I started at the bar. *Mavis*

Releasing the tension that holds back the fears and becoming aware of their own worth and abilities often gives Survivors renewed energy and a feeling they can control their lives again.

When you're worried and stressed you have no energy. Now I feel full of life and energy. I could conquer anything at the moment. I think much more of myself and have more confidence. I've got so many things I want to do now. I can't see I'll have time to fit everything in. I feel like making a fresh start. I want to go to the Technical College and take a course. *Claire*

Becoming aware of their own self-worth and learning to take control of their lives often helps Survivors rid themselves of problems with drugs, alcohol or eating.

A lot of the problem was my weight and once I lost weight I felt a lot better about myself. But I could never have done it without the group. I began to feel I was worth something—that I had something to offer as a person. People were interested in me and I could have pride in myself. Before the group there didn't seem to be any point in losing weight and I was frightened of men so it worked in keeping them away. If I hadn't come to the group I would have lacked the confidence to say to myself: You're doing this for you because you want to lose weight and feel more confident. *Colleen*

Assertiveness training helps Survivors understand that they have rights and teaches how to express them. As Survivors overcome their fears, understand why they felt so bad about themselves and come to feel they can cope with their life and stand up for their rights, the feelings of powerlessness fade.

Mainly I feel quite happy with myself and fairly confident. I'm trying to be assertive. Now I can give my opinion again. I feel as if I've got the vivacity that I had when I was 17. I feel like I can handle most situations. Obviously I have ups and downs which is good—it's just like anybody else. *Colleen*

Finding yourself

I was so scared of the change, of letting go of my image, my front. But I'm just me—released from the pain and guilt. It's so great just to feel comfortable with myself at last. *Claire*

Talking about your sexual abuse, understanding and accepting what really happened and breaking free from your problems can release the person you are underneath. Instead of hiding behind the front you present to the world you can find your true self and live your life as you want to.

Before I joined the Survivors group I felt confused about who I was. Now through opening up, being honest, revealing the secret, I have found me, and I like what I am. I am not bad, inferior, a person of no importance, or worth. The anger and frustration and hate that I thought was me, has been sorted out. It has been painful, it has been hard, but I was abused 23 years ago and since then I have been living a lie. Now I feel free, free and lighter, I have been released. This secret held me down and gradually over time it eventually dragged me down, but now it cannot hurt me anymore, I have survived it. Now I can hold my head up, I don't have to pretend anymore. I am not afraid, no one has a hold on me. The anger and frustration has gone, I feel happier, lighter, peaceful. It's the feelings inside me that have changed. I was always running away from me and I don't need to anymore. I couldn't believe that just talking would help, it did, it does. I like myself, I did nothing wrong. *Jocelyn*

17
Working Towards Prevention

YOU CAN HELP PREVENT THE SEXUAL ABUSE of children. Child sexual abuse is very common and becoming aware of the prevalence of sexual abuse may make you feel depressed and powerless. Taking action to help prevent further abuse can help you feel empowered again. It is possible for you to play an important part in the prevention of sexual abuse if you feel you want to. Before you think about carrying out any of the suggestions in this chapter it is important that you work through your feelings about your own abuse and overcome any problems the abuse has created in your life. You may want to put your energies into taking care of and trying to protect other people, but you are important too. You deserve an opportunity to be yourself and fulfill yourself in your own life. We recommend that you receive some help for yourself before you think about what you can do to help others.

The spread of sexual abuse

Sexual abuse occurs in secret. Abusers abuse children in secret and manipulate them to keep quiet so they can go on to abuse more and more children. Research and clinical work shows that abusers can abuse many children over many years. Female victims often end up feeling powerless and some go on to form adult relationships with other abusive men who physically, emotionally or sexually abuse them and may also abuse their children. The Survivor's own childhood experiences may leave her unable to protect her own children from abuse. A small number of abused children go on to abuse other children. Each abuser can therefore create a spreading wave of further abuse and distress.

How can we prevent sexual abuse

To stop the spread of sexual abuse we need to break the silence. For each child or adult Survivor who can talk about her abuse there is an abuser who can be prevented from harming other children. For each abuser who is prevented from having access to children there could be dozens of children protected from abuse and saved from years of suffering. Children who tell and receive help need not go on to develop problems that can last throughout their lives. Children who are believed and protected need not carry the feelings of shame, self-blame, betrayal and powerlessness for the rest of their lives. Adults who tell can receive help for themselves, overcome their feelings of powerlessness and learn how to protect their own children from abuse.

People can work towards the prevention of sexual abuse by teaching children how to protect themselves, looking out for signs of abuse and listening to children. It is possible to begin the process of preventing sexual abuse at a grass-roots level by breaking the secret, talking about sexual abuse, encouraging people to listen to their children, learning ways to protect children and acting to prevent abusers from having access to children.

In this chapter we suggest ways of responding to adults who disclose their own childhood abuse to you. We describe how people can protect the children in their care from sexual abuse and how they should respond if they suspect abuse or if a child tells them. We also look at what you can do to prevent your own abuser, or any abusers you are aware of, from having access to children. The work Wakefield Survivors are doing towards prevention is described. The final section of the chapter looks at wider issues involved in the prevention of sexual abuse.

Listening to adults

Most of the Wakefield Survivors begin to talk openly about their own abuse after they have been through therapy. Often their friends or other family members tell them they have also been abused. In breaking your silence you can help others to break their secret, to receive help and to prevent further abuse. Listening to adult Survivors who want to talk about their abuse is the first step in helping them break free from their pain and shame. It also means they are more likely to learn how to appropriately protect their own children and so a new generation may be saved from abuse. The Survivor may also act to prevent their abuser (or abusers) from harming other children.

I started talking with my friends and acquaintances about my own abuse and about the therapy I was receiving. More and more of them told me about their own sexual abuse. Almost every one of my women friends experienced some form of sexual abuse as a child. That was when I realized I could not remain silent. I remember too vividly my own despair when my need to be listened to and understood found nothing but deaf ears. *Ingrid*

What do you do if an adult tells you? The first thing to remember is that there is no need to panic and feel you have to do something right away. A child who is being abused needs immediate protection but with an adult Survivor the abuse has usually happened in the past. In some cases the abuse may still be continuing and the person will need support and acceptance until she is able to stop the abuse.

When people begin to talk about their own childhood abuse all you need to do is listen, believe them and accept them. Let them tell you as much or as little as they want to. Make it clear you do believe them. They may want to meet with you again to talk about it. Do not feel that you have to be responsible for the person but let them know they need to keep talking about it. Recommend they read this or another book on sexual abuse. Encourage them to get professional help. Book lists are at the end of many chapters and a Useful Addresses section at the end.

Protecting children

At least 10 percent of children are sexually abused. You can learn how to protect children around you from abuse and how to support children who have already been abused. Each child that you help in this way can be saved from a lifetime of problems. It can also be a step towards the prevention of abuse of other children because it may lead to the identification of another abuser. Some abused children also become abusers themselves. Receiving help at the time of their own abuse can stop this cycle.

The only certain way to prevent children from being abused is to ensure they are not available to an abuser. Children are sexually abused because an abuser has access to them, not because of anything that the child does. Children should never be left alone, even briefly, with anyone who is known or suspected to be an abuser.

In this section we will look at how you can watch for signs of abuse in children, how you can encourage a child to tell you about abuse, what to do if a child discloses to you and how you can teach children to protect themselves.

Signs of abuse

Children often show they are in distress by changes in their behavior. Finding out why they are behaving badly or differently from usual may uncover sexual abuse. You can encourage children to talk about how they are feeling and what is disturbing them and give them an opportunity to disclose any abuse. Children who are being sexually abused do not usually tell anyone what is happening to them. But they may show signs that they are in distress or that they are being abused. They may start bed-wetting, have nightmares, become withdrawn, have stomaches or become clingy or aggressive. Some of these signs are described in chapter 6 "Silent Ways of Telling," and listed in Table 3. It is important to remember, however, that children who show these signs are not necessarily being sexually abused. The behavior changes could be caused by some other disturbance in their lives such as a divorce or death in the family or physical or emotional abuse. Sexual abuse is suggested if a child has more sexual knowledge than you would expect for his/her age or is acting in a sexually inappropriate way. Disturbed behavior indicates that something is wrong and the child needs a trusted adult to find out what is happening to him/her. If you are concerned about a child then ask for advice from one of the telephone help lines or encourage the child to talk to you.

Listening to children

Encourage your children to talk to you, and show them you have time for them and want to listen to them. Make sure they know you will protect them and not punish them if they tell you about any inappropriate sexual behavior. Children may not talk about their abuse directly. They may say "I don't like Mr. Brown" or "I don't want to stay at Granddad's anymore." Take these comments seriously and ask them why they don't like that person or why they don't want to stay somewhere or go out with someone. If a child feels uncomfortable with someone then respect their feelings. If you are receptive your child will be more likely to talk.

This is Kate's advice on how to protect your children:

Talk and listen to your children. Their feelings count. If they don't like someone's company ask yourself "Why?" Don't force them to go with people they don't like, dismissing it by saying they're awkward or acting up. Don't put children down by calling them a baby if they are afraid of something or someone. If boys or girls are afraid there's a reason—find it out. Believe your children. Don't dismiss their worries or fears or dislikes. *Kate*

What do you do if your child tells you he or she has been sexually abused?

- Don't panic. Try not to show how upset and angry you are.
- Listen to him/her.
- Believe the child and let the child know you believe him/her.
- Tell the child he/she is right to tell and don't blame the child in any way.
- Tell him/her you will not let it happen again. Make sure the child is not left alone with the abuser.
- Tell the child you may need to tell someone else to get help to protect him/her. Explain to the child what you are going to do and why. Do not allow the child to feel they have no control over what is going to happen. Contact either the director of the local Social Services department where the child lives or the local police Child Abuse Unit or the child-protection agency.
- Do not threaten to kill or harm the abuser. This may make the child feel guilty or frightened.
- Make sure the child gets some help to work through her confused feelings about the abuse. Ask your doctor for a referral to

a Clinical Psychologist or contact Social Services or a child-protection agency.

If a child tells you, you will probably feel upset, angry or shocked. Try to get some support for yourself. Remember that with appropriate help now the child will not necessarily develop immediate or long-term problems.

When I began to talk freely about sexual abuse my daughter had the confidence to tell me that it had happened to her three years previously when she was five. Because she could tell me so early in life and because I know what help she needs to overcome her shame and guilt, I know that she will grow up without the mental scars that a continued silence would have produced. *Ingrid*

Teaching children to protect themselves

It is very difficult to identify an abuser unless you know they have abused a child. They don't look any different from anyone else and outwardly may appear to be very nice, respectable members of the community. You can't be with your children 24 hours a day for the rest of their lives so it is important to teach children how to recognize situations that are dangerous or simply difficult or uncomfortable.

I don't want to frighten my child
Many people are worried that by teaching children about the dangers of sexual abuse they will make them frightened and mistrustful of all adults. This is an understandable worry but if the subject is approached in the right way it doesn't need to be a problem. We don't need to teach children to fear and distrust people, we can teach them positive skills to help them feel safe. We can teach them that their bodies belong to themselves and they don't have to let anyone touch their bodies in a way they don't like. We teach children how to cross the road and protect themselves from the dangers of traffic without making them too fearful to ever step off the curb or get into a car. We can also teach children how to protect themselves from sexual abuse without making them fearful of every adult.

What to teach your children
You need to teach your children that they have the right to feel

safe and that they can talk to you openly whatever happens to them. Tell them that you will believe them and not be angry with them if they tell you about being touched or feeling uncomfortable with someone. Teach them their bodies belong to them and they have the right to say "No." Show them you mean this by giving them a choice about physical contact. Ask them if they want to give you or anyone else a kiss or hug but do not insist. it may be embarrassing if your children refuse to kiss someone but support them if they do this. Explain to your friends and relatives that your children have the right to choose who they kiss and hug.

Teach them the difference between surprises, like presents and parties, and secrets. Tell them they should not keep secrets, even if they are told to, and to talk to you or another trusted adult if anyone asks them to keep a secret. Make it clear that the rules apply to everyone including family members.

You can also teach them general safety rules about not talking to strangers and not going into other people's homes without permission, for example. It will be easier for them to talk about sexual abuse if they know the words for body parts and sexual acts. Teach them some basic sex education. Make clear the difference between sex and sexual assault so they do not give up afraid of touching themselves or of appropriate sexual activity.

Remember that young children take what you say literally. Be as clear as you can and check that the child has understood you.

When I was very small my mom told me not to take candy from strangers. I thought this was because they might be poison. When an old lady on a bus offered us some candy and my mom said it was all right to have one, I was really impressed that my mom could tell who had poison candy and who hadn't. *Shirley*

You can start to teach very young children about protecting themselves at a level they can understand. Show them they have rights by giving them choices about physical contact and in other ways like allowing them to choose which book to read at bedtime or which clothes to wear. Play "What if . . ." games, with questions such as "What would you do if the baby-sitter asks you to keep a secret?" Keep talking to your children about protecting themselves, don't just do it once. There are several good books on how to protect your children (see the reading list at the end of the chapter).

Some of the Wakefield Survivors drew up a list of things you can teach your children to keep them safe from abuse. This is shown in Table 9.

Stopping the abusers

Now I'm questioning myself as to whether or not I should do something about the abuser to put a stop to it all, to protect my own daughter and other children in the family. If he died I wouldn't have all these decisions to make. I ought to do something about it, but can I? Am I letting my own daughter down if I don't? What would it achieve anyway? One year in prison, then out. Could I be the one to put him in prison? Perhaps he would die in prison. He would certainly suffer, but I don't want him to suffer even though it would be his fault because he's an abuser. I would still feel responsible. But then I would feel responsible if he abuses anyone else. It could be partly my fault if he abuses any more children because I didn't do anything. But how could I hurt my mom? *Kate*

Deciding to act against your abuser can be a very difficult decision to make. Kate was racked with indecision. Her father had abused her and her nine brothers and sisters, his grandchildren, nieces and many others. She didn't want to hurt her father or her mother by exposing his activities but she couldn't sit back and let him abuse even more children.

Abusers rarely abuse one child. They may abuse dozens of children throughout their lifetime and often continue abusing in their old age. After group therapy Survivors begin to talk about their abuse to their friends and family and often find they have been abused by the same abuser. 40 percent of the women in the Wakefield Survivors groups know of at least one other child abused by their own abuser. Abusers keep on scheming, planning, and creating opportunities to abuse more children.

What can you do about it?

What can you do to prevent your abuser from abusing other children? The most important thing is to ensure that abusers do not have access to any children. You can help to protect children from abusers by informing the child-protection authorities, by confronting the abuser or by going to the police.

If you know, or have strong suspicions, that an abuser is currently abusing a child inform Social Services (ask for the Child Protection Officer or the supervisor of the area where the child

Table 9—Teaching your children to feel safe

Teach them:

They have the right to feel safe and they should tell someone if anyone makes them feel afraid or uncomfortable.

That you will believe them and not be angry if they tell you of an incident when they have been touched or felt uncomfortable.

Not to keep secrets. Not telling about surprises is OK, i.e., presents and parties.

They are allowed to disobey an adult if they are in danger or to protect themselves.

It's OK not to be polite in order to protect themselves.

How to say "NO," shout "STOP," run away.

The difference between good touch and bad touch.

Bad touch is anything that makes you feel uncomfortable, confused, uneasy.

What their private parts are (their breasts, buttocks, genitals). No one should touch their private parts unless it's a doctor or a nurse and their mother or father is with them.

It's OK for them to touch themselves.

They should not touch the private parts of an adult or older child.

They have the right to say no if anyone touches them in a way they don't like or makes them feel uncomfortable.

They don't have to kiss or hug any one young or old if they don't want to.

They have a right to say who touches them and how. "It's my body—I decide."

If a person touches them in a way they don't like or if they feel uncomfortable or uneasy about anything they should tell an adult they trust.

If that person doesn't believe them or help them, they should tell someone else and keep telling until someone does help.

To tell an adult if they think they are being followed.

Not to talk to strangers, or go anywhere withstrangers.

To be wary of special favors and bribes and blackmail.

That they can ask about other people's puzzling behavior.("Why does Uncle George want to play the funny game?")

How to use the telephone and memorize the telephone numbers of your house and another trusted person.

Rules about being invited into another person's home when playing away from their own home.

A password which can be used if an unfamiliar person has to pick them up from school.

About sex education and the difference between sex and sexual assault.

That these rules apply to everyone including the family, teachers, babysitters, etc.

lives), the police (ask for the Child Abuse Section) or the child-protection agency immediately. If you can, provide them with the date of birth of the abuser and the child and with as much other information as you can. Give your own name if at all possible. This will be kept confidential and not given to the abuser or his family. You can do this anonymously by telephone or letter but then you will not be able to provide any further information that might be needed nor will you receive any feedback on the investigations. Social services, health authorities, volunteer groups and the police are now working together in the best interests of children. Their priority is to protect children from further abuse. At the very least call one of the organizations at the back of this book and discuss the problem with one of their people.

Child sexual abuse is happening all around us. To protect the next generation we must act every time we have suspicions. You will rarely be certain that your abuser is still abusing. If your abuser has children of his own or has access to children you can inform Social Services whether or not you know for certain that he is abusing them. Social Services will then investigate the case and check all records (including doctor, visiting nurse, school) on any children involved. If anything suspicious appears they will hold a case conference and, if necessary, inform the police. If there is no indication in the records that the child is being abused then nothing else will happen at this time except that the child will be monitored for signs of abuse

In some cases the abuser is still around but there are no children in his immediate circle. In these circumstances some of the Wakefield Survivors decided to confront their abuser to let him know they are watching him, and to tell him they are informing people around him, especially those with children, of his past offenses. DO NOT confront your abuser without fully preparing yourself as described in chapter 15 on Abusers.

Some adult Survivors, like Joanne in chapter 15, give statements to the police and attempt to prosecute their abusers to prevent them from abusing others. There is no time limit on when you can prosecute for a major crime such as sexual assault on a child. There may also be difficulties finding enough supporting evidence for the case to go to court. If you want to consider prosecuting your abuser, talk to a professional about it or call the police and discuss it with someone from the child abuse unit. If you prefer, ask to talk to a female police officer.

A.C.T. (Abuse—Counseling and Training)

Wakefield Survivors help in the prevention of further sexual abuse by breaking the secrecy around their own abuse, by protecting their own and any other children around them and by ensuring that their abusers do not harm any more children. Some of the Wakefield Survivors wanted to do more than this and they formed an action group called *A.C.T.* which aims to help other people who have been abused and to do further work towards the prevention of abuse. The A.C.T. members have attended counseling courses themselves and now counsel other Survivors and work towards increasing public awareness of child sexual abuse. Being sexually abused can make you feel helpless and out of control, A.C.T. members find working towards prevention helps them feel more powerful.

Working with Survivors

There are so many women who need help, too many women still in isolation, feeling they are the only ones. I gladly picked up the suggestion by the psychologists to meet some of the women who were on their waiting lists. Before therapy starts many Survivors feel the stigma of shame and guilt very strongly and it helps them to meet another Survivor who has been through therapy and not only will understand them but also reassure them that life will be so much better after receiving the help they so desperately seek.

Many Survivors hate themselves before they receive therapy. Meeting someone and liking someone who had the same experience of being abused makes it easier for them to begin to like themselves. *Katarina*

A.C.T. members meet with Survivors who have been referred to Wakefield Clinical Psychology Service to talk to them about their own experiences and how it is possible to overcome the problems created by childhood abuse. They may continue to see a new Survivor for ongoing counseling and to support them while they are waiting for an appointment with a psychologist.

Some A.C.T. members run self-help groups for Survivors.

We set up a Survivors Support Group. Initially this was an idea Lucy and I had to help one Survivor overcome her fear of groups. We started with just two Survivors and every week added one more of the new Survivors who would be in the next therapy group. Slowly they got used to each other, slowly they lost the fear of a group, although at times it still came back. They now talk openly about the effects of the abuse and are able to encourage the new Survivors who still have to overcome their insecurities about being in a group. *Katarina*

A.C.T. members attend some of the Survivors group sessions run by the psychologists. They encourage group members to continue when they become distressed because they are facing up to their memories and feelings. A.C.T. members also attend sessions on specific topics to contribute their experiences and talk about how they learned to cope with their problems. A.C.T. members have also been involved in therapy groups for abusers—providing the abusers with a victim's perspective on abuse and challenging their beliefs.

Training workshops
In order to expand awareness of the problem of sexual abuse and increase the resources available to Survivors we run training workshops for professional and voluntary workers. These include health visitors, doctors, community nurses, police, probation officers, social workers, rape crisis and women's refuge workers, clinical psychologists, psychiatrists and any other groups involved in the care of Survivors. Members of A.C.T. attend these workshops and talk about their experiences to increase the knowledge and skill of the professionals. This also increases the self-esteem and self-confidence of the Survivors.

A.C.T. members have also run nurseries for the children of other Survivors so they could attend a group, have worked as volunteers at a local Domestic Violence resource and drop-in center and met with and advised other groups of Survivors from around Great Britain. They are also involved in campaigning for greater awareness and the prevention of sexual abuse by giving newspaper, radio and television interviews and by contributing to this book.

A.C.T. has an important role to play in helping many Survivors in the local community who have just come for help or who are thinking about coming for help and in reducing the amount of suffering that abuse causes.

You may want to join or set up a group to work towards prevention, but do not feel you have to do this. Some Survivors benefit from the therapy groups and afterwards just want to get

on with their lives. They deserve to be able to put their past
behind them at last and to fulfill their lives in any way they
choose.

Wider issues in prevention

This chapter has looked at some of the ways you can work
towards the prevention of sexual abuse. Why is the sexual abuse
of children so widespread? Why is it mostly men who abuse?
These are questions which need to be addressed if we are to
create a society which is safe for children. We can begin to try to
answer these questions by looking at wider issues such as the
general treatment of children and women in our society, the different expectations for males and females and the effects of
pornography.

In our society children are devalued. Emotional, verbal, physical and sexual abuse of children is a daily occurrence. Children
are powerless and adults feel it is acceptable to exert their power
and control over children. There are differences in the ways that
boys and girls are brought up. Girls learn that to be valued they
must be nurturing to others and not show anger. Girls and
women who are victimized therefore usually turn their anger and
distress in on themselves and become depressed, self-destructive
and vulnerable to further abuse.

Boys learn that to be valued they must appear to be powerful
and not show any weakness. Boys and men who are victimized
are more likely to turn their anger and distress outward and try
to regain their power by victimizing others, particularly those
they see as less powerful than themselves. This means men are
more likely to be abusers and women and children are more
likely to be victims.

Women have less access than men to money, jobs and influence. However, women are the ones who shoulder the emotional, practical and financial burden of child care. The lack of
legal protection afforded to women and children and the lack of
access to money, housing, child-care facilities, etc. put women in
a position where they are powerless and vulnerable. This makes
it difficult for women to leave men who are violent or sexually
abusive to themselves or their children.

Pornography, centerfold girls and the use of women's bodies
in advertising contribute to a climate in which women are not

respected and are seen as sex objects. Child pornography encourages abusers to believe it is normal and acceptable to have sex with children. Pornography, especially child pornography, is used by abusers to fantasize about abuse and this helps them to rationalize their abuse and believe they are doing no wrong.

We can begin to address these issues by making changes at an individual level in terms of how we relate to others and how we bring up children.

We can all play a small part in reshaping a society in which it is possible for children to be abused and for women to be regarded as of less importance than men. Each individual, whether she has been a victim of abuse or not, can try to influence those people close to her. It is not just the work of feminist movements or psychologists writing books and giving lectures. Parents can teach their sons to respect girls as equals and that it is not unmanly to show care, concern, sensitivity and understanding towards others, male and female alike.

They can teach their sons and daughters to value their own rights and the rights of others. Women at their workplace can begin to put a stop to being treated as nothing more than ornaments who are not to be taken seriously. Wives can insist on being treated as having equal rights. Daughters can insist on being listened to in their wishes and plans for their own future. *Ingrid*

There is also a need for change in government policies and allocation of resources. All abused children and adults need immediate help to overcome problems arising from the abuse. All professionals who work with children should be trained to recognize the signs of abuse and to deal with disclosure (telling). Schools should teach children assertiveness skills and how to protect themselves from abuse. All abusers need treatment to confront them with the damage they are inflicting on others, to help them to overcome their motivation to abuse children and to stop them from continuing to abuse children. This is particularly important for adolescents who are victimizing other children in order to stop them from embarking on a lifetime of abusing.

Summary

We can all play an important part in the struggle towards the prevention of sexual abuse. Just as individual abusers can start a spreading wave of sexual abuse and distress, the fight against sexual abuse can spread out from individuals who are aware and want to keep children safe. You can empower yourself and help in the prevention of sexual abuse by listening to and helping children and adults who have been abused, by learning how to help children remain safe and by dealing with your own abuser. You can make changes in your own life in the way you treat children and allow yourself to be treated. On a wider scale people can organize to campaign for more resources for the treatment of victims and abusers, and to control pornography and material that degrades women and children.

Survivors have suffered in silence for too long. Now it is time to speak out. Breaking the silence helps you break free from the influence of your past and can also help reshape a society where sexual abuse is common.

Suggestions

- It is important that you sort out your own problems and feelings before you try to help others so do go for help if you haven't already done so. If you feel you want to work toward the prevention of further sexual abuse follow the suggestions in the next chapter.
- If you know or suspect that a child is currently being abused follow the instructions given earlier in this chapter. Look for signs of abuse in children and listen to children who try to talk about their abuse. Teach your children how to protect them selves from abuse.
- Make sure your abuser and any other abusers you become aware of are not able to harm other children by following the suggestions given in the chapter.

Finding help

If you are a child who is being sexually abused or you suspect a child is being sexually abused contact one of the agencies or telephone help-lines listed in the further reading and Useful Addresses section at the back of the book.

If your child has been sexually abused then your doctor or social worker will be able to arrange for therapy for the child to help him or her overcome any emotional issues arising from the abuse.

Further reading

Protecting children from sexual abuse

Adams, Caren; Fay, Jennifer. *No More Secrets: Protecting Your Child From Sexual Assault.* Impact Publishers, 1981..

James, Beverly. *Treating Traumatized Children: New Insights & Creative Interventions.* Free Press, 1989.

Mandell, Joan G.; Damon, Linda. *Group Treatment for Sexually Abused Children.* Guilford Press, 1989.

Rush, Florence. *The Best Kept Secret: Sexual Abuse of Children.* Prentice-Hall, 1980.

Wurtele, Sandy K.; Miller-Perrin, Cindy L. *Preventing Child Sexual Abuse: Sharing the Responsibility.* University of Nebraska Press, 1992.

For children and teenagers

Adams, Caren; Fay, Jennifer; Loreen-Martin, Jan. *No is Not Enough: Helping Teenagers Avoid Sexual Assault.* Impact Publishers, 1984.

Cooney, Judith. *Coping with Sexual Abuse.* The Rosen Publishing Group, Inc., 1991.

Mufson, Susan. *Straight Talk about Child Abuse.* Dell Publishing Company, Inc., 1993.

Polese, Carolyn. *Promise Not to Tell.* William Morrow & Company, Inc., 1993.

Russell, Pamela; Stone, Beth. *Do You Have a Secret?: How to Get Help for Scary Secrets.* CompCare Publishers, 1986.

Further Reading
& Useful Addresses

Further Reading

General Readings

Adams, Caren & Fay, Jennifer. *Free of the Shadows: Recovery from Sexual Violence.*
  New Harbinger Publications, 1989.
Allender, Dan B. *The Wounded Heart: Hope for Adult Victims of Sexual Abuse.* NavPress
  Publishing Group, 1990.
Barnes, Patty Derosier. *The Woman Inside: From Incest Victim to Survivor.* Mother
  Courage Press, 1991.
Bass, Ellen; Davis, Laura. *The Courage to Heal: A Guide for Women Survivors of Child
  Sexual Abuse.* HarperCollins Publishers, Inc., 1993.
Bass, Ellen; Davis, Laura. *Beginning to Heal: The First Book for Survivors of Child
  Sexual Abuse.* HarperCollins Publishers, Inc., 1993.
Bronson, Catherine. *Growing through the Pain: The Incest Survivor's Companion.*
  Prentice-Hall / Parkside, 1989.
Butler, Sandra. *Conspiracy of Silence: The Trauma of Incest.* Volcano Press, Inc., 1985.
Cole, Autumn; Becca Brin Manlove. *Brother-Sister Sexual Abuse: It Happens and It
  Hurts. A Book for Sister Survivors.* Beccautumn Books, 1991.
Dolan, Yvonne M. *Resolving Sexual Abuse.* W.W. Norton & Company, Inc., 1991.
Engel, Beverly. *The Right to Innocence: Healing the Trauma of Child Sexual Abuse.*
  J.P. Tarcher, 1989.
Finney, Lynne. *Reach for the Rainbow: Advanced Healing for Survivors of Sexual Abuse.*
  The Putnam Publishing Group, 1992.
Ford, Clyde. *Compassionate Touch: The Role of Human Touch in Healing & Recovery.*
  Simon & Schuster Trade, 1993.
Gannon, J. Patrick. *Soul Survivors: A New Beginning for Adults Abused as Children.*
  Prentice Hall, 1989.
Growing through the Pain: The Incest Survivor's Companion. Parkside Publishing, 1989.
Hall, Liz; Lloyd, Siobhan. *Surviving Child Sexual Abuse: A Handbook for Helping
  Women Challenge Their Past.* Taylor & Francis, Inc., 1993.
Hindman, Jan. *The Mourning Breaks.* AlexAndria Associates, 1991.
Kritsberg, Wayne. *The Invisible Wound: Healing Childhood Sexual Abuse.* Bantam
  Books, Inc., 1993.
Kunzman, Kristin A. *The Healing Way: Adult Recovery from Childhood Sexual Abuse.*
  Harper San Francisco, 1990.
Landry, Dorothy Beaulieu. *Family fallout: A handbook for families of adult sexual abuse
  survivors.* Safer Society Press, 1991.
McClure, Mary Beth. *Reclaiming the Heart: A Handbook of Help and Hope for Survivors
  of Incest.* Warner Books, 1990.
Poston, Carol. *Reclaiming Our Lives: Hope for Adult Survivors of Incest.* Bantam Books,
  Inc., 1990.
Napier, Nancy J. *Getting Through the Day: Strategies for Adults Hurt As Children.*
  W.W. Norton & Company, Inc., 1993.
Nestingen, Signe L.; Lewis, Laurel. *Growing Beyond Abuse: A Workbook for Survivors of
  Sexual Exploitation or Childhood Sexual Abuse.* Omni Recovery, Inc., 1991.
Ovaris, Wendy. *After the nightmare.* Learning Publications, 1991.
Rutter, Peter. *Sex in the Forbidden Zone.* Fawcett Book Group, 1991.

Sanford, Linda T. *Strong at the Broken Places: Overcoming the Trauma of Childhood Abuse.* Avon Books, 1992.
Walker, Moira. *Surviving Secrets: The Experience of Abuse for the Child, the Adult & the Helper.* Taylor & Francis, Inc., 1992.

Affirmations/Meditations

Brady, Maureen. *Daybreak: Meditations for Women Survivors of Child Sexual Abuse.* Hazelden / Harper, 1991.
Farmer, Steven & Anthony, Juliette. *Healing Words: Affirmations for Adult Children of Abusive Parents.* Ballantine Books, Inc., 1992.
Thomas, T. *Surviving with Serenity: Daily Meditations for Incest Survivors.* Health Communications, Inc., 1990.
W, Nancy. *Embracing the Journey: Affirmations for Living Life as a Sexual Abuse Survivor.* Harper San Francisco, 1992.

Male survivors

Berendzen, Richard; Palmer, Laura. *Come Here: A Man Copes with the Aftermath of Childhood Sexual Abuse.* Random House, Inc., 1993.
Bolton Jr., Frank G; Morris, Larry A.; MacEachron, Ann E. *Males at Risk: The Other Side of Child Sexual Abuse.* Sage Publications, Inc., 1989.
Grubman-Black, Stephen D. *Broken Boys—Mending Men: Recovery from Childhood Sexual Abuse.* Ivy Books, 1992.
Hunter, Mic., ed. *The Sexually Abused Male, Vol. 1: Prevalence, Impact, & Treatment.* D.C. Heath & Company, 1990.
Hunter, Mic., ed. *The Sexually Abused Male, Vol. 2: Application of Treatment Strategies.* D.C. Heath & Company, 1990.
Lew, Mike. *Victims No Longer: Men Recovering from Incest & Other Childhood Sexual Abuse.* HarperCollins Publishers, Inc., 1990
Porter, Eugene. *Treating the Young Male Victim of Sexual Assault: Issues and intervention Strategies.* Safer Society Press, 1989.
Sanders, Timothy L. *Male Survivors: A Twelve-Step Recovery Program for Survivors of Childhood Sexual Abuse.* The Crossing Press, 1991.
Sonkin, Daniel J. *Wounded Men: Healing from Childhood Abuse.* HarperCollins Publishers, Inc., 1988.

For partners

Davis, Laura. *Allies in Healing: When the Person You Love Was Sexually Abused as a Child, a Support Book for Partners.* HarperCollins Publishers, Inc., 1991.
Engel, Beverly. *Partners in Recovery: How Mates, Lovers & Other Prosurvivors Can Learn to Support & Cope with Adult Survivors of Childhood Sexual Abuse.* Fawcett, Book Group, 1993.
Gil, Eliana. *Outgrowing the Pain Together: A Book for Spouses & Partners of Adults Abused As Children.* Dell Publishing Company, Inc., 1992.
Graber, Ken. *Ghost in the Bedroom: A Guide for Partners of Incest Survivors.* Health Communications, Inc., 1991.

General Readings—Canada

Bagley, Christopher R.; Thomlison, Ray J. *Child Sexual Abuse: Critical Perspectives on Prevention, Intevention and Treatment.* Wall and Emerson, Inc., Toronto, 1991.
Halliday, Linda. *Sexual Abuse: Counseling issues and concerns.* Ptarmigan, 1987.
Halliday, Linda; VanderMey, Diana. *Sexual Abuse: Court preparation manual.* Ptarmigan, 1986.
Halliday, Linda. *Sexual Abuse: Examining false allegations.* Ptarmigan, 1988.
Hallliday, Linda. *Sexual Abuse: Interviewing techniques for police and other professionals.* Ptarmigan, 1986.
Harvey, Wendy; Hunter, Robin. *Sexual offenses against children.* Butterworths, 1992.
Health Canada and Welfare Canada. *Sexual offenses against children in Canada: Summary of the report of the Committee on Sexual Offenses Against Children and Youths.* Canada Communication, 1985.

Schlesinger, Benjamin. *Sexaul Abuse of children: A resource guide & annotated bibliography.* U.T.P., 1982.
Schlesinger, Benjamin. *Sexual Abuse of children in the 1980s: Issues and annotated bibliography 1980-1984.* U.T.P., 1986.

For professionals/counselors

Briere, John. *Therapy for Adults Molested As Children: Beyond Survival.* Springer Publishing Cornpany, Inc., 1989.
Friedrich, William N. *Casebook of Sexual Abuse Treatment.* W.W. Norton & Company, Inc., 1991.
Hindman, Jan. *Step By Step—Sixteen Steps Toward Legally Sound Sexual Abuse Investigations.* AlexAndria Associates, 1987.
Nichols, William C. *Treating Adult Survivors of Childhood Sexual Abuse.* Professional Resource Exchange, Inc., 1992.
Patton, Michael Quinn, ed. *Family Sexual Abuse: Frontline Research and Evaluation.* Sage Publications, Inc., 1991.
Skirp, Cathy; Kunzman, Kristin. *Women with Secrets: Dealing with Domestic Abuse and Childhood Sexual Abuse in Treatment.* Hazelden, 1993.
Timms, Robert J. *Embodying Healing: Integrating Bodywork and Psychotherapy in Recovery from Childhood Sexual Abuse.* Safer Society Press, 1992.

Religious

Brewer, Connie. *Escaping the Shadows, Seeking the Light: Christians in Recovery from Childhood Sexual Abuse.* Harper San Francisco, 1991.
Flaherty, Sandra M. *Woman, Why Do You Weep?: Spirituality for Survivors of Childhood Sexual Abuse.* Paulist Press, 1992.
Frank, Jan. *A Door of Hope: Recognizing and Resolving the Pains of Your Past.* Here's Life Publishers, 1987.
Pellauer, Mary; Chester, Barbara; Boyajian, Jane. *Sexual Assault and Abuse: A Handbook for Clergy and Religious Professionals.* Harper & Row, 1986.
Reid, Kathryn Goering with Fortune, Marie. *Preventing Child Sexual Abuse: A Curriculum for Children Ages Nine through Twelve.* United Church Press, 1989.
Rossetti, Stephen. *Slayer of the Soul: Child Sexual Abuse and the Catholic Church.* Twenty-Third Publications, 1990.

Videos

Breaking Silence. Future Educational Films, 1628 Union St., San Francisco, CA, 94123. (415) 673-0304.
Healing Sexual Abuse: The Recovery Process. (213) 668-9541.
Incest: Speaking the Deadly Secret. Life Enrichment Therapies, 5000 Butte, #282, Boulder, CO 80301. (303) 444-7486.
"Why God—Why Me?" Varied Direction, Inc., 69 Elm St., Camden, ME 04843. 1-800-888-5236.
Incest: The Victim Nobody Believes. MTI Teleprograms Inc., 3710 Commercial Ave., Northbrook, IL 60062.
Maltz, Wendy. *Partners in Healing: Couples Overcoming the Sexual Reprecussions of Incest.* (1988) Independent Video Services, 401 E. 10th Ave., Suite 160, Eugene, OR 97401. (503) 345-3455.
The Last Taboo. MTI Teleprograms Inc., 3710 Commercial Ave., Northbrook, IL 60062.

Useful Addresses

United States

Adult Children of Sexual Abuse
3110 Merita Dr.
Holiday, FL 34691
813/938-7836

AMACU
Adults Molested as Children
United
P.O. Box 952
San Jose, CA 95108
(408) 280-5055

APSAC
American Professional Society on
the Abuse of Children
969 E. 60th St.
Chicago, IL 60637
(312) 702-9419

Association for
Sexual Abuse Prevention
P.O. Box 421
Kalamazoo, MI 49005
(216) 221-6818
(616) 349-9072

Batterers Anonymous
1269 N. E Street
San Bernardino, CA 92405
(714) 884-6809

CAIR
Child Abuse Institute of Research
P.O. Box 1217
Cincinnati, OH 45201
(606) 441-7409

CALM
Child Abuse
Listening and Meditation
P.O. Box 90754
Santa Barbara, CA 93190-0754
(805) 965-2376

Chesapeake Institute
1114 Georgia Ave.
Wheaton, MD 20902
(301) 949-5000

Children's Self-Help Center
3368 22nd St.
San Francisco, CA 94110
(415) 826-9050

Coalition Against the Sexual
Abuse of Young Children
5323 Nebraska Ave. NW
Washington, D.C. 20015
(202) 966-7183

Echoes Network, Inc.
P.O. Box 86231
Portland, OR 97206
(503) 293-2800

Incest Resources, Inc.
46 Pleasant St.
Cambridge MA 02139
(617) 492-1818

Incest Survivor
Information Exchange
P.O. Box 3399
New Haven, CT 06515

International Society for
Prevention of Child Abuse and
Neglect
1205 Oneida St.
Denver, CO 80220
(303) 321-3963

ISRNI
Incest Survivors Resource
Network, International
P.O. Box 7375
Las Cruces, NM 88006-7375
(505) 521-4260

It's P.O.S.S.I.B.L.E.
Partners of Survivors Stopping
Incest by Learning & Education
RFD 3
Box 503
Augusta, ME 04330
(207) 547-3532

M.A.L.E.
Male Assisting Leading Educating
P.O. Box 380181
Denver, CO 80238-1181
(303) 320-4365

Molesters Anonymous
c/o Batterers Anonymous
8485 Tamarind Ave., D
Fontana, CA 92335
(714) 355-1100

MOMS
Mothers Opposed to Molest
Situations, P.O. Box 70665
Eugene, OR 97401
(503) 484-7252

National Adoption Center
1218 Chestnut St.
Philadelphia, PA 19107
(215) 925-0200

National Coalition Against
Domestic Violence
P.O. Box 15127
Washington, D.C. 20003-0127
(202) 293-8860
National hotline:1-800-333-7233
National Committee for
Prevention of Child Abuse
332 S. Michigan Ave.
Chicago, IL 60604
(313) 663-3520

NCCAFV
Nation Council on Child Abuse
and Family Violence
1155 Connecticut Ave. NW
Ste. 300
Washington, D.C. 20036
(202) 429-6695

NOVA
National Organization for Victims
Assistance
717 D St. NW
Washington, D.C. 20004
(202) 393-6682

National Women's
Abuse Prevention Project
2000 P St. NW, Ste. 508
Washington, D.C. 20036
(202) 857-0216

Parents Against Molesters, Inc.
P.O. Box 3557
Portsmouth, VA 23701
(804) 363-2549

Parents Anonymous
6733 S. Sepulveda Blvd.
Los Angeles, CA 90045
(213) 410-9732
National hotline: 1-800-421-0353

Parent's United International
232 Gish Rd.
San Jose, CA 95112
(408) 453-7616 ext. 150

P.L.E.A.
Prevention, Leadership,
Education, Assistance
P.O. Box 59045
Norwalk, CA 90652
(213) 863-4824

S.A.S.A.
Sexual Abuse
Survivors Anonymous
P.O. Box 241046
Detroit, MI 48224
(313) 882-9646

SLAM
Society's League
Against Molestation
c/o Women
Against Rape/Childwatch
P.O. Box 346
Collingswood, NJ 08108
(609) 858-7800

Survivors Network for Those
Abused by Priests, P.O. Box 4487
Oceanside, CA 92052
(619) 433-3673

Survivors of Incest Anonymous
P.O. Box 21817
Baltimore, MD 21222-6817
(410) 433-2365

VOICES in Action, Inc.
(Victims of Incest Can Emerge
Survivors)
P.O. Box 148309
Chicago, IL 60614
(312) 327-1500

W.I.N.G.S. Foundation
(Women Incested Needing
Group Support)
8007 W. Colfax, CS27
Box 129
Lakewood, CO 80215
(303) 238-8660

Canada

Initiative and *Vis a Vis*
(newsletters)
The Canadian Council on
Social Development
55 Parkdale Ave.
P.O. Box 3505, Station C
Ottawa, Ontario
Canada K1Y 4G1

S.A.R.A.
Sexual Assault Recovery
Anonymous
P.O. Box 16
Surrey, British Columbia,
Canada V3T 4W4
(604) 584-2626

TRAANS
The Ritual Abuse Awareness
Network Society
P.O. Box 29064
Delamont Station
1996 W. Broadway
Vancouver, British Columbia,
Canada V6J 5C2
(604) 731-5243

Hotlines

Boys Town   1-800-448-3000

Bureau of Indian   1-800-633-5155
Affairs, Child Protection Hotline

Childhelp USA   1-800-422-4453
National Child Abuse Hotline
(Childhelp USA phone number
can also be used for Canada.)

National Domestic Violence
Hotline 1-800-333-7233

Clearinghouse on Family
Violence,Health & Welfare
1-800-267-1291

National Resource Centers and Clearinghouses

Clearinghouse on Child Abuse
and Neglect Information
P.O. Box 1182
Washington, D.C. 20013
(703) 385-3206
or
1-800-394-3366

National Resource Center for
Child Abuse & Neglect
American Humane Association
American Association for
Protecting Children
63 Inverness Dr. E
Englewood, CO 80112-5117
(303) 792-9900
Information 1-800-227-5242

The National Resource Center on
Child Sexual Abuse
107 Lincoln St., N.E.
Huntsville, AL 35801
(205) 534-KIDS
Information 1-800-543-7006

Child Protective Services Agencies

There are child protective service
agencies in each of the 50 United
States.

These agencies can be found
under headings or listings such
as the following: Department of
Human Resources, Department
of Health and Social Services.
Department of Economic
Security Administration for
Children, Youth and Families,
Department of Human Services
and Office of Child Abuse
Prevention as well as others.

Index